JUDGING
SEX WORK

Landmark Cases in Canadian Law

Since Confederation, Canada's highest court – first the Judicial Committee of the Privy Council in England and then the Supreme Court of Canada – has issued a series of often contentious decisions that have fundamentally shaped the nation. Both cheered and jeered, these judgments have impacted every aspect of Canadian society, setting legal precedents and provoking social change. The issues in the judgments range from Aboriginal title, gender equality, and freedom of expression to Quebec secession and intellectual property. This series offers comprehensive, book-length examinations of high court cases that have had a major impact on Canadian law, politics, and society.

Other books in the series are

Flawed Precedent: The St. Catherine's *Case and Aboriginal Title* by Kent McNeil

Privacy in Peril: Hunter v Southam *and the Drift from Reasonable Search Protections* by Richard Jochelson and David Ireland

The Tenth Justice: Judicial Appointments, Marc Nadon, and the Supreme Court Act *Reference* by Carissima Mathen and Michael Plaxton

From Wardship to Rights: The Guerin *Case and Aboriginal Law* by Jim Reynolds

Constitutional Pariah: Reference re Senate Reform *and the Future of Parliament* by Emmett Macfarlane

No Legal Way Out: R v Ryan, *Domestic Abuse, and the Defence of Duress* by Nadia Verelli and Lori Chambers

Debt and Federalism: Landmark Cases in Canadian Bankruptcy and Insolvency Law, 1894–1937 by Thomas G.W. Telfer and Virginia Torrie

Reckoning with Racism: Police, Judges, and the RDS *Case* by Constance Backhouse

A Culture of Justification: Vavilov *and the Future of Administrative Law* by Paul Daly

For a list of other titles,
see www.ubcpress.ca/landmark-cases-in-canadian-law.

**LANDMARK CASES
IN CANADIAN LAW**

JUDGING SEX WORK

Bedford and the Attenuation of Rights

Colton Fehr

UBCPress · Vancouver

© UBC Press 2024

All rights reserved. No part of this publication may be reproduced, stored in a retrieval system, or transmitted, in any form or by any means, without prior written permission of the publisher, or, in Canada, in the case of photocopying or other reprographic copying, a licence from Access Copyright, www.accesscopyright.ca.

33 32 31 30 29 28 27 26 25 24   5 4 3 2 1

Printed and bound by CPI Group (UK) Ltd, Croydon, CR0 4YY

Library and Archives Canada Cataloguing in Publication

Title: Judging sex work : Bedford and the attenuation of rights / Colton Fehr.
Names: Fehr, Colton, author.
Series: Landmark cases in Canadian law.
Description: Series statement: Landmark cases in Canadian law | Includes bibliographical references and index.
Identifiers: Canadiana (print) 20230488668 | Canadiana (ebook) 20230488781 | ISBN 9780774869768 (hardcover) | ISBN 9780774869799 (EPUB) | ISBN 9780774869782 (PDF)
Subjects: LCSH: Sex work – Law and legislation – Canada. | LCSH: Sex workers – Legal status, laws, etc. – Canada.
Classification: LCC KE9075 .F44 2023 | LCC KF9448 .F44 2023 kfmod | DDC 345.71025/34 – dc23

UBC Press gratefully acknowledges the financial support for our publishing program of the Government of Canada and the British Columbia Arts Council.

UBC Press
The University of British Columbia
2029 West Mall
Vancouver, BC V6T 1Z2
www.ubcpress.ca

For Marian and Avery

Contents

Introduction   1

PART 1: THE LOGIC OF *BEDFORD*

1   Setting the Stage   15

2   The Road to *Bedford*   39

3   The *Bedford* Decision   51

PART 2: ATTENUATING RIGHTS

4   Legislative Facts and the Charter   81

5   The Principles of Instrumental Rationality   95

6   Suspended Declarations of Invalidity   114

PART 3: RETHINKING *BEDFORD*

7   The Case for Upholding the Sex Work Laws   133

8   The Constitutionality of the New Sex Work Laws   157

9   Sex Work and the Criminal Law   179

    Conclusion   187

Notes   195

Bibliography   252

Index of Cases   277

Index   279

JUDGING
SEX WORK

INTRODUCTION

IN *BEDFORD V CANADA*,[1] Terri-Jean Bedford, Valerie Scott, and Amy Lebovitch – all current or former sex workers – brought an application to the Ontario Superior Court of Justice to strike down three laws restricting the practice of sex work. These laws prohibited sex workers from working out of bawdy houses[2] or communicating in public for the purpose of sex work.[3] It was also an offence for other people to live on the avails of sex work.[4] Sex workers were therefore forced to conduct their otherwise legal work in unfamiliar areas and without safeguards such as being able to screen clientele or hire protective staff. The trial judge found that these laws increased the risk of violence that sex workers face when conducting their work.[5] Given the objectives of the impugned legislation – preventing either public nuisance or exploitation of sex workers – the trial judge concluded that the sex work laws were unconstitutional since they struck an illogical or unacceptable balance between their objectives and effects.[6]

On 20 December 2013, the Supreme Court of Canada unanimously endorsed the trial judge's decision despite having upheld the same three laws two decades earlier.[7] As Chief Justice McLachlin explained, there were two important differences between the earlier constitutional challenges and the *Bedford* decision. First, the evidence submitted provided much more detail about the dangers faced by sex workers. Whereas limited evidence existed in the early 1990s, the trial judge in *Bedford* based her decision on over 25,000 pages of social science evidence.[8] Second, the legal principles pleaded in *Bedford* differed from those of its predecessors.[9] In the earlier cases, the Supreme Court considered

1

2 | Introduction

whether the sex work laws unjustifiably violated the presumption of innocence,[10] the rights to freedom of association and expression,[11] and whether the laws were unduly vague.[12] The Supreme Court in *Bedford* struck down the sex work laws by employing principles of "means-ends" or "instrumental rationality." The relevant principles of fundamental justice – prohibiting laws with overbroad (illogical) or grossly disproportionate (harsh) effects – did not have constitutional status when the earlier cases were decided.[13]

The *Bedford* decision is a landmark case in part because of the particular laws that it struck down. The sex work laws at issue were part of a controversial approach to sex work governance that many believe unduly undermined the autonomy and safety interests of sex workers. For these advocates, striking down the sex work laws constituted a major social justice victory and an important step on the road toward decriminalizing sex work. However, others believe that the criminalization of sex work in some form is necessary to deter its practice. Only by preventing sex work to the extent possible can the equality interests of women in particular be upheld. The *Bedford* case unsurprisingly served to reinvigorate political tensions surrounding the regulation of sex work. As will become evident, Parliament's response to *Bedford* should serve as a cautionary tale to those seeking to employ the Charter to create social change.

From a legal perspective, the *Bedford* case is a landmark decision for several reasons. Not only did it constitute the first time that the Supreme Court overturned its own precedent upholding a law under the Canadian Charter of Rights and Freedoms,[14] but it also dramatically affected the constitutional litigation process. The conclusion that even lower courts may overturn appellate rulings if there is a "substantial change" in the evidence or if a "new legal issue" arises has generally been met with approval.[15] The Supreme Court nevertheless also determined that appellate courts must show significant deference to a trial judge's findings of fact based on social science evidence.[16] This ruling is particularly controversial since the Supreme Court elsewhere recognized that findings of "social" or "legislative" facts are often dispositive of constitutional challenges.[17] Should a single trial judge – typically trained in law, not social science methods – be trusted to interpret competing accounts of social science evidence? Relatedly, would often indigent litigants be able to amass the necessary evidence to plead their cases? Although this occurred in *Bedford*, the lead counsel for the applicants – Alan Young – volunteered his services and convinced all expert witnesses to follow suit.

The Supreme Court attempted to address the access to justice challenge by developing constitutional principles that ease the applicant's burden of proof when challenging a law under section 7 of the Charter. That section requires any law that engages an individual's life, liberty, or security of the person to accord with the "principles of fundamental justice." In *Bedford*, the Supreme Court restructured the instrumental rationality principles of fundamental justice. When applying these principles, judges first identify the law's objective and then consider whether the law is connected to its objective. If not, then the law is arbitrary.[18] If the law is connected to its objective but applies to any individual in a manner that bears no connection to its objective, then the law is overbroad.[19] And if the law's effect on any individual is too harsh when compared to its objective, then the law violates the gross disproportionality principle.[20] This focus on a law's rationality as applied to an individual – as opposed to these principles' prior focus on a law's rationality vis-à-vis all members of society – allows litigants to use their own experiences or those of a hypothetical litigant to establish a section 7 violation. This approach greatly lessens the burden of proof on applicants because it requires the state to explain why a law's overall burdens and benefits ought to result in the law being upheld under section 1 of the Charter.[21]

The Supreme Court's restructuring of the instrumental rationality principles nevertheless had two controversial effects. First, it vastly expanded the purview of judicial review under section 7 of the Charter. Moving forward, any law that engaged the threshold interests and was not perfectly connected to its objective or had severe effects on even a single person would violate the Charter.[22] Although this change in law made it easier for constitutional issues to be raised, it also resulted in charges of "judicial activism" since judges were now much more

4 | *Introduction*

capable of finding a Charter violation.[23] Second, and less intuitively, the Supreme Court's use of the instrumental rationality principles made it possible for a legislature to sidestep judicial rulings without justifying a rights breach under section 1 or passing a reply law using the Charter's "notwithstanding clause."[24] By slightly modifying a law's objective or effects, the government can reasonably claim that any reply law is *prima facie* constitutional since it will be necessary to "rebalance" the relevant interests to determine the new law's constitutionality.[25]

Parliament provided such a response to the *Bedford* decision. Controversially, the Supreme Court granted Parliament a one-year "suspended declaration of invalidity" during which the sex work laws remained in force despite their unconstitutionality.[26] Parliament used this time to develop and ultimately pass a law – Bill C-36 – that many contend did little to improve the safety of sex workers.[27] Instead, Parliament changed the context and objective of sex work regulation. Several of the previous prohibitions were re-enacted in a narrower form. More drastically, purchasing and selling sex became illegal (though the latter was non-prosecutable), and Parliament declared that eradicating sex work was the best means to uphold the equality and dignity interests of sex workers.[28] Given this novel context, Parliament maintained that the new sex work laws did not clearly violate any Charter rights.[29] This claim was plausible since the *Bedford* case had little precedential value given the different objectives and effects of those laws. Defendants have nevertheless begun the lengthy process of constitutionally challenging the new sex work laws using the same constitutional principles invoked in *Bedford*.[30] It is only a matter of time before the Supreme Court will decide the merits of those arguments.

My aim in this book is to provide a critical take on the legal aspects of the *Bedford* case. Building on the existing literature, I contend that the Supreme Court's ruling did little to protect the safety interests of sex workers, jeopardized the ability of courts to decide rights cases implicating social science evidence coherently, rendered the most important rights provision under the Charter incomprehensible, and unduly widened the scope of judicial review while providing legislatures with an unprincipled legal means to sidestep judicial precedents. Put differently, I maintain that a decision widely considered a landmark social justice victory did much more to weaken than strengthen rights.

I nevertheless maintain that all of these results could have been avoided by viewing the constitutional challenge in *Bedford* through the lens of choice. Central to this novel response to the *Bedford* decision is the Supreme Court's recognition that some sex workers choose to engage in sex work whereas others have no "realistic choice" but to engage in the trade.[31] Given the "alarming amount of violence" faced by the latter category of sex workers,[32] I contend that they also have no realistic choice but to take basic safety precautions – such as screening clientele or setting up bawdy houses – while conducting their work. This conclusion is important for two reasons. First, the Supreme Court has observed that a person who acts without a realistic choice acts in a "morally involuntary" manner.[33] Second, it is contrary to the principles of fundamental justice to convict a person for morally involuntary conduct.[34]

The constitutionality of the sex work laws should therefore have been scrutinized based on their application to those who *choose* to perform sex work. Although I conclude that the sex work laws still caused harm to voluntarily acting sex workers, my reframing of the *Bedford* case provides important context for considering whether the sex work laws ought to have been upheld under section 1 of the Charter. In my view, the choice of some sex workers to engage in the trade suggests that any harms to them were largely caused by their choice to engage in a dangerous trade. The fact that the harms endured by voluntarily acting sex workers were largely attributable to their own behaviour dampens the impact of the social science evidence admitted in *Bedford* under the proportionality aspect of the section 1 test.

I further contend that the Supreme Court misconstrued the objectives of the sex work laws. In addition to avoiding nuisances and preventing pimps from exploiting sex workers, the sex work laws sought to deter people from choosing to enter the trade. Although ascribing multiple objectives to a law is contrary to the Supreme Court's constitutional jurisprudence, this approach ought to be abandoned since it relies on a legal fiction. As the Supreme Court writes elsewhere,

6 | *Introduction*

legislation often "does not simply further one goal but rather strikes a balance among several goals, some of which may be in tension."[35] There is no principled reason to utilize a different understanding of legislative intent in the constitutional context. I utilize my conception of choice in relation to sex work and the broader objectives of the sex work laws to bolster my view that each law was justifiable under section 1 of the Charter.

In making this argument, I do not intend to take a side in the increasingly polarized debate about the best means for regulating sex work. My analysis – which I suspect might raise some eyebrows – should nevertheless signal the need to consider a more fundamental question concerning the relationship between criminal law and constitutional law: Is it constitutional to criminalize sex work at all? This important question has received inadequate attention in Canadian law. I contend that this result derives from the Supreme Court's refusal to constitutionalize any of the principles typically thought to delineate the permissible scope of criminal law. By filtering the Supreme Court's constitutional analysis in *Bedford* through the lens of criminal defences, my analysis not only affirms the importance of the Anglo-American structure of criminal law when conducting constitutional analysis but also encourages criminal lawyers to unpack their grievances with sex work regulation in a way that reveals their true constitutional concern: whether the impugned activities of sex workers are a proper object of criminal prohibition. This path, I suggest, can serve to open the door to more meaningful regulatory reform than that achieved in *Bedford*.

The book unfolds in three parts. Part 1 reviews the *Bedford* case and the Supreme Court's prior precedents upholding the sex work laws. In Chapter 1, I identify the two main gaps in the Supreme Court's early jurisprudence that resulted in the sex work laws being upheld: limited social science evidence and inadequate judicial engagement with the "principles of fundamental justice." In Chapter 2, I detail the changing social and legal landscape that allowed the applicants to re-raise the constitutionality of the sex work laws a mere decade and a half after they were upheld.[36] In so doing, I draw from a personal interview with Alan Young, who shed light on his litigation strategy and the barriers

Introduction | 7

that he faced in bringing the constitutional challenge. In Chapter 3, I summarize the social science evidence submitted in *Bedford* and the legal arguments for and against striking down the sex work laws. I distinguish the empirical record and legal arguments in *Bedford* from the Supreme Court's earlier decisions, enabling readers to gain a clearer sense of the deficiencies underlying the latter cases and the subsequent controversy underlying the *Bedford* decision.

In Part 2, I take aim at the logic of *Bedford* and explain how the decision – contrary to its intent – served to attenuate rights. I contend in Chapter 4 that the Supreme Court's decision to defer to the trial judge's findings of fact pertaining to social science evidence risks undermining constitutional rule. This follows for two reasons. First, trial judges are highly susceptible to making questionable findings of fact because of their well-documented struggle to understand social science evidence.[37] Second, social science evidence is frequently dispositive of constitutional issues.[38] As such, showing deference to the trial judge's factual findings subjects democratically enacted legislation to the trial judge's ability to understand that evidence as opposed to constitutional principles. Absent legislative prescriptions to address this issue, allowing an increased number of appellate justices to screen factual findings is the most promising means to minimize the chance that a law's constitutionality will be decided based on faulty evidence.

In Chapter 5, I then explain how the Supreme Court's decision to "individualize" the instrumental rationality principles gave rise to controversy for both those who support and those who oppose judicial review. Those who charged that the Supreme Court's decision unduly expanded judicial review failed to channel their criticisms at the substance of the law. Put differently, it is questionable whether the Supreme Court's favoured principle – overbreadth – qualified as a principle of fundamental justice. The Supreme Court's insistence that the instrumental rationality principles "presume" that the law achieves its objective also gave rise to challenges. Although this presumption ensures that litigants need not submit voluminous empirical evidence to establish a rights infringement, it also rendered the arbitrariness and gross disproportionality principles either unworkable or unduly protective of

8 | *Introduction*

state legislation in readily identifiable scenarios. Finally, the Supreme Court's preference for employing the instrumental rationality principles made it easier for legislatures to evade judicial rulings. By slightly modifying a law's objective or effects, the government can reasonably claim that it is necessary to "rebalance" the relevant interests even though the new law has a similar impact on section 7 interests.

In Chapter 6, I consider the implications of the Supreme Court's decision to suspend the sex work laws' declaration of invalidity. In a few short paragraphs, the Supreme Court determined that a suspended declaration of invalidity was warranted, and the sex workers just afforded protection under section 7 of the Charter were required to endure another year of those laws to allow Parliament adequate time to respond. This aspect of the judgment has been criticized for ignoring the substantial effects of a suspension of invalidity on the security interests of sex workers. It is also a questionable practice based on the text of the Constitution, which arguably does not permit courts to suspend a declaration of invalidity.[39] The fallout from *Bedford* illustrates the need to develop a principled framework for suspending declarations of invalidity especially when serious harm is likely to result from such a declaration.

In response to these problems, I contend that it is best to require legislatures to suspend declarations of invalidity using constitutional tools readily available to them and that courts should suspend a declaration of invalidity only in rare circumstances in which an unwritten constitutional principle compels such action. Even in those circumstances, however, it is necessary to suspend a declaration of invalidity only for as long as it might take the affected legislature to invoke the same unwritten constitutional principle as a means of determining the duration of the suspension. This approach is prudent since I maintain that courts are ill equipped to determine the appropriate lengths of suspended declarations of invalidity.[40] Applying this approach to the *Bedford* case, I contend that there was no principled basis for the Supreme Court to suspend the sex work laws' declaration of invalidity.

In Part 3, I offer a rethink of the *Bedford* decision and consider the implications of the legal framework that I provide for the future of sex work regulation in Canada. I begin in Chapter 7 by outlining the choice-based argument for upholding the sex work laws at issue in *Bedford*. I maintain that my approach would have better respected the will of Parliament to restrict voluntary sex work while protecting those who engage in sex work in a morally involuntary manner.

In Chapter 8, I contend that my choice-based framework applies with equal force to several of Parliament's new laws. Parliament responded with both narrower versions of the sex work laws at issue in *Bedford* and new prohibitions against advertising and procuring sexual services. More controversially, Parliament also decided to criminalize the purchase of sex. The choice-based framework for assessing the constitutionality of the sex work laws should prevent the former prohibitions from being struck down. However, the constitutionality of the key provision of the new sex work laws – the criminalization of purchasers – will turn uncomfortably on the trial judge's interpretation of the social science evidence concerning the efficacy of the new sex work laws. Given the limited available evidence and the difficulties courts face in interpreting social science evidence, I maintain that courts ought to show the new sex work legislation deference at this early stage of its adoption.

In Chapter 9, I respond to anticipated objections to my choice-based analysis by reframing the constitutional question for future litigants. Drawing from the section 7 jurisprudence, I contend that the *Bedford* case was pleaded using the instrumental rationality principles because of the Supreme Court's unwillingness to utilize constitutional law to meaningfully delineate the boundaries of what may be criminalized. Framing the argument in this way resulted in the analysis being divorced from the theory underlying criminal law. Although filtering the constitutional analysis through the law of defences might give rise to objections – the unfairness of requiring vulnerable sex workers to endure the criminal process to obtain an acquittal – I contend that these retorts do not undermine my doctrinal critique. Instead, any unfairness resulting from the Anglo-American structure of criminal law should bring litigants back to first principles of criminal law. Put differently, my hope is that my critique of *Bedford* results in litigants

10 | *Introduction*

asking whether the impugned sex work laws further any of the legitimate aims of the criminal law.

I conclude by unpacking a peculiar aspect of the *Bedford* decision: it was unanimous. The various controversial legal rulings in *Bedford* belie the conclusion that nine critical-thinking justices were in perfect agreement about the merits of the case. In my view, the unanimity in the *Bedford* case was a result of the judicial culture cultivated by Chief Justice McLachlin during her tenure on the Supreme Court. By fostering a culture of cooperation among justices, concurring and dissenting reasons became much less frequent.[41] Such a perspective nevertheless would have been valuable to guide litigants in future Charter challenges, especially those currently arising in response to Bill C-36. I therefore maintain that the *Bedford* decision casts doubt on the high value that the former Chief Justice placed on cooperation and emphasizes the need to encourage more robust concurring and dissenting reasons on the bench.

Before proceeding, I want to make two further observations. First, I use the terms "sex work" and "sex worker" – terms coined by the recently deceased Carol Leigh – instead of "prostitution" and "prostitute" except when directly quoting courts or scholars using the latter terms. The distinction between these terms is in part political. As the trial judge explained in *Bedford,* the term "sex worker" is typically employed to avoid the stigma associated with the term "prostitute."[42] Debra Haak also observes that a more robust understanding of the two terms can help to bring conceptual clarity for legal decision makers.[43] The term "sex work" is typically used to refer to those who sell sexual services "bearing certain characteristics, most notably that they are adults, who engage as a matter of consent and in the absence of third party coercion."[44] These characteristics are contrasted with those underlying prostitution, which connotes coerced and nonconsensual activity.[45]

The question therefore arises whether the political purpose underlying use of the term "sex work" can be preserved without glossing over the important distinction between "prostitution" and "sex work." In my view, allowing "sex work" to serve as an umbrella term need not result in the distinction being lost. In its place, some scholars distinguish between categories of sex work, identifying it as either "voluntary" or "survival."[46] This terminology is more appropriate since it serves the laudable goal of lessening the stigma faced by sex workers while also recognizing that many of them do not act in a normatively voluntary manner. Although this distinction is contested,[47] the Anglo-American criminal law has long drawn a line between voluntary and involuntary actions. As I contend in Part 3 of the book, it is both acceptable and prudent to rely on a distinction that operates as a central piece of the criminal law when structuring the relationship between it and sex work.

Second, and despite the political underpinnings of my preferred terminology, I have not written this book as an advocate of any form of sex work regulation. Nor have I written it as a social scientist deeply immersed in the empirics of sex work. I necessarily engage with the empirical evidence as it was understood by the various levels of courts in *Bedford*. It is also important to engage with the history of sex work regulation in Canada. Without such a review, it is difficult to appreciate fully the moral, political, and social gravity of the judicial decisions considering the constitutionality of the sex work laws. My aim, however, is not to turn my analysis into an empirical review of sex work regulation or its history. Instead, this is a book about a landmark case in Canadian law and why I think that the case was misguided in its reasoning. With the purpose of the book set out, I turn now to an overview of the Supreme Court's early cases engaging with the constitutionality of the sex work laws.

PART 1

THE LOGIC OF
BEDFORD

1

Setting the Stage

THE PLIGHT OF SEX workers in Canada is intrinsically tied to the regulation of sex work and other forms of sexual morality. A review of this history can help to explain why sex workers – typically women and often women of colour – are among the most disadvantaged populations in Canadian society. As Constance Backhouse explains, "[d]iscriminatory laws ... were used to attack a social problem that was itself a reflection of a discriminatory society."[1] Put differently, social and economic discrimination against women explained why many turned to sex work. The state in turn used the criminal law to stigmatize and ostracize these women for "choosing" their "unvirtuous" occupation. By reinforcing discrimination with more discrimination, sex workers were destined to become an increasingly marginalized population.

This history can also help to explain the judicial failure to strike down the sex work laws when they were first constitutionally challenged in the early 1990s. It is likely that society's prejudice against sex workers hampered the investigation of the perils of sex work. Although limited research existed, it was insufficient to establish that the dangers of sex work were intricately connected to the sex work prohibitions. The fact that the "principles of fundamental justice" protected under section 7 of the Canadian Charter of Rights and Freedoms were underdeveloped when the sex work laws were first challenged also helps to explain why

16 | *The Logic of* Bedford

these laws were initially upheld. Limited engagement with section 7 unfortunately rendered courts ill equipped to account for the harms caused by the sex work laws.[2] To develop these arguments, I review the historical governance of sex work in Canada, the Supreme Court of Canada's interpretation of the impugned sex work laws, the relevant provisions of the Charter as they were then understood, and the Supreme Court's reasons for initially upholding the sex work laws.

THE GOVERNANCE
OF SEX WORK PRE-CHARTER

Governance of sex work in Canada during the nineteenth and twentieth centuries took on various forms depending on the political and social attitudes of the day. Canada's experiment with a noncriminal, regulatory form of governance around the time of Confederation was brief. Attempts to employ rehabilitative principles to "reform" sex workers were similarly unsuccessful in early Canada. Instead, the criminal law – guided by Victorian morality – constituted the dominant method of governing sex work. No matter the approach to governance, gender, race, and class discrimination permeated the law.

The passing of the *Contagious Disease Act (CDA)*[3] in Upper and Lower Canada in 1865 is illustrative of the Canadian experience with sex work regulation. The *CDA* permitted "diseased" sex workers to be detained for up to three months upon any person swearing before a judge that the sex worker suffered from a venereal disease and was conducting sex work in a prohibited place.[4] As the full title of the legislation confirmed,[5] the *CDA* was passed to slow the spread of venereal disease among the many military and naval men who hired sex workers in the newly united province of Canada. Importantly, the *CDA* was passed as a result of lobbying not only by military and naval men but also by upper-class citizens who accepted that sex work was a "necessary social evil" to satisfy the insatiable sexual appetites of men.[6] The law's double standard was well illustrated by the fact that a similar law in place for screening military men for venereal disease was repealed half a decade earlier because the procedure was considered "unpopular" with soldiers and "distasteful" to the medical officers performing the inspection.[7]

The *CDA*'s implicit endorsement of Victorian attitudes toward sexual morality was defended by numerous journalists who noted that sex workers provided married men with an outlet when their wives were unwilling to have sex. Sex work also provided unmarried men with a means to satisfy their sexual desires in a more socially acceptable way than other forms of sexual conduct, such as masturbation or seduction.[8] For these reasons, Judith Walkowitz concluded, the *CDA* represented "the high water mark of an officially sanctioned double standard of sexual morality, one that upheld different standards of chastity for men and women and carefully tried to demarcate pure women from the impure."[9] Fortunately, a lack of approved medical facilities made the *CDA* difficult to enforce, and the legislation's natural expiration five years after its enactment passed with little debate on the legislation's merits.[10]

Underenforcement of the *CDA* and changing political tides nevertheless brought Canada's brief experiment with sex work regulation to an end. Near the time of Confederation, social puritans began widely condemning the practice of sex work as immoral.[11] Begrudging the decline of family values, many calls for reform centred on preserving women's historical role within the family. Sexual passivity was viewed as a key means of preserving female virtue and thus the family unit.[12] Organizations such as the Women's Christian Temperance Union, the Young Women's Christian Association, and the National Council of Women led this purist crusade alongside various religious bodies.[13]

The impetus for law reform was also heavily influenced by concerns about women being forced into the sex trade, a practice known as "white slavery."[14] Although for some scholars this phenomenon captured the practice of sex work more generally, others used the phrase to refer to sex workers who were physically coerced or tricked into participating in the trade.[15] As Ruth Rosen explained, these women entered the sex trade for various reasons, including "false promises of marriage, mock marriages that had no legal status, and deliberate attempts to entangle a woman in foreign debt or emotional dependency."[16] Although this latter category of sex worker existed, records show that most sex workers

18 | *The Logic of* Bedford

engaged in the practice out of economic necessity, a fact underappreciated by social purists.[17]

Culminating with Canada's first *Criminal Code* in 1892, various federal laws restricted the practice of sex work in response to its perceived social ills. In 1869, Parliament passed *An Act Respecting Vagrants,*[18] which not only criminalized sex workers merely for *being* sex workers but also prohibited anyone from keeping a bawdy house, frequenting a bawdy house, and living on the avails of sex work.[19] The same year Parliament passed *An Act Respecting Offences of the Person,*[20] which criminalized procuring the "defilement" of any woman under the age of twenty-one.[21] The criminalization of sex work further expanded during the decades leading up to the enactment of the *Criminal Code.* For example, it became an offence to entice a woman to a bawdy house for the purpose of sex work or to conceal a woman in such a house.[22] Men were also prohibited from seducing women of "previously chaste character" between the ages of twelve and sixteen.[23] Furthermore, it became illegal to procure women for "unlawful carnal connection" or for parents or guardians to promote the defilement of their daughters.[24] By the end of the nineteenth century, these and other related laws criminalized "every aspect of prostitution except the ... act of commercial exchange for sexual services."[25]

During the same time period, other reformers adopted a rehabilitative approach to sex work. The premise of this approach was that sex workers were "blameless ... because they had been entirely duped by the deceit and predatory wiles of evil men."[26] As a result, it was possible for these sex workers to be fully reformed and reintegrated into society. Their children could also be raised in such a manner that they would refuse to enter the sex work trade. To achieve these ends, charitable organizations were tasked with providing religious, moral, and economic instruction to sex workers who "volunteered" to stay at their institutions for lengthy periods of time.[27] Unfortunately, the moral and religious instruction was offensive to many women, and the typical economic training provided – domestic service – was often redundant and generally viewed as inadequate to gain economic independence given its poor remuneration.[28]

Setting the Stage | 19

As it became apparent that women were not consenting to stays at reformatory houses, the rehabilitative model shifted its focus to the prison context. Many women began receiving lengthy sentences in reformatory prisons – a minimum of five years in some instances – upon being convicted of a vagrancy offence.[29] Some reformatory prisons even permitted indefinite detention if a woman contracted a "contagious or infectious disease."[30] Lengthy prison terms were considered desirable since they provided sufficient time for individual reform.[31] Predictably, these tactics were unsuccessful. As Backhouse opines, "[i]t was practically useless to attempt to reform prostitutes without simultaneously altering the various factors which drove them to prostitution – poverty, restricted employment options, sexual victimization ... lack of access to birth control and abortion, and the all-pervasive sexual double standard."[32] Failure to regulate the johns who purchased sex also ensured that demand for sexual services remained high, thereby rendering sex work one of the most viable options for many of these women upon their release from prison.[33]

Renewed concerns about white slavery and lax enforcement of the existing sex work laws nevertheless fuelled a continued call for law reform early in the twentieth century.[34] Amendments to the *Criminal Code* in 1913 dropped the twenty-one-year age restriction for committing the procurement offence and permitted whipping as a punishment for any person convicted of multiple procurement offences.[35] Parliament also added prohibitions against concealing women in a bawdy house, encouraging new immigrants to join bawdy houses, and "exercising control, direction or influence over a female for purposes of prostitution."[36] The modern iteration of the living on the avails offence was also adopted. This provision prohibited "living wholly or in part on the avails of prostitution" and was bolstered by a presumption of guilt if the accused either lived with or was "habitually in the company of prostitutes with no visible means of support, or residing in a house of prostitution."[37] The bawdy house provisions were also amended by adding a presumption of guilt when a person "appeared to be a master or mistress."[38] Furthermore, the amendments treated landlords as keepers of bawdy houses if they permitted a property to be used as such and prohibited anyone from being "found in" a bawdy house.[39]

20 | *The Logic of* Bedford

The only other major legal change after the amendments in 1913 was the repeal in 1972 of the offence of "being" a sex worker. The requirement that sex workers provide a satisfactory account of themselves to avoid conviction was increasingly criticized for its inconsistency with the common law privilege against self-incrimination, which had recently received legislative protection under the *Canadian Bill of Rights*.[40] As a result, the status offence was replaced by a prohibition against "soliciting" sex work in public places. Since the narrow judicial interpretation of the term "solicit" is relevant to the first constitutional challenge of the sex work laws, I undertake a more detailed account of the initial iteration of the soliciting offence below when reviewing the judicial interpretation of the sex work laws.

Throughout its history, application of the sex work laws by the authorities was exceedingly gendered.[41] Not only did the police primarily enforce the sex work laws against women, but also trial judges commonly ordered women to pay significant fines and serve lengthy sentences of hard labour for what would be considered a minor infraction today.[42] As Harvey Graff observed, sex workers were specifically targeted by the state because they "were seen as failing in the society's expected standards of feminine behaviour" since they "were not at home nurturing a family or properly domesticated; their perceived deviance endangered the maintenance and propagation of the moral order, the family, and the training of children."[43]

There were also important racial dimensions in the application of the sex work prohibitions. Although sex workers of various minority backgrounds were disproportionately affected,[44] the treatment of Indigenous sex workers constitutes the most egregious and sustained form of discrimination against any group of sex workers. Despite contact during the fur trade between white settlers and Indigenous communities resulting in many family unions, more sustained colonization during the early nineteenth century relegated Indigenous women to "second status."[45] As settlement increased, many Indigenous women were sexually exploited by settlers and Indigenous men who sold the sexual services of their female relatives.[46] The persistent overrepresentation of Indigenous women in sex work, and street sex work in particular, is now understood to have direct ties to colonialism and its attendant consequences, such as poverty, familial violence, childhood abuse, racial discrimination, addiction, homelessness, and lack of education.[47]

Appellate courts in early Canada nevertheless provided what might be viewed as a check on majoritarian biases toward sex workers.[48] In various cases, appellate courts provided narrow interpretations of the elements of sex work offences to avoid using the criminal law as a means of compelling social reform.[49] The decision in *R v Levesque* is illustrative.[50] A woman found engaged with a soldier in a barrack yard was convicted at trial for being a "common prostitute" unable to provide a "satisfactory account of herself." The conviction followed from eyewitness evidence of her conduct during the day in question and hearsay evidence of her poor moral character. The court not only found the hearsay evidence to be inadequate proof of her status as a common prostitute but also questioned whether the evidence showed that the sexual act took place in public, thus implying a narrow interpretation of a "public place."[51] The court also restrictively interpreted the requirement that evidence exist whether the accused could provide a "satisfactory account of herself." Wandering the streets without any accompanying harmful or indecent conduct was held to be insufficient proof of the offence despite its gravamen constituting the mere state of *being* a sex worker in a public place.[52]

In *R v Clark*,[53] the Ontario Court of Queen's Bench provided a similarly narrow interpretation of the requirement for proving the early offence of "frequenting" a bawdy house. To meet the elements of the offence, Justice Armour required that the Crown prove that the accused person "habitually" frequented the bawdy house.[54] Justice McMahon of the same court later expanded this requirement in *R v Remon*.[55] Before a conviction could follow, the police must also have asked the client or sex worker "to give an account of himself or herself; for it may be that the person charged as being a 'frequenter' is there for a lawful purpose ... who might readily give a satisfactory account of his or her presence in such a house."[56] Read together, these requirements ensured that police would need to prove both numerous and illegitimate occupations of a bawdy house before a conviction could be sustained.

22 | *The Logic of* Bedford

Other courts originally provided a narrow interpretation of the term "prostitution."[57] In *R v Gareau*,[58] Justice Dorion of the Quebec Court of Appeal overturned the accused's conviction for keeping a disorderly house because it was based on providing sexual services to only one man. Without broader evidence of indiscriminate sexual intercourse, the court refused to find that the appellant's action constituted "prostitution."[59] The Quebec Court of Queen's Bench came to a similar conclusion in *The Queen v Rehe*.[60] A mistress paid by a married man to provide sexual services was acquitted of engaging in "prostitution" on appeal. Justice Wurtele reasoned that "prostitution in the general sense of a woman submitting herself to illicit sexual intercourse with a man may have existed[, but] prostitution in a restricted and legal sense did not exist."[61] In his view, the purpose of the sex work laws was "the repression of acts which outrage public decency and are injurious to public morals."[62] The woman's private behaviour in the case "did not outrage public decency nor violate any provision of the criminal law of the land."[63]

These and similar judgments[64] must nevertheless be read alongside other types of cases implicating women's rights during this time period. Although appellate judges seemed to be empathetic toward sex workers,[65] Backhouse persuasively contends that the judicial sympathy shown toward sex workers was motivated by a broader acceptance of the pervasive double standard in sexual morality.[66] This intent is inferable when one considers the infamous sexual stereotypes of the day that permeated sexual assault law and family law. If appellate courts were truly concerned about women's rights, then they would have shown a similar empathy in these and other areas of law relevant to gender equality.[67] Their failure to do so suggests that the driving rationale for narrowly interpreting the sex work laws was to facilitate "a significant range of male access to the sexual services of women."[68]

The above review of sex work governance in Canada provides necessary context for understanding the ensuing constitutional challenges. Importantly, it suggests that the sex work laws served multiple purposes. Although Parliament's laws endorsed traditional roles for women, the impetus for imposing these roles arose from demands by social puritans to deter development of the sex trade via the criminal law.[69] Although appellate courts interfered with Parliament's attempts to criminalize sex work, their motivation for doing so was to perpetuate the pervasive double standard of sexual morality. Without providing a meaningful check on legislatures, it was unlikely that the social conditions for many sex workers would improve. With the adoption of the Charter, litigants were given a new tool to compel social change. It did not take long before litigants attempted to use that tool to shape sex work governance. The most important early cases are the *Sex Work Reference*[70] and *R v Downey*.[71] Before describing these cases, however, I provide a more nuanced review of the relevant sex work laws when they were constitutionally challenged.

THE SEX WORK LAWS POST-CHARTER

As the *Criminal Code* was revised in 1985, the sections at issue in the *Sex Work Reference* and *Downey* were numbered differently from those in *Bedford*, though the substance of the provisions remained constant after 1985.[72] Subsection 193(1) (subsequently subsection 210(1)) prohibited "keeping" a common bawdy house. Subsection 193(2) (subsequently subsection 210(2)) further made it an offence to be an inmate of a bawdy house, to be found in a bawdy house without lawful excuse, or knowingly to permit one's property to be used as a bawdy house. The former prohibition constituted an indictable offence punishable by a maximum of two years of imprisonment, whereas the latter prohibition was a less serious summary conviction offence and subjected offenders to a maximum of one year of imprisonment.

The term "bawdy house" was defined in section 179 of the *Criminal Code* (subsequently section 197) as a place "frequently or habitually" used "by one or more persons for the purpose of prostitution or the practice of acts of indecency."[73] To be a "keeper" of a bawdy house, the accused must have exercised "some degree of control over the care and management of the premises" and "participate[d] to some extent ... in the 'illicit' activities of the common bawdy-house."[74] However, it was not required that the accused's participation be sexual in nature. Instead,

24 | *The Logic of* Bedford

the accused must have "participate[d] in the use of the bawdy house as a bawdy house."[75] As for acts of "prostitution" that rendered a place a "bawdy house," the Supreme Court defined the term as any exchange of sex for money.[76]

The various modes of liability for the summary conviction offences listed under subsection 193(2) of the *Criminal Code* were also defined by the courts. The term "inmate" was defined as a "resident or regular occupant" and typically referred to sex workers.[77] To be "found in" a bawdy house, the person – usually a client or pimp – must have been seen by someone at the bawdy house. Other proof that the person was present on the premises was insufficient to warrant a conviction.[78] The "permitting" offence was directed at the owner of the premises, regardless of whether they were running the bawdy house as a business. An owner was therefore liable if they knew that their premises was being used as a bawdy house and failed to "intervene forthwith" to prevent such use, and their failure could be "considered as the granting of permission to make such use of the premises as and from the time [they] gained such knowledge."[79]

Subsection 195.1(1)(c) of the *Criminal Code* (later subsection 213(1)(c)) prohibited communicating in public for the purpose of sex work. As mentioned previously, an earlier version of this provision criminalized "every person who solicits any person in a public place for the purpose of prostitution."[80] In *R v Hutt,*[81] the Supreme Court interpreted the term "solicits" as requiring that the sex worker engage in "pressing and persistent" communications.[82] The Supreme Court's decision was extensively criticized for making street prostitution easier to practise since the public believed that the communication prohibition failed to provide police with adequate power to regulate the sale of sex in public.[83]

Parliament responded by amending the communication offence in 1985.[84] The new provision criminalized anyone in a place open to public view who "stops or attempts to stop any person or in any manner communicates or attempts to communicate with any person for the purpose of engaging in prostitution or of obtaining the sexual services of a prostitute." The relevant communication need not specify the particular sexual services or money to be paid. Nor was it required that an agreement be reached between the negotiating parties. A conviction would enter if a court found that the communication was "for the purpose" of selling sex,[85] which included nonverbal communications.[86] Subsection 195.1(2) further defined "public place" broadly as "any place to which the public have access as of right or by invitation, express or implied, and any motor vehicle located in a public place or in any place open to public view." Such an offender would be guilty of a summary conviction offence and subject to a maximum of six months of imprisonment.

Finally, subsection 195(1)(j) of the *Criminal Code* (subsequently subsection 212(1)(j)) prohibited "liv[ing] wholly or in part on the avails of prostitution of another person." The scope of the provision was limited to those who provided a service or good to a sex worker because they were a sex worker. Thus, those who provided common services such as grocers and doctors were excluded from the provision.[87] The phrase "wholly or in part" was also interpreted narrowly. Those who ran a business such as an escort agency were found to be living parasitically on the avails of sex work.[88] However, courts would not convict a person merely for living with a sex worker. As the Ontario Court of Appeal observed in *R v Grilo*,[89] "the proper question is whether the accused and the prostitute had entered into a normal and legitimate living arrangement which included a sharing of expenses for their mutual benefit or whether, instead, the accused was living parasitically on the earnings of the prostitute for his own advantage."[90]

Despite the different contexts within which a person could run afoul of the living on the avails prohibition, the provision required that courts presume that a person who "lives with or is habitually in the company of a prostitute" is living on the avails of sex work.[91] This presumption was included to make it more difficult for pimps to escape conviction by masquerading as nonexploitive acquaintances of sex workers.[92] Despite the provision's laudable objective, it also required that spouses, partners, roommates, drivers, and bodyguards who lived with or were habitually in the company of sex workers prove that they were in legitimate living arrangements. These nonexploitive parties could be

26 | *The Logic of* Bedford

convicted unless they were able to raise a reasonable doubt about the nature of their relationship with the sex worker.[93] If they failed to do so, then they were liable to a maximum of ten years of imprisonment.[94]

APPLYING THE CHARTER

The constitutional challenge in the *Sex Work Reference* arrived on the Supreme Court's docket in a manner different from that of most cases. As opposed to a legal dispute between opposing parties, reference decisions are sent directly to a court via the legislature. The case was instituted by the Manitoba government pursuant to the *Constitutional Questions Act.*[95] The decision to send the reference question arose from an earlier decision by the Manitoba Provincial Court that found the communication provision unconstitutional and suggested that the bawdy house provision meet a similar fate.[96] The Manitoba Court of Appeal disagreed.[97] At the Supreme Court, the appellant maintained that the sex work laws violated two provisions of the Charter: first, the right to freedom of expression under section 2(b); second, the principles of fundamental justice preserved under section 7 because of the laws being both impermissibly vague and sending out conflicting messages about the legality of sex work.

Shortly after the Supreme Court upheld the Manitoba Court of Appeal's judgment, two further constitutional challenges arrived on the Supreme Court's docket. The first case, *R v Skinner,*[98] challenged the communication provision based on the rights to freedom of expression and association, protected in sections 2(b) and 2(d) of the Charter. However, the Supreme Court found that the freedom of association challenge depended on the argument pertaining to freedom of expression.[99] Since the latter argument was addressed in the *Sex Work Reference,* the *Skinner* case is of little moment. The second case, *Downey,* challenged the constitutionality of the third law at issue in *Bedford:* the prohibition against living on the avails of sex work. The applicant maintained that the impugned prohibition unjustifiably violated the presumption of innocence, constitutionally enshrined in section 11(d) of the Charter.

Below I review each rights challenge as well as whether any infringements were justifiable under section 1.

Section 2(b)

The right to freedom of expression serves three purposes: increasing democratic discourse, truth finding, and self-fulfillment.[100] Given these broader objectives, the term "expression" has been defined expansively to include any activity that "attempts to convey meaning."[101] The Supreme Court nevertheless devised one exception to this rule: violence can never constitute expression.[102] As a result, any restriction on nonviolent conduct that expresses meaning will violate the Charter, raising the more pressing question of whether the impugned law constitutes a justifiable infringement under section 1.

Since the Manitoba Court of Appeal rendered its decision before the Supreme Court interpreted the right to freedom of expression, it was afforded significant latitude in determining whether the communication provision violated the Charter. A unanimous Court of Appeal answered this question in the negative. In its view, "when a prostitute propositions a customer, or *vice versa,* we are not dealing with the free expression of ideas, nor with the real or imagined factual data to support an idea."[103] The Manitoba Court of Appeal's understanding of expression solely as a means to forward the pursuit of knowledge necessarily excluded more mundane forms of interaction.[104] Since the Supreme Court determined in the *Sex Work Reference* that a proper interpretation of the right to freedom of expression protected any attempt to convey meaning, it had little difficulty concluding that a sex worker propositioning a customer or vice versa constituted a form of expression.[105]

Section 7

The text of section 7 of the Charter provides that "[e]veryone has the right to life, liberty and security of the person and the right not to be deprived thereof except in accordance with the principles of fundamental justice." Upon first reading, the inclusion of the second conjunction "and" suggests that section 7 provides multiple rights: first, a

28 | *The Logic of* Bedford

general right to "life, liberty and security of the person" and, second, a right not to be deprived of those interests "except in accordance with the principles of fundamental justice." Although the Supreme Court has not ruled out this reading,[106] the "rights" to "life, liberty and security of the person" are consistently applied as threshold interests that do not themselves establish a breach of the Charter. A breach arises only when the state deprives an individual of a threshold interest in a manner inconsistent with a principle of fundamental justice.[107]

In the *Sex Work Reference,* Chief Justice Dickson, writing for a unanimous court on this point, concluded that the impugned laws clearly engaged the liberty interests of sex workers because those laws could result in a prison sentence.[108] Given this conclusion, he did not entertain broader arguments related to sex workers' economic freedoms or security of the person interests.[109] In his concurring reasons, Justice Lamer considered the latter arguments. The appellants maintained that the liberty interests of sex workers were violated because they were not allowed to participate in a legal profession.[110] Similarly, they contended that their security of the person interest was engaged because the impugned laws prevented sex workers from working in a legal trade to earn the basic necessities of life.[111]

The appellants' broader interpretation of liberty derived from both legal philosophy and American jurisprudence. John Stuart Mill famously proclaimed that harm to others was the only basis on which a citizen's actions could be restricted.[112] Building on this understanding of liberty, the American Supreme Court, in *Lochner v New York,*[113] found that the Fourteenth Amendment of the American Constitution provided a right to contract.[114] Justice Lamer nevertheless disagreed that the terms "liberty" and "security of the person" ought to be defined so broadly. The Fourteenth Amendment prohibits depriving "any person of life, liberty, or property, without due process of law." The decision to exclude "property" from section 7 of the Charter strongly implied that the threshold interests were "not synonymous with unconstrained freedom."[115] This interpretation was bolstered by a purposive reading of the Charter. Although section 7 protects individual liberty and security of the person, more specific rights – such as freedom of expression, religion, conscience,

Setting the Stage | 29

and association – were explicitly provided elsewhere in the Charter.[116] This strongly implied that the threshold interests in section 7 were meant to be circumscribed by the context within which that section sought to govern: the justice system.[117]

Despite Justice Lamer's narrow interpretation of the threshold interests, the unanimous conclusion that the liberty interest was engaged made it necessary to determine whether the two principles pleaded in the *Sex Work Reference* constituted principles of fundamental justice. The first principle requires that laws not be unduly vague. As Chief Justice Dickson observed, "where a person's liberty is at stake it is imperative that persons be capable of knowing in advance with a high degree of certainty what conduct is prohibited and what is not."[118] Lamer similarly concluded that "[i]t is essential in a free and democratic society that citizens are able, as far as is possible, to foresee the consequences of their conduct, in order that persons be given fair notice of what to avoid."[119] The Supreme Court nevertheless found "that the terms 'prostitution,' 'keeps' a bawdy house, 'communicate' and 'attempts to communicate' are not so vague, given the benefit of judicial interpretation, that their meaning is impossible to discern in advance."[120]

The second proposed principle of fundamental justice would prohibit legislatures from "send[ing] out conflicting messages whereby the criminal law says one thing but means another."[121] Although sex work was legal, the impugned provisions rendered almost every aspect of it illegal. The bawdy house provision prohibited operating from a fixed indoor location, and the communication provision made it impossible to negotiate in public for the sale of sex. The applicant therefore contended that the legislative scheme attached the stigma of criminalization to one "lawful activity (communication) directed at the achievement of another lawful activity (sale of sex)."[122] Although the Supreme Court recognized that Parliament's laws made it practically impossible to sell sex legally,[123] it did not agree that the principles of fundamental justice require direct criminalization of an activity. Although it was a "circuitous" path to criminalizing sex work, Chief Justice Dickson found it "difficult to say that Parliament *cannot* take this route."[124] He continued, observing that "[u]nless or until this court is faced with the direct

30 | *The Logic of* Bedford

question of Parliament's competence to criminalize prostitution, it is difficult to say that Parliament cannot criminalize, and thereby indirectly control, some element of prostitution."[125]

Section 11(d)

Section 11(d) of the Charter provides that any person charged with an offence has the right "to be presumed innocent until proven guilty according to law in a fair and public hearing by an independent and impartial tribunal." Interpreting this provision in *Downey,* the Supreme Court concluded that the presumption of innocence is violated if an accused might be convicted despite the Crown's case giving rise to a reasonable doubt about whether the offence was committed.[126] Thus, any provision that requires the accused to prove some fact to avoid a finding of guilt will violate the presumption of innocence.[127]

There is nevertheless one exception to this general rule. As the Supreme Court held in *R v Whyte,*[128] "substituting proof of one element for proof of an essential element will not infringe the presumption of innocence if, upon proof of the substituted element, it would be unreasonable for the trier of fact not to be satisfied beyond a reasonable doubt of the existence of the essential element."[129] In other words, "[o]nly if the existence of the substituted fact leads inexorably to the conclusion that the essential element exists, with no other reasonable possibilities, will the statutory presumption be constitutionally valid."[130]

The Supreme Court in *Downey* concluded that the living on the avails provision violated the presumption of innocence. Although the two accused were charged with running an escort agency, the constitutional challenge relied on a hypothetical scenario related to a person who cohabits with a sex worker. As the Supreme Court observed, a self-supporting spouse or companion of a sex worker could live with the sex worker without relying on the latter's income.[131] For the Supreme Court, "[t]he fact that someone lives with a prostitute does not lead inexorably to the conclusion that the person is living on avails."[132] Since hypothetically the accused person could be convicted if they failed to raise a reasonable doubt about their living arrangement, the living on the avails provision was found to violate the presumption of innocence.[133]

Section 1

Since the communication and living on the avails offences infringed rights, the Supreme Court in both the *Sex Work Reference* and *Downey* was asked to consider whether each provision could be upheld under section 1 of the Charter. Section 1 provides that the rights and freedoms in the Charter are guaranteed "subject only to such reasonable limits prescribed by law as can be demonstrably justified in a free and democratic society." In *R v Oakes,*[134] the Supreme Court concluded that a law justifiably infringes a Charter right if two criteria are established.[135] First, the law must promote a "pressing and substantial" objective.[136] Second, in forwarding that objective, the law must constitute a proportionate infringement of the right.[137] To do so, the law must be rationally connected to its objective. In other words, the law must not be arbitrary, unfair, or based on irrational considerations.[138] In addition, the law must impair the constitutional right as minimally as reasonably possible.[139] Finally, the law's salutary and deleterious effects on Charter interests must be proportionate.[140] As the Supreme Court concluded in *Oakes,* "[t]he more severe the deleterious effects of a measure, the more important the objective must be if the measure is to be reasonable and demonstrably justified in a free and democratic society."[141]

Communication Offence

The prohibition against communicating in public for the purposes of sex work was upheld by the majority of the Supreme Court, consisting of Chief Justice Dickson (Justices La Forest and Sopinka concurring) and Justice Lamer. Dickson found that the purpose of the communication provision was to avoid the societal nuisances caused by sex work.[142] As he explained, such activity "is closely associated with street congestion and noise, oral harassment of non-participants and general detrimental effects on passers-by or bystanders, especially children."[143] Later in his judgment, he also maintained that the law sought to curtail street solicitation more generally.[144] These objectives were found to be pressing and substantial, thereby satisfying the first branch of the *Oakes* test.[145] Given the law's likely ability to deter such conduct, the law was also found to be rationally connected to its objective.[146]

32 | *The Logic of* Bedford

Chief Justice Dickson further found that the law minimally impaired the right to freedom of expression. He maintained that communicating in public for the purpose of sex work was primarily motivated by the desire to make money.[147] For Dickson, such a purpose does not lie anywhere near the core guarantees of the right to freedom of expression: promoting democratic discourse, truth finding, and self-fulfillment.[148] The fact that the prohibition on communicating in public for the purpose of sex work caught conduct that might not give rise to a social nuisance if done in a remote public place did not render the law unjustifiable. For Dickson, "[t]he notion of nuisance in connection with street soliciting extends beyond interference with the individual citizen to interference with the public at large, that is, with the environment represented by streets, public places and neighbouring premises."[149] The impugned law's ability to curtail solicitation more generally therefore rendered it minimally impairing of the right to freedom of expression.[150]

Similarly, the fact that the law applied to any communication – even one that does not require making noise – did not render it unjustifiable because the definition of "communication" was qualified by the phrase "for the purpose of engaging in prostitution or of obtaining the sexual services of a prostitute."[151] Even though the law might apply to some nonvisible sexual communications, Chief Justice Dickson's conclusion that it also sought to curtail street solicitation resulted in it adequately pursuing its objective.[152] In passing a new law, Parliament took into account various alternatives – including the narrower communication offence repealed following the Supreme Court's decision in *Hutt* – and found that the broader definition of communication best balanced the need to curtail street solicitation and sex workers' economically motivated expression interests. As Dickson concluded, the legislation "challenged need not be the 'perfect' scheme that could be imagined ... Rather, it is sufficient [since] it is appropriately and carefully tailored in the context of the infringed right."[153]

In considering whether the law balanced its salutary and deleterious effects, Chief Justice Dickson weighed its ability to curtail street solicitation and avoidance of the social nuisances that it targeted against the economic interests of those who sell sex in public. Although Dickson

Setting the Stage | 33

did not explain precisely the deleterious effects arising from street solicitation, Justice Wilson later summarized the government's concerns as related to "the harassment of women, street congestion, noise, decreased property values, adverse effects on businesses, increased incidents of violence, and the impact of street soliciting on children who cannot avoid seeing what goes on."[154] When weighed against the minimal constitutional value inherent in economic expression, Dickson concluded that the law struck an appropriate balance between its objective and effects.[155]

Justice Lamer took a broader view of the legislation's objective. As opposed to reading each provision individually, the fact that Parliament made sex work practically impossible to practise meant that the objective of the laws was to eradicate sex work more generally.[156] His rationale for this conclusion was tied to the history of sex work governance. As he observed, "[t]his rather odd situation wherein almost everything related to prostitution has been criminalized save for the act itself gives one reason to ponder why Parliament has not taken the logical step of criminalizing the act of prostitution."[157] For Lamer, the most plausible explanation was "that, as a carryover of the Victorian Age, if the act itself had been made criminal, the gentleman customer of a prostitute would have been also guilty as a party to the offence."[158] Put differently, criminalizing the sale of sex also would have resulted in the criminalization of purchasing sex, unlikely to sit well with a voting population who supported the notion that men needed sex workers to satisfy "natural" sexual urges.[159]

Justice Lamer also provided more detailed evidence of legislative intent with respect to the solicitation offence. In particular, he cited the broader work of the legislative committee considering Bill C-49 and numerous working papers from the Department of Justice in support of the view that the solicitation offence was directed at more than curbing "nuisances."[160] As Lamer explained, these and other pieces of evidence bolstered his conclusion that the communication prohibition possessed an "additional objective of minimizing the public exposure of an activity that is degrading to women, with the hope that potential entrants in the trade can be deflected at an early stage."[161]

34 | *The Logic of* Bedford

In upholding the legislation under section 1 of the Charter, Justice Lamer concluded that prohibiting a basic element of sex work – communicating for the purpose of selling sexual services – was readily connected to the solicitation offence's deterrence-based objective.[162] Since the law applied only to sex workers and their customers communicating in a public place, Lamer also agreed that the impugned provision's effects minimally impaired the right to freedom of expression.[163] Finally, given the law's pressing objective and the tenuous connection between the communication at issue and the purposes underlying freedom of expression, Lamer found that the provision readily balanced its salutary and deleterious effects.[164]

Justice Wilson came to the opposite conclusion. In her view, the law's objective was simply to avoid social nuisances, not to eradicate sex work more generally.[165] As with Chief Justice Dickson, however, minimal evidence was put forward to justify this narrow reading of the sex work law's objective.[166] Although Wilson agreed with the other members that the law's objective was pressing and substantial and that its effects were rationally connected to its objective,[167] she found that the law did not minimally impair its objective because its broad definition of "public place" caught activity that could not plausibly give rise to a nuisance.[168] As an example, she noted that a person would commit an offence while communicating in a remote public park late at night for the purpose of sex work. For Wilson, "[s]uch a broad prohibition as to the locale of the communication ... [goes] far beyond a genuine concern over the nuisance caused by street solicitation."[169] Relatedly, the law was not minimally impairing because it did not require proof that the accused's communication gave rise to an actual nuisance to ground a conviction.[170] Wilson therefore would not have upheld the communication provision.

Living On the Avails Offence

In considering whether the living on the avails prohibition was justifiable under section 1 of the Charter, the Supreme Court relied heavily on two studies commissioned by the federal government commonly cited as the Fraser and Badgley Reports.[171] The Fraser Report found that pimps typically control groups of women within a defined territory.[172] It further found that, in cases in which a sex worker speaks out against a pimp, "physical violence, forced acts of sexual degradation and subtle forms of coercion ... were used by the pimps to keep them on the streets."[173] The relationship between sex workers and pimps was therefore "most closely analogous to slavery."[174] The Badgley Report similarly found that sex workers feared for their lives if they spoke to law enforcement about their pimps.[175] The level of control that pimps exercised over sex workers also gave rise to significant psychological dependency, resulting in some sex workers having extreme difficulties functioning without their pimps.[176]

Given the available evidence, Justice Cory, writing for a majority of the Supreme Court, concluded that the purpose of the living on the avails offence was to prevent the exploitation of sex workers.[177] The law was rationally connected to its objective because it gave rise to a reasonable inference – even if not always true – that the person living with a sex worker was doing so in an exploitive manner.[178] Although it is difficult to determine the prevalence of this social problem, this was largely because pimps control, abuse, and threaten sex workers to deter them from discussing these relationships with others. The need to draw an evidentiary presumption was therefore necessary to combat the practice of pimping.[179]

The majority further found that the presumption at issue in *Downey* minimally impaired the infringed right because there were no other alternative means of pursuing Parliament's pressing and substantial objective in as effective a manner. To eliminate the presumption completely "would reward [pimps] for the intimidation of vulnerable witnesses in a situation where it has been demonstrated that just such intimidation is widespread."[180] The majority also observed that Parliament could have adopted a more extreme policy and reversed the onus of proof, requiring that accused persons prove on a balance of probabilities that they were innocent. This approach, however, would operate unfairly for those who live with sex workers in a nonexploitive manner.[181] Parliament

36 | *The Logic of* Bedford

therefore struck a middle ground by requiring only that the accused raise a reasonable doubt about whether they were living on the avails of sex work.[182]

Finally, the majority of the Supreme Court concluded that the presumption struck a reasonable balance between the competing societal and individual interests at stake. Society's interest in prosecuting pimps is severely hampered by their ability to control sex workers either via intimidation tactics or by creating psychological dependency. A presumption in favour of those living with sex workers for exploitive purposes therefore makes prosecuting pimps feasible in many scenarios in which otherwise they would be untouchable. At the same time, an accused who does not live on the avails of sex work should have little difficulty providing evidence to raise a reasonable doubt about this fact.[183]

The minority justices refused to uphold the law under section 1 of the Charter. Writing for himself, Justice La Forest concluded that the prohibition against living on the avails of sex work was not minimally impairing for two interrelated reasons. First, the provision was drafted broadly enough to catch many "people who have legitimate, non-parasitic living arrangements with prostitutes."[184] Second, and more importantly, the Crown provided inadequate empirical evidence that it was necessary for Parliament to cast the prohibition so broadly to attain its objective of facilitating the prosecution of pimps.[185]

Justice McLachlin (Justice Iacobucci concurring) went further and found that the prohibition against living on the avails of sex work was not rationally connected to its objective. For a law to be connected to its objective, she maintained, it must be both internally and externally valid.[186] The law was internally illogical because it was not *likely* that the presumed fact would follow from the fact substituted by the presumption.[187] There were simply too many exceptions to make the impugned presumption reasonable. As McLachlin observed, "[s]pouses, lovers, friends, children, parents, room-mates, business associates, [and] providers of goods and services" could all fall into this category.[188]

A law's external rationality turns on whether the law furthers its purported objective.[189] For Justice McLachlin, it was unlikely that the law actually served to protect sex workers from exploitation by pimps.

As she observed, "[t]he effect of the presumption is to compel prostitutes to live and work alone, deprived of human relationships save with those whom they are prepared to expose to the risk of a criminal charge and conviction and who are themselves prepared to flaunt that possibility."[190] As such, sex workers cannot live with friends and family members or enter into protective arrangements with others. McLachlin therefore inferred that the living on the avails offence forced sex workers onto the streets and into the hands of exploitive pimps, thereby undermining Parliament's purpose. Legislation that undermines its own purpose cannot be rationally connected to its objective.[191]

LEGAL AND EVIDENTIARY GAPS

The Supreme Court's early jurisprudence rightly has been criticized for failing to consider the various harms posed to sex workers by the impugned sex work laws. As Maria Powell suggests, "[t]he issue of harms and the wealth of evidence supporting the fact that the impugned provisions of the *Criminal Code* aggravate the harms faced by sex workers were not put forward in the *Prostitution Reference*."[192] In her view, "[a]part from the recommendations of the Special Committee on Pornography and Prostitution [the Fraser Committee] which were released in 1985, much of the evidence relied upon in the *Bedford* case was not available at the time of the *Prostitution Reference*."[193]

Alan Young agrees that there was limited evidence before the courts pertaining to the harms caused by the sex work laws.[194] Citing various documents related to the legislative history of Bill C-49, Young nevertheless observes that Parliament was clearly "aware of the risk of harm increasing [from outdoor sex work] but mistakenly concluded that moving inside was an available legal option to mitigate the risks of working on the streets."[195] Since some evidence was before the Supreme Court, Young maintains, the primary problem was that the evidence was not tied to appropriate constitutional principles.[196] Yet, as he concedes, it is unlikely that the Supreme Court would strike down a law without a substantial amount of empirical evidence.[197] The limited evidence cited therefore renders it doubtful that the Supreme Court

38 | *The Logic of* Bedford

had sufficient evidence to base its decision on any harms that accrued to sex workers.[198]

Young is nevertheless correct that the underdeveloped nature of the Charter is partially responsible for the sex work laws initially surviving constitutional scrutiny.[199] The relatively young age of the Charter resulted in the section 7 challenge considering only whether the impugned laws were unconstitutionally vague. Given the ability of judges to interpret legislation, it is difficult to prove that a law is so vague that courts cannot understand it.[200] Yet a more detailed assessment of the law's effects on sex worker safety raised the prospect of a broader legal challenge. Unfortunately for the applicants, the two principles used to strike down laws based on flawed means-ends rationality – overbreadth and gross disproportionality – had not yet been recognized as principles of fundamental justice.[201]

A final explanation of the limited evidence and constitutional arguments relates to the parties that participated in the proceedings. One of the most important and long-standing Canadian feminist organizations – the Women's Legal Education and Advocacy Fund (LEAF) – was not involved in the litigation. When asked why LEAF did not apply for intervenor status, Kathleen Mahoney replied that the organization was very busy at the time.[202] More illuminating, she stated that, "no matter what these women say about themselves, they are all 'tortured, drug-addicted, extremely unhappy, abused people.'"[203] As Janice McGinnis later observed, LEAF happily contributed to a variety of anti-pornography cases but was unwilling to engage with women's rights in the sex work context.[204] This was because LEAF explicitly viewed sex workers as victims, not as autonomous agents. The emphasis from a law reform perspective was therefore to control pimps and johns, which might have distracted from LEAF's ability to listen to the concerns of sex workers. Without representation from LEAF, it was much less likely that the various feminist perspectives on sex work regulation would be raised.[205]

2

The Road to *Bedford*

THE SUPREME COURT's decisions upholding the communication, bawdy house, and living on the avails prohibitions were disappointing to many sex work advocates. They knew that changing the sex work laws would be formidable given the relative recency of the Supreme Court's decisions and the political unpopularity of sex workers more generally. When the constitutional challenge in *Bedford* was filed in 2007, the applicants and their counsel believed that the evidentiary and political tide had shifted adequately to justify bringing a second constitutional challenge. Utilizing a "shoestring Legal Aid budget," the applicants convinced a network of sex work advocates to volunteer their services to help convince the courts to reconsider the constitutionality of the sex work laws.[1]

Foremost among those volunteers was Alan Young, lead counsel for the applicants in *Bedford* and long-time advocate for the marginalized and politically unpopular. Drawing from a personal interview with Young and other publicly available materials,[2] I offer insights into the sociolegal rationale for bringing the *Bedford* challenge a mere decade and a half after those laws were upheld. As Young explains, he was motivated to bring the case because of a personal belief that the state was inefficaciously using the criminal law to address what is often a consensual transaction. For Young, however, it was the availability of improved evidence of the dangers faced by sex workers and the evolution

40 | *The Logic of* Bedford

of section 7 of the Charter that created a promising atmosphere for rechallenging the sex work laws. Amassing the relevant evidence and convincing the courts to hear the novel constitutional challenge nevertheless posed significant barriers to striking down the sex work laws.

EMPIRICAL EVIDENCE

Apart from several limited studies of the health implications[3] and history of sex work in Canada,[4] little research existed on sex work by the mid-twentieth century.[5] As the topic became more popular in the 1970s, researchers began using social science research methods to understand sex work better. This early interest was largely influenced by the public's perception that sex work was becoming an increasingly pressing social problem. Decisions by municipal police departments in Vancouver and Toronto to close off sex work venues pushed sex work onto the streets, where it became more visible to the public.[6] At the same time, the Supreme Court's narrow interpretation of the term "solicit" in *R v Hutt*[7] raised public fears about sex workers overtaking the streets and turning them into "sexual supermarkets."[8]

Public pressure to respond to the nuisances arising from sex work resulted in the federal government commissioning both the Badgley Report and the Fraser Report.[9] The Badgley Report provided the first national survey of Canadian sex workers and included findings from interviews with over 200 street workers. The Fraser Report also conducted interview-based research on the effects of the sex work laws on street workers.[10] Shortly after the adoption of the communication offence in 1985, the federal government funded several further studies on the efficacy of the communication provision.[11] Academic researchers were also conducting local and regional studies of sex workers during this time.[12] As John Lowman explains, this early research collectively revealed that street workers typically enter the trade as minors, are disproportionately Indigenous, and frequently have backgrounds of sexual abuse.[13] It also revealed that sex workers enter and continue in the trade for a variety of reasons, including pressures exerted by pimps, drug addiction, and the provision of basic necessities of life.[14]

The Road to Bedford | 41

Although this early research provided a limited basis for understanding some of the dangers faced by sex workers, Young maintains that it was the discovery of dozens of sex workers' remains on Robert Pickton's pig farm in Port Coquitlam, British Columbia that solidified the dangerous nature of sex work in the public eye. Beginning in 2002, police began investigating a man who would end up being the most heinous serial murderer in Canadian history.[15] While conducting a search warrant for illegally stored firearms, the police found various belongings of female sex workers who had gone missing from the Downtown Eastside of Vancouver.[16] This evidence elevated Pickton to the status of prime suspect in an investigation known as Project Even-Handed, a joint RCMP–Vancouver Police task force investigating missing sex workers from the region. Using the victims' belongings as a basis to secure a broader warrant to search Pickton's farm, the police were eventually able to identify the remains of thirty-three sex workers.[17]

As the trial judge warned the jury, the facts in the Pickton case were "as bad as a horror movie."[18] Among the more egregious evidence disclosed during the trial was the discovery of "two women's heads in a freezer, cleaved in two and packed with their hands and feet."[19] Other bodies were also disposed of in a gruesome fashion.[20] News spread that many of the bodies were fed to Pickton's pigs or butchered and ground into meat, some of which was sold to the public.[21] Although initially Pickton was only tried and found guilty on six counts of second-degree murder, he was charged with the deaths of twenty more women. Unfortunately, these charges were stayed because Pickton had already received the maximum allowable sentence for murder: life in prison with no possibility of parole for twenty-five years.[22] The inability to identify the seven other known victims prevented any further charges, and evidence suggests that Pickton killed sixteen more sex workers whose bodies were not recovered.[23]

As the trial judge observed in *Bedford,* the Pickton murders were not the first to target sex workers. Expert testimony demonstrated that sex workers in various foreign jurisdictions are often targeted by serial killers because they are vulnerable, marginalized, and therefore less likely to be reported missing.[24] For instance, "Jack the Ripper" murdered

42 | *The Logic of* Bedford

between five and eleven sex workers in late-nineteenth-century London. Around the same time, Thomas Cream – also known as the "Lambeth Poisoner" – killed nine people, most of whom were sex workers. In the 1970s, the "Yorkshire Ripper," Peter Sutcliffe, killed at least thirteen women, many of whom were sex workers. Arthur Shawcross – the "Genesee River Killer" – and Joel Rifkin independently committed similar atrocities in the 1980s and 1990s. More recently, Gary Ridgway, known as the "Green River Killer," confessed to killing forty-eight women, most of whom were sex workers.[25]

Yet it would be misleading to suggest that sex workers going missing in Canada began with Pickton. Although the appalling nature of his murders greatly increased public awareness of the harms endured by sex workers,[26] police knew of similar atrocities occurring on a stretch of Highway 16 in northern British Columbia called the "Highway of Tears." As many as forty-three women – many of whom were sex workers and/or Indigenous – went missing or were found murdered along this highway.[27] Project KARE in Alberta is similarly investigating over eighty cases in the Edmonton area, where a serial murderer is suspected of targeting sex workers.[28] The recently disbanded Project Devote in Winnipeg underwent a similar investigation of twenty-eight missing and murdered persons.[29]

Parliament's unwillingness to reform the sex work laws in light of these various murders provided one of the strongest motivations to re-litigate the constitutionality of those laws. For Young, more concrete evidence that the laws contributed materially to these risks – evidence that I review when detailing the *Bedford* decision in the next chapter – made it imperative for the safety of sex workers that the laws be struck down. The Supreme Court in *Bedford* agreed. As Chief Justice McLachlin would later observe, "[i]f screening could have prevented one woman from jumping into Robert Pickton's car, the severity of the harmful effects is established."[30] In other words, no matter the degree of nuisance avoided by the sex work laws, their ability to contribute materially to the loss of a single life would impose effects inconsistent with fundamental justice.

The Road to Bedford | 43

EVOLUTION OF THE CHARTER

The second major development that Young maintained opened the door to re-challenging the sex work laws concerned the "principles of fundamental justice" under section 7 of the Charter. During the first few decades of litigation under section 7, the courts relied heavily on principles of criminal law theory when constitutionalizing principles of fundamental justice. Near the turn of the century, however, the Supreme Court increasingly began to overturn judgments constitutionalizing new principles of criminal law theory. Foremost among these judgments was *R v Malmo-Levine,*[31] a case that Young also brought to the Supreme Court. Unlike in *Bedford,* Young lost the case in spectacular fashion since the Supreme Court refused to constitutionalize John Stuart Mill's harm principle: a prohibition against state interference with conduct that does not harm another person.[32] Failure to constitutionalize this arch-liberal principle strongly suggested to Young that he would need to look elsewhere for relevant constitutional principles when challenging the constitutionality of the sex work laws.

Fortunately for Young, courts interpreting section 7 of the Charter had also begun to slowly develop a different method of judicial review shortly after the *Sex Work Reference* was decided. These principles of fundamental justice are commonly referred to as the principles of "means-ends" or "instrumental rationality." Beginning in 1994, the Supreme Court developed a principle requiring that any law that engages an individual's life, liberty, or security of the person interests must not be overbroad. Explaining this principle in *R v Heywood,*[33] the Supreme Court observed that, if a law's effects were not reasonably necessary to obtain its objective, then the law would be inconsistent with fundamental justice.[34]

Although the Supreme Court in *Malmo-Levine* rejected the harm principle, it nevertheless confirmed the constitutional status of a further instrumental rationality principle. This principle provides that a law's effects must not be "grossly disproportionate" compared with its ability to achieve its objective.[35] Unlike the prohibition against grossly

44 | *The Logic of* Bedford

disproportionate punishment in section 12 of the Charter,[36] gross disproportionality under section 7 considers any nonpunitive effects of a law on an individual's threshold interests.[37] For Young, this principle was vital to constitutionally challenging the sex work laws. As he aptly put it, "gross disproportionality is having a human skull in some predatory criminal's kitchen."[38] Since the purpose of the bawdy house and communication prohibitions was to avoid minor social nuisances, his argument that these effects were unconstitutional compared with the laws' objectives seemed to be "incontrovertible."[39]

The Supreme Court's adoption of the overbreadth and gross disproportionality principles marked an important shift in the types of principles that the court employed under section 7 of the Charter. By changing the emphasis from constitutionalizing principles of criminal law theory to principles that measured a law's instrumental rationality, section 7 jurisprudence sought to make the task of challenging a law's constitutionality easier.[40] As opposed to offering an often-complex theoretical critique of a law, the applicant need only do two things. First, the applicant had to determine the impugned law's objective. That could be done by reading the law's substance and delving into parliamentary debates and other records on why the law was enacted. Second, the applicant had to devise scenarios outlining the law's effects on the life, liberty, and security of the person interests of those affected by the law. Fundamental justice would be violated if those effects were adequately disconnected from the law's objective or imposed too severe consequences.

As the Supreme Court recognized in *Bedford,* despite the instrumental rationality principles being simple to apply in theory, they nevertheless imposed a significant burden of proof on the applicant. The overbreadth and gross disproportionality principles originally measured the law's effects against its objectives in a "holistic" manner. In other words, the applicant was tasked with proving that the law's effects on *all* citizens were overbroad or grossly disproportionate when measured against the law's ability to obtain its objective.[41] To conduct such a challenge in the sex work context, it was therefore necessary to amass thousands of pages of reports, studies, and expert evidence testing

The Road to Bedford | 45

the attainability of the government's objectives and the effects of the sex work laws.[42] This reality gave rise to a further barrier.

THE COST OF LITIGATION

Various legal scholars have written about the high cost of litigating Charter issues. As Benjamin Berger observes, "the great promise of *Charter* jurisprudence is dependent upon a litigant clearing the practical hurdle of costs."[43] Kent Roach similarly identifies the cost of litigation as "[o]ne of the main impediments to obtaining effective and meaningful *Charter* remedies."[44] Robert Sharpe echoes this sentiment, noting that, "[w]hile our system of justice delivers quality results, it often does so at a cost that shuts the courtroom door to all but the well-to-do."[45] For Andrew Petter, "[c]osts like these represent a formidable obstacle to disadvantaged and even middle-income Canadians who wish to pursue their *Charter* rights in the courts."[46]

Drawing from his vast experience litigating Charter issues, Young estimates that the cost of a constitutional challenge will exceed $1 million in cases in which the applicant must present extensive social science evidence.[47] For the *Bedford* case, Young was able to obtain funds only from Legal Aid Ontario's Test Case Program and only after reapplying for those funds.[48] The program initially provided him with $45,269 to fund the trial and to reply to the Crown's appeal.[49] Young later received a stipend of $26,500 to cover administrative costs related to the case's eventual appeal to the Supreme Court. In addition, he received funding to hire a co-counsel at the Supreme Court.[50] Legal Aid Ontario's compensation for senior counsel was $136.43 per hour, a fee less than half of what most senior counsel charge.[51] The co-counsel's salary nevertheless increased the cost of the Supreme Court hearing to $85,876, nearly double the initial funds provided for the combined lower court hearings.[52]

As Young explains, the allotted funding was "modest ... for a case involving over 60 witnesses (most of whom were cross-examined), 27,000 pages of documentary evidence, 7 days to hear the application

46 | *The Logic of* Bedford

and 5 days of argument ... in the Court of Appeal," as well as a hearing at the Supreme Court. Even charging at a significantly reduced rate for senior counsel services, Young estimates that his legal fees would have totalled $450,000 to run the trial alone.[53] Fortunately for the applicants, he did not charge any legal fees. He nevertheless required funding for various disbursement expenses, including $11,720 for transcribing the cross-examinations of the Crown's thirty witnesses and $5,749 for photocopying the eighty-eight-volume evidentiary record.[54] Although Young was able to convince the various experts who testified on the applicants' behalf to volunteer their services, he was also required to pay for various costs related to their travel and accommodations, taking a further $11,963 from his budget.[55]

Fortunately for Young, his position as a law professor at Osgoode Hall Law School allowed him to lower the costs of litigation in other ways. Importantly, he was able to recruit approximately three dozen students either to volunteer their services or to work as research assistants for fifteen dollars an hour. These students significantly reduced the amount of work that Young was required to invest in preparing for trial. He subsequently concluded that he spent approximately 500 hours preparing the *Bedford* application and that without extensive student assistance his preparation would have been approximately 1,500 hours.[56] Young also noted that a major part of the students' workload involved drafting affidavit evidence from expert witnesses. He maintained that if the experts were required to write their own affidavits – as opposed to proofread the work of law students – then many of them would have been much less likely to volunteer their services.[57]

GETTING THE CASE TO COURT

A final and more practical obstacle also arose: Under which circumstances would a court agree to hear the applicants' challenge? It was highly unlikely that any government would send another reference to the courts. It would also be difficult to convince a litigant charged with the relevant offences to allow an advocacy lawyer to constitutionally challenge the impugned laws. This left one final procedural avenue for bringing the case: an application based on public or private interest standing. To bring such an application, Young joined forces with Terri-Jean Bedford, Valerie Scott, and Amy Lebovitch and ultimately was successful in convincing the courts to reconsider the constitutionality of the sex work laws.

Finding a Litigant

As the Supreme Court observed in *Canada (Attorney General) v Downtown Eastside Sex Workers United against Violence Society*[58] – a case involving parallel litigants seeking standing to constitutionally challenge the sex work laws – the "practical realities" of such a constitutional challenge made it "very unlikely that persons charged under these provisions would bring a claim similar to the respondents."[59] The first major barrier relates to the economic realities of constitutional litigation. Individual sex workers charged with a nonserious criminal offence are much more likely to plead guilty and receive a light sentence than expend personal time and resources challenging the constitutionality of an offence. Indeed, many sex workers viewed the fines that they typically received for violating the sex work laws as a "licensing fee."[60] Clients also face similar economic barriers. For instance, the only post–*Sex Work Reference* constitutional challenge of the communication prohibition lacked an evidentiary record to prove the harms alleged to accrue to sex workers as a result of that provision.[61] This was likely because of the high cost of calling expert evidence to prove a Charter violation.

The Supreme Court in *Downtown Eastside* further noted that the inherent unpredictability of the litigation process made bringing a traditional constitutional challenge to the sex work laws less practical. Citing a post–*Sex Work Reference* challenge to the communication offence, *R v Hamilton*,[62] the Supreme Court noted that the Crown stayed the proceedings without providing any explanation to the court set to hear the challenge.[63] Young observed that this Crown strategy had also been used against him on multiple occasions when he had instituted a constitutional challenge on behalf of a person charged with an offence. Often the state would rather let an accused person go free

48 | *The Logic of* Bedford

than expend significant time and energy defending a complex constitutional challenge.

Convincing those charged with a sex work offence to challenge the laws constitutionally is also less likely given the nature of the sex work trade. As the Supreme Court noted in *Downtown Eastside,* "there were no sex workers in the Downtown Eastside neighbourhood of Vancouver willing to bring a comprehensive challenge forward."[64] Many sex workers "feared loss of privacy and safety and increased violence by clients."[65] A sex worker's privacy would be infringed if their spouse, friends, or family members discovered that the applicant was a sex worker. This likely would occur since a constitutional challenge to the sex work laws is highly likely to be covered by the media. Such exposure can also limit a sex worker's "current or future education or employment opportunities" and feasibly could be insulting to clients, which could increase the potential for future violence.[66]

These various barriers justified employing a different procedure for challenging the constitutionality of the sex work laws. That procedure, known as an application for "declaratory relief" in Ontario,[67] allows sufficiently affected applicants to challenge the constitutionality of a law without being charged with an offence. As Young observed, employing this procedural method could avoid some of the obstacles identified in *Downtown Eastside.* This is because an application for declaratory relief need not rely on a current sex worker to challenge the sex work laws. Instead, it is possible to convince former sex workers to be representative plaintiffs.

The first of the applicants in *Bedford* fit precisely this profile. Young knew Valerie Scott through her sex workers' rights advocacy. Given her advocacy work and the fact that she was no longer a sex worker, she was open about her experience in the sex work trade. As Young observed, Scott was also an intelligent and articulate person who could withstand the publicity that likely would come along with the case. Amy Lebovitch was also a sex workers' rights advocate and thus public about her experience as a sex worker. Young learned about Lebovitch by asking Scott whether she could find a current sex worker to participate in the constitutional challenge. As I explain below, the law was unclear about

The Road to Bedford | 49

whether a group of former sex workers would be permitted to launch a constitutional challenge on their own, and Young wanted to avoid losing the case on procedural grounds.

The relationship between Terri-Jean Bedford and Young was more complex. Young met Bedford during a criminal hearing in 1999 as a result of her being charged with running a bawdy house, and he volunteered to help with her case. Although Bedford was ultimately convicted,[68] the case attracted a significant amount of media attention since the main issue was whether BDSM (bondage, discipline, sado-masochism) constituted sexual activity for the purposes of the bawdy house offence. Bedford – dubbed by the media as the "Bondage Bungalow Dominatrix" – proved to be popular with the media, as she recounts in her memoirs.[69] This made her an ideal person to be the face of a constitutional challenge that surely would attract similar if not greater media attention than her previous encounters with the law.

Bedford did not disappoint, and even the highest echelons of government did not escape her criticism. After winning at trial, Bedford responded to the trial judge's decision to stay the proceedings pending appeal by telling Prime Minister Stephen Harper to "fight like a man" and address the issues with legislation as opposed to hiding behind the courts.[70] Harper jokingly responded by noting that he had "never been called upon to respond to a dominatrix before."[71] Displeased with Harper's response, Bedford, while awaiting the Ontario Court of Appeal's decision, promised to take her "riding crop to Parliament Hill and get that dead horse, Stephen Harper, moving."[72] After winning at the Supreme Court, Bedford even offered her services to Harper as a "government whip" in the Senate.[73] For Young, the media attention that Bedford was able to generate was valuable not only for bolstering the case but also for generating awareness of the dangers faced by sex workers in the post-*Bedford* legal environment.

Private Interest Standing
Receiving standing to raise a constitutional issue when the person is not charged with the relevant offences requires that the applicant demonstrate either private or public interest standing.[74] To achieve the

50 | *The Logic of* Bedford

former, each applicant must demonstrate a "special interest" in the challenged legislation.[75] The Crown conceded that one of the applicants – Lebovitch – had private interest standing because she was a sex worker at the time of the application and therefore maintained a special interest in the constitutionality of the laws.[76] As Young predicted, the Crown nevertheless maintained that Bedford and Scott did not have standing because they were former sex workers.[77] In the Crown's view, the suggestion by the latter applicants that they would return to sex work if barriers to engagement in such work were removed was inadequate to grant them a "special interest" in the proceedings.[78]

The trial judge in *Bedford* disagreed. As she observed, "[a]ll three applicants allege that they are prevented from engaging in their livelihood, either safely or at all, by the provisions. This gives all three applicants a direct, personal interest in the outcome of this application that is different than the general member of the public."[79] The appellate courts demurred. The reality was that one of the applicants was currently a sex worker and therefore had private interest standing. As a result, the constitutional issues raised in the case were properly before the courts. The Ontario Court of Appeal therefore declined to address whether the other two applicants also had private interest standing,[80] and the Supreme Court did not raise the issue. Instead, the appellate courts focused on the substantive merits of the constitutional challenge.

3

The *Bedford* Decision

THE APPLICANTS IN *BEDFORD* were successful in their application to the Ontario Superior Court of Justice to strike down the three sex work laws. This constituted the first time that a trial court overturned a Supreme Court decision upholding a law under the Charter of Rights and Freedoms. However, because of the *stare decisis* principle, the trial judgment was not binding on other provinces' courts. It was therefore imperative that the *Bedford* decision be appealed through the regular court process. Despite the Ontario Court of Appeal partially overturning the trial judge's decision,[1] the Supreme Court upheld the trial decision and rendered the laws of no force or effect across the country subject to a one-year suspended declaration of invalidity.

The Supreme Court's rationale for overturning its prior precedents is plain on the surface. The court isolated the two problems identified with the *Sex Work Reference* and *Downey:* limited social science evidence and underdeveloped constitutional principles. The broader evidentiary record pertaining to the harms endured by sex workers resulted in the Supreme Court concluding that each law violated the instrumental rationality principles of fundamental justice. Given the Supreme Court's earlier ruling that violations of section 7 of the Charter are practically impossible to justify,[2] the Crown did not explicitly attempt to uphold

52 | *The Logic of* Bedford

the laws under section 1. Instead, it settled for obtaining a suspended declaration of invalidity.

THE EVIDENTIARY RECORD

The main difference between the evidence submitted in the *Sex Work Reference, Downey,* and *Bedford* was that the former cases did not focus on the experiences of sex workers. It became apparent from their testimony that sex workers were not concerned about the "vagueness" of the laws or whether an evidentiary onus violated the presumption of innocence. Instead, they were concerned about the dangers that these laws posed to them and in particular to street workers. The record illuminating these perspectives at trial was voluminous.[3] In addition to hearing lay witnesses' personal experiences of sex work, the parties provided a detailed review of social science research linking the harms incurred by sex workers to the sex work laws.

The Applicants

Terri-Jean Bedford left her sexually, physically, and psychologically abusive home at the age of sixteen. She was subsequently sent to a boarding house in Windsor, where she was introduced to drugs by an older male companion. Shortly thereafter, she began engaging in sex work to pay for their drug addiction. This was the beginning of her fourteen years of experience as a sex worker in various cities across Canada.[4] During this time, she worked as a street worker, escort, massage parlour attendant, and dominatrix, and at one point she owned and managed an escort agency. In an affidavit filed with the trial court, Bedford stated that she was "raped and gang-raped too many times to talk about" and that she was beaten on the head with a baseball bat as well as tortured both physically and psychologically.[5]

Bedford further testified about her experience working indoors – both as a manager and as a sex worker – and contrasted this experience with working on the street. In her experience, indoor sex work was much safer, though she admitted that the safety of any bawdy house depends primarily on the precautions taken by those in charge. Speaking to her experience of employing eighteen escorts, Bedford testified that she was not aware of a single incident of violence during the two years that she ran the bawdy house.[6] She described a variety of safety procedures, which included ensuring that someone was present during in-calls with unfamiliar clients; that escorts were accompanied during calls; that the client's name, number, and credit card information were recorded; and that appointments with intoxicated clients were cancelled.[7]

Unfortunately for Bedford, her escort service was raided by the police, and she was charged with several sex work–related offences. Initially, she absconded to Calgary and Vancouver to work as a street worker and escort, but eventually she returned to Windsor to face the charges. She was sentenced to fifteen months in prison as a result.[8] After being released, Bedford worked briefly as an administrative assistant but was quickly laid off. Given her lack of marketable skills, she returned to work at various massage parlours and was charged multiple times with being an inmate in a bawdy house.[9] She subsequently set up a bondage house that offered sado-masochistic services but did not engage in explicitly sexual actions or "extreme sado-masochistic role play." Despite the absence of penetrative sex, the *Criminal Code* definition of "prostitution" – exchanging sexual services for money – was broad enough to catch Bedford's conduct and resulted again in her being convicted for bawdy house–related charges.[10] Bedford expressed a desire to resume working as a dominatrix in a secure, indoor location, but given the potential for criminal liability she abstained from such work.[11]

Unlike Bedford, Amy Lebovitch grew up in a normal and supportive home. She finished high school with high academic standing and had various employment opportunities but chose to be a sex worker to obtain money quickly and gain independence. Lebovitch worked as a street worker and escort and in a fetish house, and she was a sex worker at the time of the application to strike down the sex work laws. She moved off the streets after seeing other street workers "black and blue" and hearing their many horrifying accounts of violence that they had endured.[12] She testified that working indoors was much safer than

54 | *The Logic of* Bedford

working on the street, though indoor sex work could become dangerous if poorly managed.[13]

After two years of sex work, Lebovitch attended the University of Ottawa to study criminology and psychology. To support her studies, she worked at an indoor fetish house performing BDSM and other traditional sexual services. During this time, she experienced a single instance of violence in which she was tied up and raped by one of the clients. She attributed that experience to poor management of the bawdy house arising from a lack of screening clientele.[14] Shortly after this experience, Lebovitch moved to Toronto, where she attended Ryerson University's social work program. During this time, she transitioned to independent work from her home and limited outcalls to hotel rooms. She did so because she feared conviction under the bawdy house provision. She also feared that her partner would be charged with living on the avails of sex work since the two cohabited.[15]

Lebovitch was also employed as a spokesperson for an organization called the Sex Professionals of Canada (SPOC). The group was described by Justice Himel, the trial judge in *Bedford,* as "a political group that works towards decriminalization through political activism, community building and public awareness."[16] In that capacity, Lebovitch gave numerous talks at Canadian universities and to the media about the nature of sex work in Canada. She also sought, recorded, and distributed information from sex workers reporting "bad dates." This term is slang for "incidents which ended in violence or theft at the expense of prostitutes." As Lebovitch observed, several sex workers' rights organizations keep lists of "bad dates" and distribute them to sex workers.[17]

Valerie Scott began "dabbling" in sex work when she was fifteen years old.[18] At first, she worked in a massage parlour, then as an erotic dancer, and later as a sex worker. At various points in her life, she provided sexual services on the street, in massage parlours, from her home, or in hotel rooms. She also ran a small escort business for four and a half years.[19] While working from home, she screened clients on her own before engaging in sexual relations with them. During this time, Scott maintained that she never experienced "significant harm."[20]

The Bedford *Decision* | 55

While working as a street worker, however, she was often subjected to threats of violence as well as verbal and physical abuse. Fortunately for Scott, she worked on the streets only for four months, after which time she returned to providing sexual services indoors.[21] She eventually left sex work in 1993 because of chronic pain but wanted to rejoin the profession if barriers to safe practice were removed from the *Criminal Code.*[22]

Throughout her time as a sex worker, Scott consistently advocated for the legalization of sex work. She first joined the Canadian Organization for the Rights of Prostitutes in the mid-1980s, a group that advocated publicly for the decriminalization of prostitution. As a result of her involvement, Scott provided submissions to the Legislative Committee on Bill C-49 that ultimately proposed a broader communication provision contrary to her advice. As discussed earlier, Bill C-49 was passed in response to the Supreme Court's decision in *R v Hutt*[23] and significantly narrowed the applicability of Parliament's first ban on communicating in public for the purposes of sex work. Scott warned that Bill C-49's broadly proposed communication provision "would result in the death and injury of street prostitutes," but her warning went unheeded.[24] Following the adoption of Bill C-49, Scott joined the National Action Committee on the Status of Women. In that capacity, she called for the repeal of the new communication provision as well as the bawdy house and living on the avails offences.[25]

Scott also helped to establish Maggie's, a drop-in and phone centre for sex workers operating in Toronto. In her first year in this position, she spoke to approximately 250 sex workers who expressed serious concerns about client violence and the legal and social consequences arising from being arrested for sex work. While at Maggie's, Scott also began compiling and distributing "bad date" lists to local sex workers. Later in her career, she founded SPOC. She continued developing "bad date" lists with other sex workers, including Lebovitch. As the executive director of SPOC, Scott testified in 2005 before the House of Commons Subcommittee on Solicitation Laws about the need for law reform. Leading up to her appearance, she estimated that she had

56 | *The Logic of* Bedford

spoken with approximately 1,500 sex workers during her time as a sex worker and working at Maggie's and SPOC.[26]

Lay Witnesses

Various other lay witnesses were called by both the applicants and the Crown to buttress or undermine the applicants' experiences.[27] The applicants first called eight other former sex workers to corroborate their observations. They generally affirmed that indoor sex work is much safer than street sex work, though they recognized that indoor work could become dangerous with poor management.[28] The Crown also called several sex workers as witnesses in an attempt to paint all sex work as inherently dangerous. These witnesses confirmed that violence happened indoors as well as on the street. However, they did not explain the management policies of the bawdy houses where high risks of danger were present.[29] Both the applicants' and the respondent's evidence from sex workers was corroborated by various lay witnesses selected to echo each party's particular narrative. These witnesses included sex work advocates, politicians, a journalist who had written extensively on the sex trade, and a social worker.[30]

The Crown also submitted evidence from nine police officers with experience investigating sex work offences. Although the officers testified that most sex work occurs indoors, the vast majority of their experience was limited to investigating street workers for violations of the communication provision.[31] Recalling data from Toronto, one officer testified that between 2005 and 2007 only forty-nine charges were laid under the living on the avails provision and eighty-two charges under the bawdy house provision, whereas 2,377 charges were laid under the communication provision.[32] Likely because their investigative experiences focused on street sex work, these officers characterized sex workers as victims typically "poverty-stricken, abused and drug-addicted" and overrepresented by Indigenous women.[33] Despite their abolitionist stance, the officers cross-examined admitted that street sex work is far more dangerous than indoor sex work since the various precautions detailed by the applicants and affirmed by their expert witnesses can be taken to avoid violent clients.[34]

Expert Evidence

Numerous Canadian and international social science experts on sex work and research methods testified for both parties in *Bedford*.[35] The expert witnesses all acknowledged various limitations to social science research on sex work. First, the research is largely qualitative, not quantitative, because of general difficulties in getting sex workers to participate in research and the limited number and fluidity of sex workers who engage in the trade. Without high numbers of research participants, it is impossible to conduct statistical analysis capable of producing conclusive results.[36] Second, drawing causal inferences is difficult because employing random sampling methods is typically not possible with sex work research. This is because the population size of sex workers is not known. Researchers must therefore limit their conclusions to the sample studied and avoid making broader generalizations.[37] Third, sex work–related research tends to focus on street workers since they are the most accessible to researchers. Indoor sex work, far more common than street sex work, is underresearched.[38]

These limitations prevented the parties from agreeing on the merits of the expert evidence provided in *Bedford*. As the trial judge observed, significant portions of each party's arguments were devoted to criticizing the various expert witnesses called at trial. These criticisms included allegations of bias, overgeneralized conclusions, and methodological errors in study designs.[39] As a result, the competing experts agreed on little about the nature of sex work. In sum, they agreed that street work is dangerous; that all sex work, including indoor work, carries some risk of violence; that significant social stigma attaches to sex work; and that multiple factors are responsible for the violence faced by sex workers.[40] Importantly, they disagreed about whether indoor sex work is or can be made safer than street sex work, whether indoor sex workers are more capable of preventing harm to themselves than street sex workers, and whether the sex work laws materially contributed to the risk of harm faced by sex workers.[41]

The applicants' expert witnesses also spoke about stereotypes and misperceptions of sex work in Canada. First, they observed that a significant number of sex workers choose to enter the trade not because

58 | *The Logic of* Bedford

they are victims but because they believe it to be better employment than unskilled labour.[42] Second, these experts maintained that homeless, drug-addicted sex workers (common traits of survival sex workers) represent a relatively small percentage of sex workers and that pimping is far less prevalent than the media suggest.[43]

The applicants' expert witnesses further concluded that indoor sex work can be made safer by employing a variety of strategies to mitigate threats from customers. These strategies echoed those discussed by the applicants, including providing sex workers with "greater control over their physical environment, close proximity to others who can intervene if help is needed, the ability to better screen out dangerous clients ... a more regular clientele, the use of drivers to get to and from appointments, and response plans for dangerous situations."[44] The applicants' experts also generally agreed that the available research suggests that how a bawdy house is run will affect sex worker safety.[45] In contrast, they noted that out-call work is inherently more dangerous because "it is difficult to assess the safety of a destination beforehand, the client may not be alone, and exit routes may not be easily identifiable or accessible."[46]

The applicants' experts also agreed that the sex work laws exacerbated the dangers faced by sex workers. The prohibition against maintaining a bawdy house forced sex workers to work on the streets or participate in out-calls. The communication prohibition resulted in sex workers being reluctant to screen their clientele by negotiating terms in advance or checking for intoxication, weapons, or the absence of door handles and lock release buttons. Although sex workers with higher incomes might mitigate these risks by hiring drivers or bodyguards, such tactics were made illegal by the prohibition against living on the avails of sex work.[47] The overall risks facing sex workers were further exacerbated because the provisions created a conflicting "victim/criminal" status in the eyes of the police. As a result, sex workers were unlikely to report instances of violence for fear of being charged with a sex work offence.[48]

The Crown's experts largely maintained that sex work is inherently harmful since it is a form of violence against women. This violence derives from the power imbalance between sex workers and their predominantly male clients.[49] The experts also maintained that sex work has a strong link to a number of other harmful activities, such as drug addiction, organized crime, and human trafficking.[50] These experts further observed that there is significant fluidity between sex workers working indoors and outdoors. Because sex workers frequently change locations, the distinction between these venues arguably is not helpful in understanding the violence faced by sex workers.[51] Despite the research of the Crown's lead expert witness conceding that there is "significantly" more violence in street sex work, the witness maintained that there is an equal amount of "psychological violence" against sex workers who work in indoor and outdoor venues.[52]

Relying on a study commissioned by the federal government in the mid-1980s commonly cited as the Fraser Report,[53] the Crown further asserted that sex work in general constituted a societal nuisance. The report noted that street sex work impedes the flow of traffic, that it results in noise in the early hours of the morning, and that many people are approached by sex workers despite having no interest in buying sex.[54] The report nevertheless failed to find any connection between sex work and organized crime.[55] It also found that sex work is a dangerous profession for all parties involved. In so concluding, however, it was clear that these dangers derive in large part from "the way in which street prostitution is currently carried out," implying that sex work could be made safer by moving indoors and taking other basic safety precautions.[56] Despite the report's recommendation to remove the communication provision, rewrite the living on the avails provision to target exploitive relationships, and allow for limited numbers of sex workers to work from bawdy houses, Parliament responded by passing Bill C-49, which ignored the latter recommendations and made the communication provision much stricter than its predecessor.[57]

Three years after Bill C-49 was adopted, Parliament commissioned another report to study the effects of the new communication law. The Synthesis Report[58] concluded that the stricter communication provision reduced sex work in some parts of the country. However, the law had

60 | *The Logic of* Bedford

little effect in larger urban centres other than to displace sex workers and significantly lengthen their criminal records.[59] The report also noted a change in bail practices in several of Canada's major cities. Judges frequently imposed bail conditions that restricted where sex workers could be located, thereby forcing them into remote areas to perform their work. The report further found that sex workers worked later at night or on weekends to avoid police. As a result, "the numbers of bad dates had increased [in Calgary], while in Vancouver, prostitutes reported being less likely to report bad dates to police for fear of being arrested themselves."[60]

The Crown also cited studies conducted after the Supreme Court decided the *Sex Work Reference* and *Downey*. First, it relied on a study conducted in Calgary and Winnipeg on the victimization of sex workers.[61] The Victimization Study acknowledged that sixty-three known sex workers were killed between 1991 and 1995, which constituted 5 percent of all female homicides in Canada. The study further observed that, though 20 percent of homicides go unsolved, that number increased to 54 percent when the homicide involved a sex worker.[62] Nevertheless, the researchers asserted that the "role of [the communication prohibition] is remote" in explaining these statistics. As they concluded, "[t]his section, along with all the other laws designed to suppress prostitution, simply make the buying and selling of sex a comparatively underground activity."[63]

The Crown also relied on a document prepared by a subcommittee of the House of Commons Standing Committee on Justice and Human Rights.[64] The Subcommittee Report recognized that only 5 to 20 percent of sex work occurred on the streets. It also noted that 75 to 85 percent of sex workers were women, and among them Indigenous women were disproportionately represented.[65] Street sex workers remained the most commonly prosecuted, and the bawdy house provisions were rarely enforced because of relatively few complaints and the high cost of police running a sting operation to prove the offence.[66] In addition, the living on the avails offence was prosecuted successfully in only 38 percent of cases. The subcommittee surmised that the offence was difficult to prosecute since it often required that sex workers testify against their

The Bedford *Decision* | 61

pimps. The report noted that sex workers are generally reluctant to do so because they fear severe beatings as a result.[67]

The Subcommittee Report further found that violence against sex workers was perpetrated by a range of actors – "clients, pimps, drug dealers, the public, and police officers" – in both indoor and outdoor settings. Speaking to indoor settings, the subcommittee found that "working conditions range from clean, respectful environments to establishments with management policies akin to slavery."[68] The subcommittee nevertheless agreed that "off-street prostitutes are generally subject to less violence."[69] In its view, however, the sex work laws were responsible in part for the violence faced by sex workers. As the subcommittee observed, "[w]hereas in the past street prostitutes frequently worked in teams in an effort to reduce the risk of violence (for example by helping take down information such as clients' licence plate numbers and descriptions), they now tend to work in isolation from one another."[70] Extensive policing of street sex workers and fear of arrest also resulted in sex workers being compelled "to move to another area, effectively separating them from friends, co-workers, regular customers and familiar places."[71]

The subcommittee also found that the bawdy house prohibition made sex work more dangerous even if the provision was rarely enforced. Sex workers worried about legal liability for being found in a bawdy house and therefore were less likely to work from a fixed, indoor setting. As one sex worker suggested, the only way to practise sex work was to do home calls. Yet the unknowns inherent in attending a stranger's home rendered sex workers highly vulnerable to predatory clients. Other sex workers concurred and added that the prohibition on bawdy houses "increases the isolation of those who engage in prostitution by criminalizing cohabitation and the establishment of an employer-employee relationship."[72]

A minority of the subcommittee members found more positive features of the sex work laws. In their view, the laws served an important denunciatory and deterrent function and therefore constituted an important means of reducing and ideally eradicating the practice of sex work. This was necessary since the minority viewed sex work as a

62 | *The Logic of* Bedford

form of violence against women, not as a legitimate form of commercial activity. As a result, "there can be no such thing as consent to prostitution or harmless sales of sexual services."[73] The minority also noted that the sex work laws facilitated an important point of contact between sex workers and the state. Without the sex work laws, it would become significantly more difficult for police to divert sex workers to state-funded programs designed to help them exit the trade. For these members of the subcommittee, the sex work laws acted "as a temporary 'wedge between the sex trade worker and her pimp,' or a tool for compelling a prostitute through 'a condition of probation that requires they meet with a counsellor who can help them develop exit strategies.'"[74]

Given their differing views on the objectives and effects of the sex work laws, the members of the subcommittee diverged with respect to its recommendations for reform. Whereas the majority was in favour of repealing the impugned sex work laws, the minority "advocated for legal reform criminalizing pimps and clients, who would pay hefty fines upon conviction, while largely decriminalizing prostitutes, who would benefit from programs funded by the fines paid."[75] The response in 2007 from the federal government – which had changed from a Liberal to a Conservative government since the report was commissioned – sided with the minority view and refused to repeal the sex work laws in response to the majority's concerns about these laws' impacts on the safety of sex work.[76]

International Evidence

The parties in *Bedford* also submitted a significant amount of evidence concerning the regulation of sex work in other liberal democracies. At the beginning of her description of this evidence, Justice Himel starkly observed that she was "struck by the fact that many of those proffered as experts to provide international evidence ... had entered the realm of advocacy and had given evidence in a manner that was designed to persuade rather than assist the court."[77] As Himel recounted, "some experts made bold assertions without properly outlined bases for their claims and were unwilling to qualify their opinions in the face of new facts provided."[78] Yet the role of the expert in Canada is the opposite:

to assist the court with objective opinions on matters outside the court's expertise.[79] As a result, the international evidence was given minimal weight in her decision.[80]

Justice Himel nevertheless cited the experiences of several international jurisdictions to shed light on some of the empirical questions at the heart of the applicants' constitutional challenge.[81] Sex work regulation in the Netherlands is exemplary of some of the benefits of decriminalizing sex work and subjecting the practice to health and safety regulations.[82] These regulations require that sex workers hold a European Union Work Permit and that anyone operating a brothel not have a criminal record.[83] Despite legalization in the Netherlands, half of sex work occurs outside the legal sector. These sex workers typically are foreign and perform out-calls set up by phone or the internet.[84] Up to 10 percent of sex workers also continue to work on the streets, and they are typically "drug addicts or suffer from mental illness, are unwanted in brothels, and unable to pay to rent a window."[85] Notably, organized crime is also thought to be involved in exploiting nonregulated sex workers.[86]

Despite the poor state of nonregulated sex work, the Dutch government commissioned various reports that found that decriminalization was "moderately successful in improving working conditions and safety in the legal practice of prostitution."[87] The reports suggest that those working in the licensed sector are not exploited or underage and that sexually transmitted diseases are less prevalent among sex workers than among the population as a whole.[88] Moreover, the Dutch government's studies found that "[a]pproximately 90 per cent of reported incidents of violence against prostitutes are against women working illegally."[89] This provides support for the applicants' suggestion that working in well-regulated indoor locations can drastically reduce violence against sex workers.

Other jurisdictions have taken a different approach to governing sex work. After decades of decriminalization, Sweden criminalized the purchase of sex and the act of pimping. However, the act of selling sex remains legal.[90] The objective of this policy is to deter sex work because it constitutes an act of predominantly male violence against

64 | *The Logic of* Bedford

women and children. As representatives of the Swedish government observe, "[g]ender equality will remain unattainable as long as men buy, sell and exploit women and children by prostituting them."[91] During the first three years of the policy, the number of sex workers in Sweden was estimated to have decreased by 33 percent.[92] More importantly, the number of street workers was found to have decreased by approximately 25 percent.[93] Government reports further suggest that few foreign sex workers remained as street workers and that human traffickers might now find Sweden an unattractive destination.[94]

The positive changes brought about by what is often referred to as the "Nordic Model" for regulating sex work were attributed to more than just a change in law. The Swedish government accompanied its legal changes with other policies targeting male demand for sex work. They included a national poster campaign raising awareness of the detrimental effects of sex work and trafficking on women. The Swedish government developed additional training programs for police to increase their understanding of why sex workers are susceptible to entering the trade and typically are incapable of leaving it without significant aid. Following this additional training, complaints from law enforcement that the sex work laws were difficult to enforce ceased and were followed by a 300 percent increase in arrests of clients and pimps.[95] Convictions under the new laws nevertheless remain rare.[96]

Findings of Fact

After weighing the extensive evidentiary record before her, Justice Himel made the following findings of fact germane to her constitutional ruling:

1 Prostitutes, particularly those who work on the street, are at a high risk of being the victims of physical violence.
2 The risk that a prostitute will experience violence can be reduced in the following ways:
   a Working indoors is generally safer than working on the streets;
   b Working in close proximity to others, including paid security staff, can increase safety;

The Bedford *Decision* | 65

c Taking the time to screen clients for intoxication or propensity to violence can increase safety;

d Having a regular clientele can increase safety;

e When a prostitute's client is aware that the sexual acts will occur in a location that is pre-determined, known to others, or monitored in some way, safety can be increased;

f The use of drivers, receptionists and bodyguards can increase safety; and

g Indoor safeguards including closed-circuit television monitoring, call buttons, audio room monitoring [and] financial negotiations done in advance can increase safety.

3 The bawdy-house provisions can place prostitutes in danger by preventing them from working in-call in a regular indoor location and gaining the safety benefits of proximity to others, security staff, closed-circuit television and other monitoring.

4 The living on the avails of prostitution provision can make prostitutes more susceptible to violence by preventing them from legally hiring bodyguards or drivers while working. Without these supports, prostitutes may proceed to unknown locations and be left alone with clients who have the benefit of complete anonymity with no one nearby to hear and interrupt a violent act, and no one but the prostitute able to identify the aggressor.

5 The communicating provision can increase the vulnerability of street prostitutes by forcing them to forego screening customers at an early and crucial stage of the transaction.[97]

Himel's findings of fact were upheld at the Ontario Court of Appeal and later at the Supreme Court.[98] The above summary of facts was therefore used at all levels of court to determine the merits of the applicants' constitutional arguments.

Missing Pieces

Although Justice Himel's findings are thorough, they are also incomplete, given her limited engagement with the impacts of the sex work laws on certain minority groups. The impacts on transgender people

66 | *The Logic of* Bedford

in particular received sparse mention at trial.[99] Although the Ontario Court of Appeal recognized that some sex workers are transgender, it relegated this point to a brief footnote.[100] The Supreme Court did not even mention the impacts of the sex work laws on transgender people.[101] This is unfortunate but perhaps unsurprising given the limited progress of transgender rights in Canada when *Bedford* was decided.[102]

Although research on the impacts of sex work regulations on transgender people remains sparse, it is important to recognize that transgender sex workers face an additional layer of discrimination.[103] This in turn has been shown to result in many transgender sex workers working on the streets compared with their cisgender counterparts.[104] As a result, transgender sex workers are subject to a disproportionate amount of violence.[105] Opportunities for violence are exacerbated given the potential for clients to respond to learning of a transgender person's identity with anger.[106] Discrimination against sex workers more generally by police and fear that outing themselves as sex workers can result in criminal detention further present unique challenges. Given the higher prospect of violence while in detention, transgender sex workers understandably are less likely to contact police to seek help or report violence.[107]

The impacts of the sex work laws on the gay community also received negligible attention in all three judgments in *Bedford*.[108] Nor did the factums at the Supreme Court so much as mention the impacts of the sex work laws on gay persons.[109] As Prime Minister Justin Trudeau observed in his apology to the 2SLGBTQ+ communities, the bawdy house provision in particular was used to criminalize the sexual conduct of gay men found in bathhouses, gay bars, and private homes.[110] It has been subsequently reported that more than 1,300 gay men were charged under this provision between 1968 and 2004.[111] Although most of those criminally charged were not selling sex – they were mostly charged for acts of "indecency" or being "found in" a bawdy house[112] – the dramatic impacts of the bawdy house laws on the gay community provide important context for understanding the widely discriminatory nature of the sex work laws.

As with transgender sex workers, it should also be recognized that there is a lack of academic study of male sex work.[113] This deficiency likely exists because male sex work was intertwined historically with the criminalization of homosexuality as deviant sexual behaviour.[114] As John Scott observes, the fact that gay sex was directly criminalized and harshly punished resulted in policy makers and law enforcement officials failing to distinguish the two activities.[115] The lack of attention to male sex workers in the *Bedford* case, however, might be explained by the lower tendency for violence as a result of sexual transactions between gay men. Some studies conclude that male sex workers face significantly less violence because they often work discreetly indoors, their clients are less confrontational because they want to avoid undue attention, and male sex workers typically are less physically vulnerable than their female counterparts.[116] Other studies nevertheless find that male sex workers can endure significant amounts of violence.[117] In my view, it is more likely that the impacts of the sex work laws on gay men were overlooked because they did not fit the predominant narrative of sex work involving men exploiting women. Regardless of the reason, the failure to adequately acknowledge the impacts of the sex work laws on minority groups disproportionately affected by the sex work laws suggests that the evidentiary record was either incomplete or inadequately engaged with by the courts.

LEGAL ISSUES

The *Bedford* case raised five legal issues. First, each court considered the extent to which prior Supreme Court precedents are binding on lower courts. Second, the appellate courts determined whether a trial judge's findings of "social" or "legislative" facts were owed deference on appeal. Third, all courts grappled with a novel application of section 7 of the Charter assessing whether the sex work laws engaged sex workers' security of the person interest in a manner that violated fundamental justice. Fourth, each court briefly considered the application of section 1, even though justificatory arguments were not

68 | *The Logic of* Bedford

explicitly made by the Crown with respect to any violation of section 7. And fifth, each court was asked to suspend any declaration of invalidity to afford Parliament time to respond to the various rulings.

Stare Decisis

The *stare decisis* principle requires that lower courts render decisions consistent with those of higher courts. Thus, the *ratio decendi* of a case – the part of a judge's reasoning necessary to decide the issues presented to the court – will bind lower courts. Judicial pronouncements not necessary for deciding the case before the court – referred to as *obiter dicta* – are merely meant to persuade lower courts. By requiring that lower courts follow the ratio decendi of higher courts, the *stare decisis* principle promotes important values central to the rule of law such as certainty, predictability, and consistency. It also increases "the legitimacy and acceptability of judge-made law, and by so doing enhances the appearance of justice."[118] Yet strict adherence to *stare decisis* can also undermine important values. As Justice Himel observed, "a rigid adherence might lead to 'injustices in individual cases, continued application of legal principles long since outdated as society has changed, and uncertainty bred by judges who draw overly fine distinctions to avoid *stare decisis*.'"[119]

To decide whether the Supreme Court's prior precedents were binding on the lower courts, it was therefore necessary to determine what was decided in those cases. On its face, the Supreme Court's decision in the *Sex Work Reference* concluded that the communication and bawdy house offences did not violate section 7 of the Charter and that the communication provision constituted a justifiable infringement of section 2(b) of the Charter. Because the *Bedford* case involved the same sections, it was plausible that *stare decisis* barred lower courts from reconsidering the constitutionality of these offences. However, given the unique structure of section 7 of the Charter, the Supreme Court affirmed that the interests of "life, liberty and security of the person" are to be treated as distinct.[120] Since the majority's decision in the *Sex Work Reference* was based on the liberty interest, a challenge based on the laws' infringement of sex workers' security of the person was adequate to distinguish the *Sex Work Reference*.[121] More importantly, the *Sex Work Reference* considered only whether the sex work laws were inconsistent with the vagueness principle of fundamental justice. Because the applicants in *Bedford* employed three novel principles of fundamental justice – arbitrariness, overbreadth, and gross disproportionality – the trial judge was required to conduct a fresh analysis.[122]

The same conclusion did not follow with respect to the Supreme Court's decision that the communication provision was a justifiable infringement of the right to freedom of expression.[123] The Ontario Court of Appeal held that the *Sex Work Reference* could not be "displaced by recasting the nature of the expression at issue as promoting safety, and not merely commercial expression," for this change in perspective had "not altered the *ratio decidendi*" of the *Sex Work Reference*.[124] Although the Ontario Court of Appeal conceded that a novel perspective could influence the section 1 analysis, it determined that such a question "is a matter for the Supreme Court to decide for itself."[125] To conclude otherwise would undermine the rule of law, for every time a litigant came across new evidence they would be able to ask a trial judge to overturn Supreme Court precedent.[126]

Summarizing its ruling, the Supreme Court observed that a trial judge may overrule a higher court's decision in the Charter context in two circumstances: when the relevant provisions were not raised in the prior case or "if there is a change in the circumstances or evidence that fundamentally shifts the parameters of the debate."[127] To disallow these exceptions would subordinate the Charter to the common law principle of *stare decisis* and render the trial judge a "mere scribe" in proceedings raising new constitutional issues.[128] Since the Charter is part of the supreme law of Canada, it would be incongruous for a common law principle to prevent a novel argument from being considered by lower courts.[129] However, since the Supreme Court was able to resolve the constitutional questions under section 7 of the Charter, it chose not to address whether the Ontario Court of Appeal correctly refused to hear the applicants' freedom of expression challenge to the sex work laws.[130]

70 | *The Logic of* Bedford

Appellate Review of Legislative Facts

The appellate courts further dealt with an important issue that will arise in cases in which an applicant attempts to strike down a law based on social science evidence: to what extent is a trial judge's findings of fact subject to appellate review? Relying on prior Supreme Court precedent, the Ontario Court of Appeal affirmed that facts derived from social science evidence are not subject to any form of deference by appellate courts.[131] The Supreme Court reversed course.[132] As with adjudicative facts (the "what, when, where, and whom" of a case), the Supreme Court concluded that appellate courts may overturn a trial judge's findings related to social science evidence – a category of facts often referred to as "legislative" facts – only if there is a "palpable and overriding error."[133]

The Supreme Court provided two main reasons for this conclusion. First, allowing for robust appellate review "would require the appeal court to duplicate the sometimes time-consuming and tedious work of the first instance judge in reviewing all the material and reconciling differences between the experts, studies and research results."[134] The need for judicial economy therefore militated against allowing expansive appellate review of legislative facts. Second, the Supreme Court concluded that legislative facts "may be intertwined with adjudicative facts ... and with issues of credibility of experts."[135] Separating and applying different standards of review to each category of facts "would immensely complicate the appellate task."[136]

Section 7 of the Charter

As discussed in Chapter 1, section 7 of the Charter employs a two-stage analysis. First, the applicant must prove that the impugned law engages a person's life, liberty, or security of the person interest. Second, if so, then the analysis requires that the law be consistent with the "principles of fundamental justice." The Supreme Court in *Bedford* applied and, in an important way, overhauled the law under section 7 to place the focus of the second stage of the inquiry on a law's means-ends rationality as it applies to a single individual.

Threshold Interests

As the Supreme Court affirmed in the *Sex Work Reference,* the availability of imprisonment is sufficient to engage the liberty interest and require that an impugned law be consistent with the principles of fundamental justice.[137] However, the essence of the constitutional harm raised by the applicants in *Bedford* did not concern the liberty interest. Instead, the harms facing sex workers jeopardized their security of the person by making what was a legal form of work more dangerous. The Supreme Court has consistently held that this threshold interest protects everyone's physical and psychological integrity.[138] Although the sex work laws did not cause direct harm, the applicants maintained that they contributed to the dangers faced by sex workers. The Crown opposed this argument by maintaining that a "direct causal connection" between the law and any effect was required before an applicant's security of the person interest could be engaged. In rejecting this argument, the Supreme Court affirmed that the governing standard requires only that the connection be "real" as opposed to "speculative."[139]

Justice Himel found it probable that the dangers facing sex workers could be reduced by removing the current restrictions on sex work. The applicants' evidence was primarily adopted by the court to support this conclusion.[140] Thus, the trial judge agreed that two factors contributed to the threat of violence: venue of work and individual working conditions.[141] Working indoors significantly reduced the risk of violence, especially if the indoor location was fixed and run competently. Hiring nonexploitive staff could also increase safety. Likewise, allowing street workers to screen clients could reduce instances of violence against them.[142] As a result, all court levels in *Bedford* concluded that the sex work laws materially contributed to the dangers faced by sex workers, thereby engaging sex workers' security of the person interest.[143]

Principles of Fundamental Justice

The first step in an instrumental rationality analysis requires interpreting the impugned law's objective. Each level of court in *Bedford* affirmed that the objectives of the sex work offences were those previously

72 | *The Logic of* Bedford

determined by the majorities in the *Sex Work Reference* and *Downey*. The bawdy house provision sought to avoid various nuisances – neighbourhood disruption and disorder – arising from operating such a business.[144] The prohibition against communicating in public for the purposes of sex work was similarly designed to prevent nuisances related to noise and public exposure to sex work.[145] Finally, the objective of the prohibition against living on the avails of sex work was to prevent sex workers from being exploited, notably by pimps who live parasitically off sex workers.[146]

The relevant principles of fundamental justice pleaded were those prohibiting arbitrary, overbroad, and grossly disproportionate laws.[147] Before the Supreme Court's decision in *Bedford*, these principles considered the effects of a law on all people and compared those effects with the law's ability to achieve its objective. Under this "holistic" approach,[148] a law is arbitrary if "it bears no relation to, or is inconsistent with, the objective that lies behind [it]."[149] A law violates the overbreadth principle if its means are not reasonably necessary to achieve its objective.[150] Finally, a law violates the gross disproportionality principle if its effects on all people are too harsh compared with its ability to achieve its objective.[151]

The Supreme Court's "individualistic" approach to the instrumental rationality principles adopted two important changes. First, the individualistic approach requires that the law have only an arbitrary, overbroad, or grossly disproportionate effect on a single, real or hypothetical, person.[152] Second, the approach requires courts to presume that the impugned law achieves its objective.[153] Both changes served the same laudable purpose: preventing applicants from being required to submit voluminous evidence to support a constitutional challenge. As Chief Justice McLachlin observed, "[t]o require s. 7 claimants to establish the efficacy of the law versus its deleterious consequences on members of society as a whole ... would impose the government's s. 1 burden on claimants under s. 7. That cannot be right."[154]

Applying the individualistic approach, the Supreme Court found that the bawdy house and communication provisions violated the gross disproportionality principle. In essence, the bawdy house provision resulted in grossly disproportionate effects because it required sex workers to forgo the "safety benefits of proximity to others, familiarity with surroundings, security staff, closed-circuit television and other such monitoring that a permanent indoor location can facilitate."[155] When balancing the risks posed to the security interests of sex workers against the law's nuisance abatement objective, the Supreme Court concluded that the law's effects were grossly disproportionate compared with its purpose.[156] Similarly, preventing sex workers from taking basic safety precautions to avoid the nuisance inherent in street sex work struck a grossly disproportionate balance between the law's means and ends.[157] Finally, the living on the avails provision violated the overbreadth principle since sex workers' security interests were impinged in a manner inconsistent with the law's objective of preventing sex workers from being exploited. This followed because the provision applied to many types of workers – such as security guards, drivers, and receptionists – who did not seek to exploit sex workers but were employed to protect them.[158]

Section 1 of the Charter

The Supreme Court's early jurisprudence set an unusually high bar for a law that infringes section 7 of the Charter to be justified under section 1. Writing in *Reference re Section 94(2) of the Motor Vehicle Act,*[159] Justice Lamer observed that section 1 justifications of section 7 rights are appropriate only "in cases arising out of exceptional conditions, such as natural disasters, the outbreak of war, epidemics, and the like."[160] Similarly, Justice Wilson wrote in her concurring reasons that she could not conclude that "the guaranteed right in s. 7 which is to be subject *only* to limits which are reasonable and justifiable in a free and democratic society can be taken away by the violation of a principle considered fundamental to our justice system."[161] Given these conclusions, it is unsurprising that the Supreme Court has never upheld a law that infringes a principle of fundamental justice under section 1.

As a result of this high standard, the Crown in *Bedford* did not contend that any of the impugned laws were justifiable under section 1.[162] The Supreme Court nevertheless briefly considered a potential

74 | *The Logic of* Bedford

justification of the living on the avails provision because some of the Crown's section 7 arguments were relevant to the section 1 analysis.[163] In effect, the Crown argued that the provision must be drafted broadly to capture all exploitive relationships that can be difficult to identify because pimps can masquerade as any number of potential employees.[164] The Supreme Court retorted that "the law not only catches drivers and bodyguards, who may actually be pimps, but it also catches clearly non-exploitative relationships, such as receptionists or accountants who work with prostitutes."[165] As a result, it concluded that the law was not minimally impairing and failed to strike a reasonable balance between its salutary and deleterious effects.[166]

Despite not seriously engaging with potential justifications under section 1 of the Charter, the Supreme Court recognized that its adoption of the "individualistic" conception of the instrumental rationality principles required it to soften its view on whether section 1 may operate to justify a breach of section 7.[167] Although individualizing the instrumental rationality principles more fairly aligned the burden of proof in constitutional challenges,[168] it also made it much easier to prove a violation of the principles of fundamental justice. By requiring only an illogical or harsh effect on a single person, the Supreme Court's new conception of section 7 demanded that legislatures pass perfectly logical laws. Setting the standard this high required that infringements of section 7 be open to policy justifications.[169]

Remedy

Section 52(1) of the *Constitution Act, 1982* provides in relevant part that a law "inconsistent with the provisions of the Constitution is, to the extent of the inconsistency, of no force or effect."[170] In considering which remedy to order, courts must both consider the need to uphold the purposes underlying the Charter and respect the role of the legislature in a democracy.[171] In balancing these aims, the Supreme Court concluded that it was necessary to strike down the communication and living on the avails offences and strike the term "prostitution" from the definition of "bawdy house" in section 197 of the *Criminal Code.*[172]

The latter remedy was necessarily limited because the bawdy house offence was challenged only insofar as it applied to "prostitution." To the extent that the provision applied to "acts of indecency," it continued to have the full force of law.[173]

Each level of court further considered whether to accede to the Crown's request to suspend the declaration of invalidity. The Supreme Court concluded in *Schachter v Canada*[174] that such a remedy constitutes "a serious matter from the point of view of the enforcement of the *Charter*" since such a delay "allows a state of affairs which has been found to violate standards embodied in the *Charter* to persist for a time despite the violation."[175] As such, the Supreme Court initially identified three limited scenarios in which suspending a declaration of invalidity might be appropriate: when declaring legislation invalid without enacting legislation in its place would "pose a danger to the public," "threaten the rule of law," or "result in the deprivation of benefits from deserving persons," such as when a piece of legislation is "deemed unconstitutional because of underinclusiveness."[176]

In considering whether these limited exceptions applied, the trial judge observed that many *Criminal Code* provisions remained in place to ensure the safety of sex workers and to allow police to ensure that nuisances arising from sex work do not go unpunished. To protect sex workers from exploitation and harm, section 212(1)(a)–(i) prohibits various components of procuring and concealing sex work. The prohibition against uttering threats in section 264.1 has been used against abusive pimps,[177] as has the prohibition against intimidating a person to perform a nonconsensual act.[178] Abusive clients and pimps have also been prosecuted for sexual assault, assault, theft, extortion, torture, human trafficking, and unlawful confinement, among other offences.[179] Sexual exploitation of minors is also prohibited under sections 151, 152, and 153. Sections 170 and 171 further criminalize procuring minors, section 172.1 prohibits child luring, and section 280 criminalizes nonparental child abduction.

To combat societal nuisances pertaining to sex work, Justice Himel observed, sections 213(1)(a) and (b) prohibit sex workers from attempting

76 | *The Logic of* Bedford

to stop a motor vehicle as well as impeding or redirecting pedestrian or vehicular traffic for the purposes of sex work. Section 175 more generally prohibits causing a nuisance in public, "including fighting, indecent exhibition, [and] loitering."[180] Section 177 further prohibits loitering at night on another person's property, and section 180 creates a more general offence of common nuisance. Any repeated and unwanted communications can also be prohibited by the prohibition against criminal harassment in section 264. Section 173(2) bans indecent public exposure, thereby prohibiting sex workers from performing sexual acts in public view, and section 174 criminalizes such conduct by prohibiting public nudity.

Given the various available provisions to combat the harms and societal nuisances arising from sex work, the trial judge refused to grant a suspended declaration of invalidity. In further support of her position, the trial judge found that the impugned prohibitions related to bawdy houses and living on the avails of sex work were rarely enforced, and the communication prohibition was only minimally effective in curbing societal nuisances.[181] Any danger to the public therefore paled in comparison with the harms facing sex workers as a result of the sex work laws remaining in effect. Citing Kent Roach, Justice Himel agreed that "[d]elayed declarations of invalidity will not be appropriate if they expose individuals and groups to irreparable harm caused by the continued operation of a law that has been found unconstitutional."[182]

Without referencing Justice Himel's reasons, the Supreme Court overturned her decision declaring the sex work laws immediately invalid. Although the Supreme Court recognized that, "[w]hether immediate invalidity would pose a danger to the public or imperil the rule of law ... may be subject to debate," it also maintained that "moving abruptly from a situation where prostitution is regulated to a situation where it is entirely unregulated would be a matter of great concern to many Canadians."[183] With only brief mention of the increased risks posed to sex workers by leaving the laws in place, the Supreme Court concluded that the declaration of invalidity should be suspended for one year.[184]

CONCLUSION

For those who opposed the impugned restrictions on sex work, the *Bedford* decision was an occasion to celebrate. The substance of the decision strongly suggested that sex workers could expect the sex trade to be made safer. The decision nevertheless has been subject to criticism from both those who think the laws were unconstitutional and those who support criminal restrictions on sex work. Building on this literature, I contend in the remainder of this book that the legal analysis in *Bedford* did not meaningfully further rights. Instead, its development and application of the law served to weaken not only the immediate safety interests of sex workers but also the position of future rights claimants pleading an infringement under section 7 of the Charter. After defending this thesis in Part 2, I explain in Part 3 why the Supreme Court could have avoided all this controversy by utilizing the structure of the Anglo-American criminal law to uphold the sex work laws while ensuring that those who do not realistically choose to engage in sex work could take basic safety precautions while conducting their work. Although such a criticism cannot revive the prior sex work laws, viewing the new sex work laws through a similar lens should result in constitutional arguments similar to those made in *Bedford* failing to prove a violation of section 7 of the Charter.

PART 2

ATTENUATING RIGHTS

4

Legislative Facts and the Charter

KENNETH CULP DAVIS famously distinguished between adjudicative and legislative facts.[1] Adjudicative facts concern the "immediate parties – what the parties did, what the circumstances were, what the background conditions were."[2] Legislative facts inform a court's judgment on questions of law and policy.[3] The latter facts often derive from social science research and help to explain how litigants relate to the broader society.[4] For my purposes here, the relevant distinction between these categories is that adjudicative facts are subject to appellate review based on "palpable and overriding error,"[5] whereas legislative facts historically were "entitled to little deference" from appellate courts.[6]

The Supreme Court of Canada's decision in *Bedford* to subject legislative facts to the same deferential standard of review as adjudicative facts relied on two main arguments. First, given the voluminous nature of legislative facts, requiring appellate justices to review the trial record anew would be inefficient.[7] As opposed to reviewing a case for an error of law or a "palpable and overriding" error of fact – the traditional role of appellate courts – appellate justices would devote significant time and resources to comprehending social science evidence.[8] Second, the Supreme Court maintained that reviewing findings of legislative fact would "immensely complicate the appellate task" since it might be

82 | *Attenuating Rights*

difficult for appellate justices to distinguish issues of credibility and adjudicative facts from legislative facts.[9]

Although one scholar has briefly expressed support for this deferential approach,[10] the evidentiary rule deriving from *Bedford* has received surprisingly little critical discussion. In my view, showing deference to a trial judge's findings of legislative fact can be expected to undermine constitutional rule. This follows for two reasons. First, trial judges are generally underqualified to interpret scientific evidence. Second, they have inadequate means to educate themselves about the area of science at issue in a particular trial. These facts are concerning since the Supreme Court recognizes that findings of legislative fact frequently will be dispositive of constitutional issues.[11] Without meaningful prescriptions to address the trial judge's knowledge deficit, showing deference to the judge's understanding of legislative facts subjects democratically enacted legislation to the judge's capacity to understand scientific evidence as opposed to constitutional principle. Absent broader change to the adversarial system, ensuring that a greater number of justices fully scrutinize the record serves to minimize the chance that a law's constitutionality will be decided based on faulty evidence.

DECONSTRUCTING DEFERENCE

It is useful to consider whether appellate courts should show deference to a trial judge's findings of legislative fact by first unpacking the rationale underlying why appellate courts defer to findings of adjudicative facts. The latter rule is sensible since the trial judge can view and hear the witness testify and therefore assess the demeanour of the witness. These sorts of observations are difficult to replicate on appeal.[12] Even if replication were possible, appellate justices should still defer to the trial judge's findings of adjudicative facts given the latter's expertise in adjudicative fact finding. As the Supreme Court observed in *R v Buhay*,[13] "the sifting and weighing of this kind of evidence is the particular expertise of the trial court. The further up the appellate chain one goes, the more of this institutional expertise is lost and the greater the risk of a decision which does not reflect the realities of the situation."[14]

Showing deference to the trial judge's findings of fact also promotes the efficient operation of the judicial system. As the Supreme Court observed in *Schwartz v Canada*,[15] "[u]nlimited intervention by appellate courts would greatly increase the number and the length of appeals generally."[16] Given the scarcity of judicial resources, limiting appeals based on adjudicative facts promotes the efficiency of the justice system. The Supreme Court in *Bedford* made a similar observation with respect to appellate courts reviewing voluminous records of social science evidence. Not only would such a review take a substantial amount of time, but it would also arguably be difficult for appellate justices sifting through the record to distinguish between each category of facts and isolate issues pertaining to the credibility of experts.[17]

Limiting appeals based on adjudicative facts can also promote greater fairness in the justice system. As the Supreme Court concluded in *Housen v Nikolaisen*,[18] allowing broad appeals based on such factual disagreements would enable resource-rich parties to use the appellate process to relitigate a case to the prejudice of resource-poor parties.[19] A similar rationale can be applied to legislative facts in constitutional cases. If the Crown loses at trial because its legislative facts were rejected, then a broad appeal based on those facts would permit the Crown to relitigate the constitutionality of a piece of legislation. Since the Crown can regularly be expected to spend significant resources on litigation, allowing for a broad review of legislative facts can disadvantage the average litigant who cannot financially afford to support an appeal.[20]

Finally, limiting appeals based on adjudicative facts improves the integrity of the justice system. As the Supreme Court observed in *Housen*, "[f]requent and unlimited appeals would ... weaken public confidence in the trial process."[21] This follows because allowing full review of the factual record sends the message that the initial trial process was a dress rehearsal. This in turn will likely have a negative effect on the reputation of trial courts. A similar argument could be made with respect to the impact of *de novo* review of legislative facts. If the trial judge's findings of fact are readily overturned, then the public might view the trial process as having little import when rendering constitutional decisions.

84 | *Attenuating Rights*

Each of these rationales for showing deference to a trial judge's factual findings has limited appeal with respect to legislative facts. As for the trial judge's ability to assess demeanour, it is unclear why this is necessary with respect to witnesses who testify about legislative facts. As John Monahan and Laurens Walker observe, "[t]he sweating, shifty-eyed witness to a criminal's alibi may indeed be less credible than is the calm and self-assured witness; but observable nervousness on the part of an expert presenting social science data is more likely to reflect unfamiliarity with courtroom procedures than it is to indicate that the underlying data are invalid."[22] Indeed, often it will be unnecessary to view the testimony of an expert witness since its merits will be apparent when learning its substance. The *Bedford* case is illustrative since the trial judge did not view any of the expert witnesses testify. This occurred because the rules governing applications for "declaratory relief" allow witnesses to be examined by the parties outside court under the supervision of a master, not the trial judge.[23]

Even if there is value added by deferring to the trial judge's credibility findings, there is no reason in principle that the appellate court could not show deference to those findings but still review findings of legislative fact de novo. The Ontario Court of Appeal in *Bedford* took this approach without any apparent difficulty.[24] In rejecting this procedure, the Supreme Court reiterated its efficiency concerns.[25] More importantly, it added that reviewing factual evidence de novo is inconsistent with the role of the appellate courts. In its view, the "appellate task is not to review evidence globally, but rather to review the conclusions the first instance judge has drawn from the evidence" and apply the law to those conclusions.[26]

It is unclear why the role of appellate courts must remain static in light of novel and pressing legal challenges. The phenomenon of social science evidence being submitted in constitutional cases is relatively new in Canada. As Benjamin Perryman recently observed, "[i]n less than two decades, we have moved from a constitutional jurisprudence that could find serious psychological harm on the basis of a brief affidavit of the applicant, to a jurisprudence that frequently relies on, if not requires, massive social science records."[27] Barring some reason to think that trial judges' limited experience with legislative fact evidence places the judges at an advantage vis-à-vis appellate courts, it is not sensible to effectively exclude the latter courts from considering the record afresh.

Those who study the ability of judges to understand legislative facts suggest that their limited experience has not translated into expertise. As Justice Binnie observes, Canadian judges typically have no background in the sciences, let alone the nuanced scientific subject matter that arises in the case before any given trial court.[28] The structure of adversarial proceedings perpetuates this disadvantage. Whereas the lawyers in a proceeding spend a significant amount of time preparing their cases, "the judge hits a dispute cold and is expected to get 'up to speed' within a few days."[29] Absent a background in the area of fact raised by the parties' evidence, it will be extremely difficult for the judge to understand the relevant expert testimony.

The structure of the adversarial system is also likely to result in experts who exhibit explicit or implicit biases.[30] As the Supreme Court recognized in *R v DD*,[31] "although not biased in a dishonest sense, [expert] witnesses frequently move from the impartiality generally associated with professionals to advocates in the case."[32] Explaining this phenomenon, David Paciocco observes that expert witnesses are often chosen specifically because their opinions align with the party's case. It is difficult for opposing lawyers who lack equivalent knowledge to reveal such partiality by way of cross-examination.[33]

Experts are also partial because of "association bias," defined as "the natural bias to do something serviceable for those who employ ... and adequately remunerate [a person]."[34] As Paciocco explains, this type of bias "includes the litany of conscious and unconscious pressures on experts to work in the interests of those they are associated with in litigation."[35] Similarly, experts also exhibit "professional" and "noble cause" biases. The former type of bias arises when an expert's opinion is distorted to maintain an image of being on a particular side, such as the Crown or defence.[36] The latter form of bias arises when the expert believes that their work supports a fundamentally just cause.[37] As Paciocco maintains, such "crusading expert witnesses ... may be prone to see what they want to see."[38]

86 | *Attenuating Rights*

Judges therefore will be required as a matter of course to determine which evidence is reliable based on biased accounts of evidence while under significant time constraints and without the necessary educational background to scrutinize the evidence. For these reasons, scholars have long expressed concern about the capacity of judges to determine legislative facts.[39] Summarizing these views, Jodi Lazare contends that the judiciary's "limited capacity to critically evaluate social science data ... means that judges may misinterpret the evidence or prefer evidence from one witness over another for reasons unrelated to the validity or reliability of the evidence."[40]

This does not mean that individual appellate justices are necessarily better than individual trial judges at deciphering the meaning of scientific evidence. The advantage of appellate courts rests in their numbers. As a case works its way through the appeals process, "the evidentiary record is scrutinized by increased numbers of judges at each level of court, creating a sense of safety in numbers and consensus."[41] The increase in justices at appellate hearings – typically three at the provincial appellate court and nine at the Supreme Court – increases the likelihood that "the evidence will be examined by a judge with the requisite awareness of the risks and challenges associated with expert evidence from the social sciences."[42] As a result, "the risk of uncritical reliance on unsound evidence, or of misapprehension of complex scientific evidence, is minimized."[43]

It is equally unlikely that the integrity of the justice system will be improved by showing deference to a trial judge's findings of legislative fact. Reasonably informed members of the public are aware that trial judges are typically trained in law, not in social or natural sciences.[44] Showing deference to a single trial judge with respect to a matter in which the judge is not trained would reduce public confidence in the administration of justice. Although relying on appellate justices is not a perfect solution, it does increase the chance that errors in legislative facts will be corrected. As Justice Binnie suggests, any decreased risk of judges misunderstanding facts should correspondingly increase the public's faith in the judicial system.[45]

Finally, the potential observed earlier for the Crown to be unduly advantaged if findings of fact are readily overturned on appeal need not result in increased costs to litigants. Assuming that appellate courts show deference to findings of credibility, these courts would be assessing legislative fact evidence based on the evidentiary record alone. I see no reason why the appellate courts could not substitute their own findings of fact for those of the trial judge since that evidence typically will not change materially upon rehearing the same evidence from the same expert witnesses. The appellate court therefore would not have to order a new trial to the detriment of constitutional litigants. The case could simply proceed through the appellate process by applying the relevant constitutional principles to the appellate court's findings of legislative fact.

It might be prudent nevertheless in some circumstances to order a new trial because of a trial judge's assessment of legislative facts. In those cases, it is also necessary to take into account how evidence was submitted in recent Canadian constitutional challenges. As Alan Young observes, "[t]he recent flurry of section 7 challenges were not simply accompanied by a modest selection of contextual studies and research, but rather were cases in which dozens of expert and experiential witnesses testified and countless studies were tendered."[46] Thus, litigants are finding ways to submit the relevant social science evidence despite financial barriers. As Perryman explained, litigants are taking group approaches that bring together (often on a volunteer basis) affected people, organizations, academics, and experts to put together an informed evidentiary record.[47] These actors will likely still be motivated to testify at a retrial. Existing epistemic communities therefore provide at least some assurance that the high costs of litigation will not thwart meritorious constitutional challenges even in cases in which a retrial is ordered.

It is also notable that other legal mechanisms are available to mitigate the costs of litigation in cases in which counsel and experts do not volunteer their services. As Young observes, it is possible to receive advanced costs for litigation in some cases, though in reality these grants are rarely issued.[48] It is also possible for "special costs" to be awarded by a court upon completion of a trial. In a challenge to the euthanasia

88 | *Attenuating Rights*

laws, the Supreme Court awarded over $1 million to the applicants to mitigate costs similar to those that would have been incurred in the *Bedford* case.[49] Such costs are not guaranteed upon bringing a constitutional challenge, but in a case like *Bedford* Young predicts that he too would have received similar compensation if he and the expert witnesses did not agree to volunteer their services.[50] Although the availability of such funding post-trial is never guaranteed, it can make advocacy lawyers more likely to take on or continue a case based on a contingency fee arrangement.

ALTERNATIVES TO APPELLATE REVIEW

Although allowing appellate justices to reconsider legislative facts is no panacea, this prescription must be viewed in light of alternative means for improving judicial understandings of expert evidence. Several prescriptions to improve legislative fact finding can be adopted. They include encouraging counsel to submit "Brandeis briefs," increasing judicial education, and recruiting judges with backgrounds in the sciences. However, the most effective prescriptions will require legislative amendments to modify the adversarial system in a manner that reduces the potential for biased expert witnesses and increases the likelihood that experts will testify in a way that judges can understand. Since the judicial remedies are inadequate, and the legislative remedies nonexistent, I contend that the Supreme Court erred by not allowing appellate justices to review a trial judge's findings of legislative fact.

Brandeis Briefs

For Justice Brandeis of the American Supreme Court, "it was essential ... that legal analysis proceed through an understanding of social facts."[51] As counsel in *Muller v Oregon*,[52] Brandeis filed a brief at the Supreme Court that included a range of social science materials supporting the constitutionality of an impugned law. The key feature of Brandeis briefs is that they are not presented by a witness at trial. Instead, they are attached to the written submissions that a lawyer files as part of a case. Although Canadian law was initially hostile to Brandeis briefs, the Supreme Court began admitting them in the mid-1970s.[53] As the Supreme Court reasoned, "[m]aterial relevant to the issues before the court ... and not inherently unreliable or offending against public policy should be admissible."[54]

Brandeis briefs are useful because they allow the parties to save significant time and resources by admitting evidence by way of written arguments as opposed to calling costly expert witnesses at trial.[55] If the applicant is impecunious, then this method of providing expert evidence can mitigate disadvantages inherent to the adversarial system.[56] Brandeis briefs are also valuable on appeal. The malleable nature of legislative fact evidence and the slow progression of any appeal to an apex court could result in some evidentiary records becoming outdated.[57] Topics such as the harms caused by the sex work laws or the efficacy of the prohibitions pertaining to sex work are precisely the type of empirical questions in which evidence could feasibly evolve over a relatively short period of time.

Writing in the American context, Allison Orr Larsen agrees that many of the Brandeis briefs submitted to American courts are insightful and written by leading experts. Yet she also finds that the American courts are "inundated with eleventh-hour, untested, advocacy-motivated claims of factual expertise."[58] Alan Young makes a similar point.[59] Although less factual support exists in the Canadian context, the fact that a similar jurisdiction has experienced partiality problems when relying on Brandeis briefs strongly suggests that Young's concerns are meritorious. Because judges have difficulty deciphering which expert evidence is reliable during the course of a trial, it is reasonable to conclude that they will have similar difficulties determining which legislative fact evidence to rely on when that evidence is submitted by way of Brandeis briefs. For this reason, a liberal approach to admitting Brandeis briefs is unlikely to make legislative fact evidence more understandable to courts, though it can mitigate the financial challenges that applicants face when challenging a law implicating legislative facts.

Legal Education

Improving legal education with respect to the sciences is also a potential strategy that courts and law schools can employ to mitigate the negative

90 | *Attenuating Rights*

impact of complex scientific evidence on the justice system. As Justice Binnie suggests, law schools can teach courses on scientific method and the law to better ensure that lawyers are capable of presenting complex scientific evidence.[60] Similarly, Perryman more recently suggested that "[t]here is an important role ... for law schools and professional development organizations to train future lawyers and current lawyers to become literate and effective consumers of social science research."[61] For Perryman, however, this potential is "currently under realized" since law schools do not appear to be prioritizing a better understanding of legislative fact evidence.[62]

Judicial programs, such as those provided by the National Judicial Institute, might also offer training sessions to judges to give them a grounding in the sciences. However, offering such education will not necessarily result in judicial enrolment. A plethora of evolving legal issues exists for which judges can seek education, and given their personal experiences, it might be that better understanding of the sciences is low on their lists of priorities. Creating broader cultural change via education requires a deep-seated and long-term commitment from law schools and legal education programs to improving the capacities of lawyers and judges to understand scientific evidence. Such a change will not happen quickly and, by all accounts, is only beginning to gain some momentum in the legal literature.

It is nevertheless notable that some judiciaries have proven to be capable of engaging with scientific evidence. In comparing the Canadian and German experiences, Jula Hughes and Vanessa MacDonnell observe that "the study of law tends to be somewhat more interdisciplinary in Germany [because] legal sociologists, criminologists and legal historians form part of most law faculties or work closely with legal academics."[63] For Hughes and MacDonnell, this different relationship between the legal profession and the sciences "may reduce the sense of splendid academic isolation that is so often palpable in Canadian law faculties."[64] Relatedly, the authors note that almost all judges on the German Constitutional Court "hold concurrent professorial appointments ... [and] have doctoral and professorial degrees in law."[65] Legal academics in Germany also "have the opportunity (frequently exercised) to sit as part-time judges[.] ... [which] results in a legal discourse that is informed by daily contact between judges and fellow academics from law as well as ... other disciplines."[66]

Hughes and MacDonnell also note that the structure of the German Constitution[67] facilitates better understanding of scientific evidence. Article 26 of the German Constitutional Court's enabling statute provides that the court has a "general obligation to discover the truth through independent and self-initiated investigation."[68] Moreover, Article 27a provides the German Constitutional Court with "the power to invite third party experts to comment on issues before the court."[69] For Hughes and MacDonnell, "[t]he combined effect of these investigatory powers is that the German Constitutional Court has both an opportunity and an obligation to augment the evidentiary record through independent inquiry."[70] The different judicial culture and broader available constitutional powers can help to explain why the German Constitutional Court is rarely criticized for its understanding of social science evidence.[71]

Recruiting Scientifically Trained Judges

Justice Binnie further suggests that it would be appropriate for the governments who appoint justices to recruit those with requisite training in the sciences.[72] When allocating particular judges to hear cases, the more qualified judges can be appointed to cases likely to include extensive scientific evidence. Since constitutional cases require a notice of constitutional question to be filed with the courts at an early stage,[73] the courts will have time to assess which of their justices will be most capable of deciphering a vast and complex scientific record. Such availability would have been beneficial in a case such as *Bedford*. Although Justice Himel did an admirable job, she was appointed originally as the case management judge. It is only because no other judge was willing to take the case that she became the trial judge.[74]

Yet, whenever a type of expertise is prioritized in judicial appointments, it is likely that judges with other desirable qualities will be passed over. It is thus difficult to predict how Justice Binnie's proposal might impact the judiciary more broadly. More pressingly, this type of change requires

92 | *Attenuating Rights*

significant time to develop a broad swath of lawyers capable of being judges with the relevant scientific and legal skills necessary to preside over these complex matters. It is unlikely that there is a sufficient number of these types of lawyers given the educational priorities of law schools and judiciaries. Waiting for properly equipped judges to enter the judiciary is therefore an inadequate response to a currently pressing problem.

Modifying the Adversarial System

There is also a variety of legal reforms that Parliament could adopt to aid courts in deciding constitutional challenges implicating legislative facts. First, it is possible to permit courts to appoint their own expert witnesses, as occurs in many inquisitorial justice systems.[75] Research shows that judges "have less trust in party-appointed experts whose statements are often considered to have low credibility due to the risk of partiality,"[76] whereas they afford court-appointed experts "a greater degree of trustworthiness."[77] Allowing courts to appoint their own experts mitigates the issue of impartial experts raised earlier. In turn, the expert evidence is more likely to be communicated in a neutral and clear way to the trial judge if the expert feels no loyalty to a particular side of a legal dispute. As long as judges approach the court-appointed expert's evidence with as much rigour as they otherwise would approach expert testimony, this reform would make it less likely that judges are deciding constitutional issues based on a distorted picture of the empirical evidence.[78]

A similar reform would require the parties to agree on joint experts. In the United Kingdom, for instance, parties are required to agree on which expert will testify, and, if they cannot agree, then the judge may decide which expert to appoint.[79] The *Federal Court Rules*[80] in Canada similarly allow litigants to appoint a joint expert but only if all parties consent.[81] However, there is no safeguard allowing the judge to appoint an expert in the absence of agreement by counsel. Although this proposal can be useful when appointing experts to inform the trial judge on some scientific facts,[82] it is much less likely that counsel will agree on witnesses in cases in which expert evidence is dispositive of the

Legislative Facts and the Charter | 93

constitutional issue and the relevant experts typically take clear political stances. The sex work laws are illustrative. As Justice Himel concluded, many of the experts called by the parties in *Bedford* eschewed their role as neutral witnesses and advocated for a particular resolution of the case based on their preferred model of sex work regulation.[83]

A more meritorious legislative amendment would require that the expert witnesses of all parties testify concurrently.[84] This is more likely to be an effective means of communicating evidence for several reasons. First, it is more efficient than calling each expert individually since there is almost certainly overlap in testimony even among competing experts.[85] Second, experts can be required to deal with contentious issues one at a time. This approach to testifying would be less confusing for the trial judge since it avoids the need to sort out competing accounts of various issues based on expert testimony typically spanning several days.[86] Finally, concurrent testimony deters advocacy-based testimony.[87] As Justice Binnie explains, "[e]xperts testifying in the presence of one another are likely to be more measured and complete in their pronouncements, knowing that exaggeration or errors will be pounced upon instantly by a learned colleague, as opposed to being argued about days later, perhaps by unlearned opposing counsel."[88]

The *Federal Court Rules* currently allow for expert witnesses to "comment on the views of other panel members" and "pose questions to other panel members."[89] Several provinces also allow for concurrent expert testimony in pretrial proceedings to aid in resolving key issues before trial.[90] Although requiring experts to provide testimony concurrently in criminal proceedings poses dangers – notably those arising from the panel of experts saying something inadmissible before a jury – this problem is nonexistent in constitutional cases since such cases are heard by a judge alone. However, proceedings related to the constitutionality of laws considered outside the Federal Court and Federal Court of Appeal do not permit concurrent testimony.[91] This is unfortunate since such an approach is most likely to help judges understand the complex legislative fact evidence that they frequently encounter in the criminal law context.

94 | *Attenuating Rights*

CONCLUSION

Trial judges are currently ill equipped to render decisions based on complex and voluminous expert evidence outlining legislative facts. Although it is possible that legal culture will adapt to the need to educate lawyers and judges on scientific evidence, constitutional decisions must be decided when they are raised. These circumstances have resulted in an urgent need to help judges better understand legislative fact evidence. This issue is especially pressing since the Supreme Court recognizes that legislative fact evidence is frequently dispositive of constitutional issues.[92] Adopting innovative procedures to increase the efficiency and efficacy of calling expert witnesses to testify about legislative facts in constitutional cases is a promising means to reform the process of adjudication for determining legislative facts. However, such proposals have not been adequately adopted. Although allowing robust appellate review of legislative fact evidence is not a perfect solution, it currently constitutes a least-worst option capable of preventing some laws from being struck down or upheld based on erroneous evidence.

5

The Principles of Instrumental Rationality

THE SECOND MAJOR LEGAL change undertaken in *Bedford* involved a reconceptualization of three principles of fundamental justice: arbitrariness, overbreadth, and gross disproportionality. These principles collectively assess a law's "means-ends" or "instrumental rationality."[1] Put differently, the principles consider whether a law has any illogical or severe effects on an individual's life, liberty, or security of the person interest. Prior to *Bedford*, these principles weighed a law's overall effects against its ability to achieve its objective.[2] The Supreme Court in *Bedford* replaced this "holistic" conception of the instrumental rationality principles with an "individualistic" one. Under the new approach, courts must presume that the law achieves its objective and ask whether the law has an arbitrary, overbroad, or grossly disproportionate effect on a single individual. If so, then the law violates fundamental justice, and the court must determine whether the ability of the law to achieve its objective can justify the infringement of rights.[3]

The individualization of the instrumental rationality principles was necessary given the overlap between the holistic conception of those principles and the proportionality test for justifying a law under section 1 of the Charter. As several commentators observed, the holistic conception of the arbitrariness principle parallelled the "rationale connection" inquiry; overbreadth's prior assessment of whether a law is

96 | *Attenuating Rights*

"necessary" to obtain its objective duplicated the minimal impairment analysis; and gross disproportionality was similar to the final stage of the proportionality test considering whether a law's salutary and deleterious effects strike a reasonable balance.[4] Carving out a distinct role for the instrumental rationality principles vis-à-vis section 1 therefore made the relationship between sections 1 and 7 more coherent.

Yet the Supreme Court's new understanding of the instrumental rationality principles caused a variety of other problems. First, the individualistic approach made it unclear whether it is necessary to preserve all three principles of fundamental justice given the substantial overlap among them.[5] Second, it is questionable whether the Supreme Court's favoured principle of overbreadth meets the requirements to qualify as a principle of fundamental justice.[6] Third, the Supreme Court's requirement that judges presume the law achieves its objective at the section 7 stage of analysis rendered the arbitrariness principle moot[7] and unjustly raised the burden of proof for gross disproportionality.[8] Finally, and most concerning, the individualization of the instrumental rationality principles rendered cases decided based on these principles of negligible precedential value.[9] These effects suggest that the Supreme Court's reconfiguration of the instrumental rationality principles in *Bedford* was a failure.

OVERLAPPING RIGHTS

The fact that all three instrumental rationality principles compare a law's means and ends raises a question: Was it necessary to constitutionalize three distinct principles? Early commentators suggested that the individualistic conception of the overbreadth principle crowded out the arbitrariness and gross disproportionality principles.[10] There was some intuitive appeal to the suggestion that arbitrariness was unnecessary in light of the broad reach of the overbreadth principle. As the Supreme Court explained in *Bedford,* a law is arbitrary if it does not have *any* connection to its objective.[11] Because overbreadth requires only that a law is arbitrary as applied to a *single* individual, it is plausible that any law that violates the arbitrariness principle also infringes the overbreadth principle.

This argument must be considered in light of the different ways that a law can violate the arbitrariness principle. Early in its jurisprudence, the Supreme Court acknowledged that a law is arbitrary if it has no logical connection to its objective. Thus, a law that claims to accomplish X but really achieves Y would violate fundamental justice. In *Bedford*, however, the Supreme Court affirmed that a law can also be arbitrary if the law cannot achieve its objective.[12] In other words, despite the law's objective and text being aligned, a law will be arbitrary if there is no evidence demonstrating that it is capable of achieving its objective. I will refer to the former conception of arbitrariness as a *logical* failure and the latter conception as an *empirical* failure of instrumental rationality.[13]

The individualization of the instrumental rationality principles rendered the logical conception of arbitrariness moot. Overbreadth concerns itself with laws that apply in a manner divorced from the law's objective in part (a partial logical failure).[14] It must follow that a complete logical failure – breaches of the arbitrariness principle – can be divided into individual failures of logical rationality.[15] As I observe elsewhere, "[a] litigant faced with proving that a law fails logically to further its aim to a single individual (overbreadth) as opposed to all individuals (arbitrariness) would reasonably choose the former path."[16] This choice is sensible because it requires that "the state bear the heavier onus of showing that the law possesses some rational connection to its objective (absence of arbitrariness) under the section 1 analysis."[17]

The same conclusion does not necessarily follow with respect to empirical breaches of the arbitrariness principle. A law that cannot achieve its objective can be tailored in a manner that provides judges with discretion in determining whether to apply the law. The general deterrence provision in section 718(b) of the *Criminal Code of Canada*[18] is illustrative. That provision allows judges to increase sentences to deter the population generally from committing a particular crime. The empirical evidence strongly suggests that mandatory minimum sentences designed to deter the population generally do not work.[19] If widely

98 | *Attenuating Rights*

publicized mandatory minimum sentencing provisions do not have a deterrent effect, then it is even less likely that a judge who increases an individual offender's sentence will be capable of generally deterring crime. It is simply unlikely that many people would know about such use of the general deterrence principle, let alone incorporate it into their reasoning when determining whether to commit a crime.[20]

As a result, it is likely that a provision with the sole purpose of allowing a judge to increase a sentence to deter the population generally has no empirical connection to its objective and therefore is arbitrary. Yet the structure of the general deterrence provision would prevent a finding of overbreadth. In imposing a sentence, a judge is permitted to choose from among the various sentencing principles to aid in crafting a fair and just sentence. If a judge is aware of a sentencing principle's inefficacy, then the judge can choose not to use that principle in crafting a sentence.[21] This discretion therefore shields the law from a finding of overbreadth since the law need not catch any conduct divorced from its objective. Such discretion cannot, however, protect the law from an arbitrariness challenge. The mere existence of such a law is contrary to fundamental justice regardless of whether judges are required to use that law.[22] Aside from this narrow exception, however, the arbitrariness principle serves little purpose post-*Bedford*.[23]

It is also likely that the overbreadth and gross disproportionality principles have significant if not complete overlap. At times, the Supreme Court has conflated the two doctrines, writing that "[o]verbreadth ... addresses the potential infringement of fundamental justice where the adverse effect of a legislative measure on the individuals subject to its strictures is *grossly* disproportionate to the state interest the legislation seeks to protect."[24] Writing a year before *Bedford,* the Supreme Court again observed that overbreadth and gross disproportionality "may simply offer different lenses through which to consider a single breach of the principles of fundamental justice."[25] The Supreme Court in *Bedford* similarly recognized that there was "significant overlap" between these principles.[26] Given the distinct methods for proving overbreadth and gross disproportionality breaches – one assessing a law's logic, the other its severity – it is more difficult to prove overlap

The Principles of Instrumental Rationality | 99

between these principles as a matter of strict logic. Nevertheless, I am unaware of a single case in which a law found to be grossly disproportionate could not also be framed as a violation of the overbreadth principle or vice versa.[27]

The Supreme Court's decision in *Bedford* is illustrative of this overlap. The grossly disproportionate effects of the prohibition against keeping bawdy houses were proven by comparing the nuisances arising as a result of keeping a bawdy house with the law's severe impact on sex workers' security interests.[28] However, as both lower courts determined, an absolute prohibition also overshot the provision's objective since it prohibited sex workers from operating discreetly in their homes.[29] Despite the complete prohibition's ability to effectively thwart many nuisances caused by sex work, it appears that the law still managed to catch individual conduct that had no connection to its objective.

A similar conclusion can be drawn with respect to the prohibition on communicating in public for the purposes of sex work. The Supreme Court found the provision to be grossly disproportionate since the risk to sex workers caused by prohibiting them from screening clientele was not a constitutionally proportionate means to address the various nuisances caused by public solicitation.[30] At trial, however, it was also contended that the provision violated the overbreadth principle.[31] The trial court rejected this argument, concluding that the prohibition was "necessary to achieve the [law's] objective of eliminating social nuisance."[32] In other words, since public solicitation generally causes a nuisance, its complete prohibition was the only realistic means for Parliament to achieve its objective.

As the Supreme Court observed in *Bedford,* the question of "necessary to achieve" is different from the question of whether a law has an arbitrary effect on a single person.[33] Applying the Supreme Court's broader conception of overbreadth, it is not difficult to imagine a sex worker communicating in isolated public places, or at least communicating with clientele discreetly, thereby not causing any public nuisance. If true, then the prohibition on communicating for the purposes of sex work catches some individual conduct divorced from its objective. Although the Supreme Court in *Bedford* was not asked to resolve this

100 | *Attenuating Rights*

question, its conclusion that "[t]he provision's negative impact ... is a grossly disproportionate response to the *possibility* of nuisance caused by street prostitution" suggests that the overbreadth argument has merit.[34]

Finally, the trial court in *Bedford* found the living on the avails prohibition both overbroad and grossly disproportionate.[35] Although the Crown claimed that the provision was designed to protect sex workers from exploitation, it also served to prevent them from hiring protective employees such as bodyguards, drivers, and receptionists and was therefore overbroad.[36] Yet the law also arguably struck a grossly disproportionate balance compared with its ability to achieve its objective. Because bodyguards and the like help to protect sex workers, the law does not achieve its objective at all when applied to those who hire nonexploitive workers. As the Ontario Court of Appeal observed in *Bedford,* a law that is incapable of achieving its objective in readily definable scenarios, yet also puts the lives of innocent citizens at risk in those scenarios, has effects grossly disproportionate to its objective.[37]

The latter instance of overlap is unique because it claims that any instance of overbreadth inherently violates the gross disproportionality principle. It does so by comparing a law's inability to fulfill its objective in a particular instance with its effect on life, liberty, and security of the person. Given the importance of the latter interests, it is reasonable to conclude that a narrow, inefficacious application of law will have grossly disproportionate effects on particular individuals. The Supreme Court's requirement that courts presume that an impugned law achieves its objective nevertheless would have prevented a gross disproportionality breach. If prohibiting sex workers from hiring employees is necessary to prevent the exploitation of vulnerable sex workers – a claim that the Crown made without much supporting evidence[38] – then it is not clear that the harm avoided would be disproportionate to the harm caused by taking away this particular option for increasing the safety of sex work.

Determining the extent of the overlap between overbreadth and gross disproportionality therefore is likely to turn in part on which conception of the gross disproportionality principle the courts endorse. As I discuss in more detail below, the extent of the overlap will also turn on whether the Supreme Court's decision to presume that an objective achieves its ends can withstand closer scrutiny. The possibility that the gross disproportionality and overbreadth principles overlap completely with each other nevertheless raises a more important question that the Supreme Court did not address in *Bedford:* Do these expansive versions of each principle meet the requirements to qualify as principles of fundamental justice?[39]

FUNDAMENTAL JUSTICE

The broad scope of the overbreadth principle opened up various types of laws to constitutional challenge under section 7 of the Charter. An illustrative case is the Ontario Court of Appeal's decision in *R v Michaud*.[40] The applicant challenged a prohibition found in the *Highway Traffic Act*,[41] and its associated regulations,[42] requiring drivers of large vehicles to install speed limiters. The applicant violated the provision by setting his speed limiter 4.4 kilometres per hour over the legal limit.[43] In challenging the provision, the applicant called expert evidence confirming that in some rare instances it is necessary to accelerate beyond the speed limit to avoid an accident.[44] Applying the individualistic approach, the Ontario Court of Appeal concluded that in those rare instances the law endangered that person's life and therefore infringed their security of the person interest. Since the objective of the speed limiter law was to make the roads safer, the Ontario Court of Appeal found that the law contradicted its objective by making the roads less safe in narrow circumstances. The law was therefore overbroad.[45]

The Ontario Court of Appeal nevertheless upheld the law under section 1 of the Charter. Since expert evidence demonstrated that the speed limiter was necessary to avoid far more accidents than it caused, the infringement on the applicant's rights was readily found to be rationally connected to its objective, to be minimally impairing of that objective, and to strike a reasonable balance between its salutary and

102 | *Attenuating Rights*

deleterious effects.[46] The Ontario Court of Appeal nevertheless expressed concern about the fact that the Supreme Court's new conception of overbreadth could so easily result in a breach of "fundamental justice." As it observed, "the regulator [often] chooses a pro-active bright-line rule in preference to a general behavioural standard, even though such a rule is usually over-inclusive and errs on the side of safety."[47] Legislatures especially employ bright-line rules as opposed to standards in areas of law that implicate human safety. In *Michaud,* for instance, it is more sensible to impose a speed limiter than to tell people driving large vehicles to "drive safely." The latter standard likely would result in many more accidents than the bright-line rule, even if in some instances that rule also causes accidents.[48]

A similar concern can be raised with respect to criminal laws employing bright-line rules. An illustrative provision is found in section 150.1 of the *Criminal Code,* which prohibits having sex with those under the age of sixteen subject to several exceptions for those close in age. As Hamish Stewart observes, the object of this prohibition is to prevent young persons from having premature sexual relations.[49] Yet it is likely that at least *some* people under the age of sixteen are capable of making responsible choices about their sexual activity.[50] As Stewart explains, "[o]ne might think of an emotionally mature complainant who is fifteen years and eleven months old and who is in a non-exploitative sexual relationship with a twenty-two-year-old accused."[51] It is likely that restricting the sexual choices of such a person intrudes on a decision of "fundamental personal importance" and therefore violates the liberty interest of the mature minor.[52] The law would also engage the liberty interests of the older partner, who could be imprisoned if convicted.[53] Because the law applies in a manner contrary to its objective of preventing premature sexual relations, Stewart reasonably concludes that it violates the individualistic conception of the overbreadth principle.[54]

Given the overbreadth principle's wide scope, the Ontario Court of Appeal in *Michaud* questioned the efficacy of the Supreme Court's individualistic understanding of the instrumental rationality principles.

The Principles of Instrumental Rationality | 103

In its view, courts ought to resort to the holistic conception of instrumental rationality when assessing regulatory laws, though it could have added criminal laws employing bright-line rules as well.[55] In defence of this position, the Ontario Court of Appeal maintained that it is "strangely incongruous to consider highway safety regulation, or any safety regulation, as 'depriving' anyone of 'security of the person' or of engaging the 'principles of fundamental justice' in the sense demanded by s. 7."[56]

Expanding this critique, I elsewhere tie the Ontario Court of Appeal's observations to a more fundamental question: Does the overbreadth principle qualify as a principle of fundamental justice? To qualify as such a principle, the Supreme Court determined, a principle must meet several requirements. Most importantly, there must be some "societal consensus" that the principle is "vital or fundamental to our societal notion of justice."[57] In making this determination, the courts are not concerned with whether there is consensus in the empirical sense. Instead, it is necessary to consider the "shared assumptions upon which our system of justice is grounded."[58] For the Supreme Court, these assumptions "find their meaning in the cases and traditions that have long detailed the basic norms for how the state deals with its citizens," and they are principles that "[s]ociety views ... as essential to the administration of justice."[59]

The "individualistic" conception of overbreadth is unlikely to garner societal consensus in this sense. In effect, the Supreme Court maintains that "it is a principle of fundamental justice that any law engaging life, liberty, or security of the person must be crafted perfectly and be aligned with its objective in all instances."[60] It is doubtful that many people would agree that such a strict standard is imperative to justice. This conclusion derives from the fact that bright-line rules are a necessary means to protect against human fallibility.[61] If given a standard to follow, then some inevitably will be incapable of achieving the ends of the law because of errors in judgment. Where human fallibility is particularly acute and likely to lead to serious consequences, bright-line rules are used in place of standards to protect the broader community.

104 | *Attenuating Rights*

Such rules therefore can be expected to routinely violate the overbreadth principle if they engage the life, liberty, or security of the person interest. It is for this reason that the Ontario Court of Appeal in *Michaud* viewed the Supreme Court's individualistic conception of overbreadth as "trivializing" the concept of fundamental justice.[62] It would have done better to put this criticism in section 7 language: the individualistic conception of overbreadth is unlikely to attract significant societal consensus given the numerous instances in which bright-line rules are prudent and necessary tools of governance.

A similar argument was successfully advanced in *R v Malmo-Levine*.[63] The applicant argued that John Stuart Mill's harm principle ought to qualify as a principle of fundamental justice. The harm principle provides that only conduct that harms another person ought to be subject to state sanction.[64] Despite the Supreme Court's recognition that Mill's conception of harm is frequently the target of criminal prohibitions,[65] the fact that it was not sufficient to capture all offences was enough to find an absence of societal consensus.[66] This followed even though the Supreme Court cited only a small number of offences in the *Criminal Code* in which harm to others does not underpin the criminal prohibition.[67] Similarly, there are numerous instances in which intuition suggests that a bright-line rule does not violate any generally accepted conception of justice.[68] Given the high bar for satisfying the societal consensus requirement exhibited in *Malmo-Levine,* it ought to follow that the individualistic conception of overbreadth also fails to qualify as a principle of fundamental justice.

A similar critique applies to the Ontario Court of Appeal's conception of the gross disproportionality principle. As explained earlier, the appellate court found that the communication and bawdy house provisions violated fundamental justice by comparing each law's effects on sex workers' security of the person interest with a narrow, inefficacious application of law. Since this understanding of gross disproportionality catches the same conduct as the overbreadth principle, it is unlikely that it would attract sufficient societal consensus to qualify as a principle of fundamental justice.

The Principles of Instrumental Rationality | 105

There is nevertheless a good case for constitutionalizing the gross disproportionality principle if its effects are simply compared with the law's objective at the section 7 stage. The Supreme Court has affirmed that the principles of fundamental justice take their shape from the other legal rights provisions in the Charter.[69] The prohibition against cruel and unusual punishment in section 12 of the Charter effectively mirrors this version of the gross disproportionality principle. Whereas section 12 prohibits any punishment grossly disproportionate to the objectives of a particular sentence, section 7 prohibits any other grossly disproportionate effects caused by a law compared with its objective. For this reason, the individualistic conception of gross disproportionality should qualify as a principle of fundamental justice.[70] However, constitutionalizing the gross disproportionality principle in this manner raises other problems with respect to the effect of presuming the efficacy of a law at the section 7 stage of analysis.

PRESUMING EFFICACY

A central feature of the individualistic conception of the instrumental rationality principles is that courts must presume that the law achieves its purpose at the section 7 stage of analysis.[71] To conclude otherwise runs contrary to the main objective of individualizing the instrumental rationality principles: ensuring a fair distribution of the burden of proof between applicants and the Crown at the sections 7 and 1 stages of analysis.[72] Under the holistic conception, applicants were required not only to prove the effects of the law on all members of society but also to demonstrate the overall efficacy of the law. As the Supreme Court rightly observed in *Bedford*, requiring constitutional applicants "to establish the efficacy of the law versus its deleterious consequences on members of society as a whole" imposed the government's burden under section 1 of the Charter on the applicant.[73]

Presuming the efficacy of the challenged law at the section 7 stage and requiring only an arbitrary, overbroad, or grossly disproportionate effect on a single litigant therefore combined to more fairly distribute the

106 | *Attenuating Rights*

burden of proof between applicants and the Crown. As Hamish Stewart observes, however, presuming the efficacy of a law's objective at the section 7 stage also renders the arbitrariness principle unworkable. For a law to be arbitrary, there must be *no* rational connection between its objective and its effects. As Stewart explains, "[i]t is unclear how a court is supposed to decide that a law has no rational connection to its objective without considering how well it achieves that objective."[74] As such, the Supreme Court's individualistic approach cannot encompass the arbitrariness principle. To the extent that arbitrariness is not crowded out by the other instrumental rationality principles, resorting to the holistic approach is therefore necessary to make the arbitrariness principle functional.

Presuming that a law achieves its objective can also dramatically affect the ability of applicants to prove that a law violates the gross disproportionality principle.[75] The Supreme Court's decision in *Canada (Attorney General) v PHS Community Services Society* is illustrative.[76] Therein, the Supreme Court considered the constitutionality of a minister's refusal to grant an exemption required to operate a safe injection site. Social science evidence established that the safe injection site saved lives by preventing overdoses without increasing drug use or crime in the surrounding area.[77] The objective of the minister's decision was to uphold public health and safety by deterring drug use.[78] This objective effectively presumed that those addicted to hard drugs will discontinue their use based on the government's strict opposition to drug use.[79] Despite the nature of addiction rendering that assumption dubious,[80] the individualistic conception would allow the Crown to argue that the lives imperilled by closing a safe injection site would be proportionate to those saved by the law's ability to deter people from taking drugs. Since *PHS* was decided pre-*Bedford*, the Supreme Court was able to avoid this conclusion by attributing little if any efficacy to the minister's decision in achieving its objective.[81]

The living on the avails offence discussed earlier is also illustrative of how presuming that a law achieves its objective can thwart an instrumental rationality analysis. If I am correct that the individualistic conception of overbreadth is not a principle of fundamental justice,

The Principles of Instrumental Rationality | 107

then the applicants in *Bedford* could only have pleaded that the law was inconsistent with the individualistic conception of the gross disproportionality principle.[82] In so doing, the court would have presumed that the law was capable of preventing the exploitation of sex workers by prohibiting all employment arrangements with them. It is not clear that grossly disproportionate effects result from the living on the avails provision given the importance of the legislation's objective. If this presumption is removed, however, then the grossly disproportionate effects can be established. The proven impact of the law on the security interest of sex workers would constitute a grossly disproportionate effect if the evidence failed to establish that the living on the avails provision had any significant effect in preventing sex workers from being exploited.

To avoid the evidentiary problem arising from presuming that the law achieves its objective, both Stewart and I have suggested separately that courts modify the burden of proof at the section 7 stage of the analysis. For Stewart, the courts under the individualistic approach should afford the litigant the opportunity to submit evidence to challenge the efficacy of an impugned law.[83] In other words, it is possible to resort to the holistic approach if the applicant thinks that the individualistic approach disadvantages their case. This prescription nevertheless overlooks the Supreme Court's concern with the holistic approach: it places the Crown's section 1 burden on the applicant.[84] Alternatively, I have proposed that the Crown and the applicant share the burden at the section 7 stage of analysis. If the applicant thinks that the law is incapable of achieving its objective, then the applicant can raise a reasonable doubt about the efficacy of the law. The Crown can then be forced to prove the extent to which the law achieves its aim. This approach would allow courts to weigh the effect of the law against its actual benefits without eschewing the main benefit of the individualistic conception of the instrumental rationality principles.[85]

Blending the individualistic and holistic conceptions of the instrumental rationality principles nevertheless raises other issues. First, the blended approach renders the section 1 analysis redundant. Because this was one of the primary reasons for abandoning the holistic conception

108 | *Attenuating Rights*

of instrumental rationality, it should weigh heavily against adopting the blended approach to the instrumental rationality principles.[86] Second, the blended approach is inconsistent with the wording of section 7 of the Charter. That provision applies if *anyone* is affected by a law inconsistent with the principles of fundamental justice. The blended approach – like the holistic conception of instrumental rationality – considers the law's impact on all citizens, not just on the individual, and compares it with the overall efficacy of the law.[87] The extent to which these inconsistencies should be tolerated depends on whether the instrumental rationality principles further what I maintain is their broader purpose: facilitating dialogue between courts and legislatures about the legitimate scope of rights.[88]

DISMANTLING THE DIALOGUE

Because judges are not elected, striking down laws enacted by the majority of the population flies in the face of a central tenet of democracy: majority rule.[89] At the same time, majorities historically have used the law to oppress marginalized peoples. The need to protect core human rights arguably requires that the judiciary – a politically independent institution – be vested with some power of judicial review.[90] To balance these competing interests, the Charter attempts to facilitate dialogue between legislative and judicial branches. Constructive dialogue on the scope of rights, the theory goes, allows judges to protect core rights while softening the critique that majority rule is undermined.[91] Although empirical study in this area is difficult to conduct, some scholars conclude that instances of "judicial activism" (the antithesis of constructive dialogue) have lessened significantly after the Supreme Court began relying on the dialogue metaphor as a means of conceptualizing the appropriate relationship between courts and legislatures in a constitutional democracy.[92]

Dialogue is facilitated under the Charter in two main ways. Where a law violates a right, section 1 of the Charter allows the government to contend that the law should be upheld for important policy reasons. Before a court can strike down the law, therefore, it must explain why

The Principles of Instrumental Rationality | 109

the government's policy reasons for infringing a right are not rationally connected to the law's objective, minimally impairing of the right, and/or fail to strike a reasonable balance between the law's salutary and deleterious effects. As Kent Roach explains, "proportionality analysis is inherently dialogic or interactional in nature [since it] allows legislatures to articulate their regulatory ambitions and explain the practical problems they face in achieving them."[93] Importantly, relying on the concept of proportionality takes courts away from the text of rights provisions and judicial precedents and requires that judges consider the government's policy reasons for infringing a Charter right.[94] As Roach observes, the Canadian experience has proven that section 1 review often leads to respectful conversations about the legitimate scope of rights between two parties with "different abilities, concerns, and perspectives."[95]

Barring a section 1 justification, the notwithstanding clause found in section 33 of the Charter allows the government to engage in dialogue with the courts on the legitimate scope of rights by overriding a judicial decision for a period of five years. By invoking the latter clause, the legislature employs its right to have the final word on a rights issue in the short term. However, after the five-year period expires, political tempers typically cool, and reasoned discourse on rights prevails. Indeed, Canadian courts and legislatures often resolve their differences either by accepting the original rights decision or by enacting a new law that strikes a compromise but is consistent with the Charter.[96] Although the notwithstanding clause is rarely used – in large part because of the popularity of courts[97] – the criminal law is an area where Parliament might feasibly employ the notwithstanding clause given the existence of strong majoritarian biases against criminal defendants in Canada.[98]

The instrumental rationality principles have nevertheless been criticized for undermining constitutional dialogue by placing too much power in the hands of judges. As Peter Hogg observes, "a judge who disapproves of a law will always be able to find that it is overbroad" because "the purpose of a law is a judicial construct, which can be defined widely or narrowly as the reviewing court sees fit."[99] The doctrine of overbreadth, Hogg contends, therefore "confers an exceedingly

110 | *Attenuating Rights*

discretionary power of review on the [Supreme] Court."[100] Outside the constitutional context, it is notable that the court maintains that legislation often "does not simply further one goal but rather strikes a balance among several goals, some of which may be in tension."[101] In the instrumental rationality context, legislation is nevertheless reduced to a singular purpose despite Hogg's observation that allowing judges to circumscribe the purpose of a law will often dictate whether the law violates the instrumental rationality principles.[102]

As I explain in Chapter 7, Hogg's criticisms – which also apply at the section 1 stage of the analysis – can be addressed by avoiding the legal fiction that laws serve only one purpose.[103] The instrumental rationality principles are nevertheless flawed for another reason: the type of "dialogue" that they promote. In their seminal article, Peter Hogg and Allison Bushell maintain that dialogue occurs when "a judicial decision striking down a law on *Charter* grounds can be reversed, modified, or avoided by a new law."[104] Despite this broad definition, not all legislative responses to judicial rulings are agreed to count as genuine dialogue. As Roach explains, instances in which legislatures explicitly overrule judicial decisions do not count as dialogue.[105] Legislative decisions claiming that the judiciary's reasoning was "wrong" should instead invoke the notwithstanding clause since this provision was designed for expressing such disagreements.[106]

Instances in which the legislature employs the dialogue metaphor to justify overruling the judiciary's application of a right with legislation is known as a "coordinate interpretation" approach to dialogue.[107] Proponents of this approach maintain that both legislatures and courts have equal power to interpret the Charter. Legislatures therefore act legitimately when they overturn judicial decisions with mere legislation.[108] Coordinate construction theorists support this understanding of dialogue because it provides a more palatable response to the criticism that judges ought not overrule democratically elected legislatures.[109] Roach nevertheless contends that this understanding of dialogue is dangerous.[110] In essence, the coordinate interpretation approach allows legislatures to undermine judicial rulings with mere legislation, which,

The Principles of Instrumental Rationality | 111

Roach persuasively maintains, "risks making a legislature a judge in its own majoritarian causes."[111]

Invoking the instrumental rationality principles as a method of judicial review serves a purpose similar to the coordinate interpretation approach to judicial review. Although legislatures cannot pass the *same* laws in response to judicial decisions, a legislature can slightly alter the law's objective or effects to sidestep a judicial precedent. Upon so doing, it is not clear that the law strikes an unconstitutional balance since it will become necessary to rebalance the law's objective and effects.[112] As will become apparent in Chapter 8, Parliament passed such a response to the *Bedford* decision. The first two judges to seriously consider the constitutionality of these laws found that many of the same harms accrued to sex workers despite the objectives of the sex work laws being altered and the protections afforded by the laws expanded slightly.[113] I have elsewhere detailed at length a similar trend with respect to legislative responses over the past decade to constitutional decisions affecting Parliament's ability to shut down safe injection sites,[114] prohibit euthanasia,[115] and place inmates in solitary confinement.[116]

The instrumental rationality principles are therefore inherently problematic since they render decisions striking down laws of negligible precedential value. Since constitutionality turns on the narrow context of a law, minor changes that do little or nothing to address the constitutional harm identified by the courts are prima facie constitutional. This in turn allows legislatures to maintain that their response law is *compliant* with Charter rights. In my view, legislatures are much more likely to feel emboldened to pass a politically charged law if they do not have to admit a rights violation and therefore need not maintain that the infringement is justified under section 1. Although the empirical evidence in support of this claim is minimal, it is notable that Parliament historically has responded to only one ruling under section 7 of the Charter in a politically charged manner. However, as illustrated above, Parliament "has made a recent habit of so responding to the Supreme Court's decisions applying the instrumental rationality principles."[117]

112 | *Attenuating Rights*

Alternatively, if the courts employed moral philosophical principles to strike down laws – either those constitutionalized as principles of fundamental justice under section 7 or those specifically enumerated in other sections of the Charter – then the courts would be able to provide much clearer guidance with respect to which effects are constitutionally impermissible. This follows because these types of principles provide more concrete, bright-line guidance to legislatures when passing laws. As I will explain in Chapter 7, the Supreme Court could have resolved the *Bedford* case by replying in precisely this way. This was possible because the most problematic aspect of the *Bedford* case – the fact that survival sex workers could not take precautions to protect themselves – infringed the principle of fundamental justice prohibiting the conviction of individuals who act in a morally involuntary manner.[118]

CONCLUSION

The instrumental rationality principles have become the most frequently invoked principles to challenge the constitutionality of legislation.[119] The popularity of these principles is understandable given the ease with which a violation can be established. Yet the Supreme Court's decision to individualize the instrumental rationality principles gave rise to a variety of conceptual challenges that the court did not identify. It is unlikely that the individualistic conception of the overbreadth principle qualifies as a principle of fundamental justice. Moreover, the presumption that a law's objective is achieved at the section 7 stage of analysis rendered the arbitrariness principle unworkable and significantly affected the ability of some litigants to prove breaches of the gross disproportionality principle. It is possible to address the latter issue by sharing the burden of proof at the section 7 stage of analysis. However, this approach effectively resorts to the holistic conception of instrumental rationality that both duplicates the section 1 analysis and is inconsistent with the text of section 7.

Even if all of these issues could be addressed, the Supreme Court's new understanding of the instrumental rationality principles allows

The Principles of Instrumental Rationality | 113

legislatures to easily move around judicial precedent by slightly modifying a law's objective or effects. The individualistic conception of the instrumental rationality principles therefore facilitates a method of judicial review similar in principle to the disavowed coordinate construction understanding of the dialogical approach to judicial review. As a result, the Supreme Court's reconceptualization of the instrumental rationality principles serves to subject rights to effective override by the regular legislative process. Although legislatures have constitutional means to overturn judicial decisions, claiming that a piece of legislation does not violate rights is more politically palatable than claiming that a right is justifiably infringed under section 1 or overriding a decision under section 33 of the Charter. As a result, I maintain, the individualistic conception of the instrumental rationality principles allows legislatures to erode rights decisions for political gain. Constitutional principles with such an incentive structure are incapable of serving the broader purpose of judicial review: protecting rights from being overrun by majoritarian biases.

6

Suspended Declarations of Invalidity

THE FINAL WAY IN which the Supreme Court in *Bedford* jeopardized rights did not involve a change in law but arose from a failure to develop the law on granting suspended declarations of invalidity. In three brief paragraphs, the Supreme Court determined that it was appropriate to postpone invalidation of the sex work laws for one year.[1] In its view, immediately invalidating the impugned provisions "would leave prostitution totally unregulated while Parliament grapples with the complex and sensitive problem of how to deal with it."[2] The Supreme Court also placed significant weight on the fact that sex work regulation is a "matter of great public concern."[3] Although the Supreme Court acknowledged that its decision would leave sex workers at an increased risk of physical harm,[4] it also maintained that its choice was "not an easy one" and that "[n]either alternative is without difficulty."[5] Without any discussion of the competing interests, the Supreme Court suspended the declaration of invalidity.

The Supreme Court's assertion that immediately striking down the sex work laws would leave sex work unregulated failed to address the trial judge's extensive review of the various laws that overlapped with the impugned sex work laws reviewed in Chapter 3.[6] The Court therefore must be taken to have prioritized a "matter of great public concern" over the constitutional rights of the applicants. According to the Supreme Court's reasons in *Bedford,* sex work regulation is of concern to the public largely because of the nuisance abatement objectives underlying two of the three prohibitions. Suspending the declaration of invalidity therefore seems to be difficult to justify since it effectively allows majoritarian desire to enforce a nonserious policy objective to trump the security interests of a vulnerable population.

Building on the existing literature, I maintain that it is necessary to overhaul the Supreme Court's framework for determining when it is appropriate to suspend declarations of invalidity.[7] Early scholars urged a more nuanced balancing between the legislature's interests in suspending declarations of invalidity and the impacts of such a remedy on constitutional rights.[8] Others suggest developing a "two-track" response that would allow courts to grant remedies to the immediate litigants but still permit suspended declarations of invalidity as a means to foster dialogue between courts and legislatures.[9] More recently, scholars have questioned whether a legal basis exists for granting suspended declarations of invalidity in cases such as *Bedford*. The text of the Constitution arguably permits *legislatures* to suspend rights decisions only by invoking the notwithstanding clause.[10] Although courts may invoke unwritten constitutional principles to suspend a declaration of invalidity, those circumstances are exceedingly rare. Moreover, there is no principled reason that legislatures could not invoke the same unwritten constitutional principles to suspend a declaration of invalidity.[11]

In my view, these critiques require that courts grant suspended declarations of invalidity only where an immediate declaration of invalidity would violate an unwritten constitutional principle. Even in those circumstances, however, any suspension should be permitted only for as long as it would reasonably take a legislature to suspend a declaration of invalidity with its own legislation. This approach is sensible since legislatures are more capable of determining how long a suspension of invalidity is required to pass a principled reply law and whether to allow for exemptions in the interim. In all other circumstances, legislatures should be required to invoke the notwithstanding clause to suspend a declaration of invalidity. Applying this approach to the *Bedford* decision leads inexorably to the conclusion that the Supreme Court was wrong to suspend the sex work laws' declaration of invalidity.

JURISPRUDENCE

Section 52 of the *Constitution Act, 1982*[12] provides that "[t]he Constitution of Canada is the supreme law of Canada, and any law that is inconsistent with the provisions of the Constitution is, to the extent of the inconsistency, of no force or effect." Read literally, this provision states that any law that violates the Charter in an unjustifiable manner must be remedied immediately.[13] The Supreme Court originally agreed with this interpretation, suggesting that suspended declarations of invalidity are a "remedial innovation" that emerged "notwithstanding the express terms of s. 52(1)."[14]

The first case to suspend a declaration of invalidity arose in *Re Manitoba Language Rights*.[15] The Manitoba government had failed over nearly a century to translate its laws into French as required by the *Manitoba Act, 1870*.[16] Since such a task cannot be completed quickly, the Supreme Court suspended the declaration of invalidity to avoid creating a "legal vacuum" and ensuing "legal chaos" in the province.[17] Despite no express legal basis for this remedy, the suspension of invalidity served to uphold a competing but unwritten constitutional principle: the rule of law. As the Supreme Court explained in *Reference re Secession of Quebec*,[18] "the rule of law requires the creation and maintenance of an actual order of positive laws which preserves and embodies the more general principle of normative order."[19] To protect the rule of law, it was necessary to keep the unconstitutional laws in force while the Manitoba government fulfilled its constitutional duty and translated each of its laws into French.

In *Schachter v Canada*,[20] the Supreme Court affirmed two additional categories for determining whether suspending a declaration of invalidity is appropriate.[21] The first concerned the need to avoid dangers to the public.[22] An illustrative case is the court's decision in *R v Swain*.[23] There the Supreme Court struck down provisions in the *Criminal Code of Canada*[24] authorizing the indefinite detention of those acquitted by reason of mental disorder. To avoid the potential danger of an immediate release of all people detained indefinitely based on mental disorder, the court suspended the declaration of invalidity for a period of six months to allow Parliament time to respond to its decision.[25]

The final category relevant to granting a suspended declaration of invalidity concerns circumstances in which a law is deemed unconstitutional because it is "underinclusive." In these circumstances, an immediate declaration would deprive worthy persons of the law's benefits.[26] An example would be a law that provides a benefit to a particular group but fails to provide the same benefit to another group for discriminatory purposes. Striking down the law in that case would deprive all people of a benefit. As the Supreme Court reasoned in *Schachter*, the "logical remedy is to strike down but suspend the declaration of invalidity to allow the government to determine whether to cancel or extend the benefits."[27]

The approach developed in *Schachter* nevertheless gave way to a different rationale for justifying suspended declarations beginning in the late 1990s.[28] Instead of relying on pre-established categories for determining whether a suspended declaration of invalidity ought to be granted, the Supreme Court began to justify such remedies by emphasizing the appropriate institutional roles of courts and legislatures.[29] If the legislature could craft multiple policy responses to alleviate a constitutional defect, then the Supreme Court automatically suspended the declaration of invalidity to ensure that the legislature was afforded the opportunity to respond to its decision. This shift in rationale unsurprisingly resulted in the Supreme Court suspending declarations of invalidity much more frequently.[30]

Writing in *Corbiere v Canada (Minister of Indian and Northern Affairs)*,[31] Justice L'Heureux-Dubé endorsed the latter rationale for issuing suspended declarations of invalidity because it promoted dialogue between legislatures and courts.[32] Unpacking this rationale, Peter Hogg and his coauthors explained that a suspended declaration of invalidity is prudent in cases in which the legislature might respond in multiple ways because "the legislature is better placed than the court to select the appropriate remedy."[33] With minimal mention of the interim effect on rights, these authors maintain that "the *Charter* is still

118 | *Attenuating Rights*

respected, because if no new law is enacted by the time the period of suspension ends, the declaration of invalidity takes effect," and any newly enacted law "must comply with the *Charter*."[34]

Sujit Choudhry and Kent Roach similarly maintain that suspended declarations of invalidity fit "into a conception of institutional relationships under the Constitution in which both legislatures and courts take joint responsibility for ensuring compliance with constitutional norms."[35] For these authors, a suspended declaration of invalidity can be analogized to "a form of legislative remand, whereby unconstitutional legislation is sent back for reconsideration in light of the court's judgment."[36] At the same time, the authors maintain that the courts do not abdicate their responsibilities to the Constitution by suspending a declaration of invalidity. Instead, the courts formulate "a remedy that will come into effect should the legislature not enact constitutional legislation by the court's deadline."[37] The dialogical function of the Charter is again used to justify interim rights infringements without any explicit balancing of the competing interests inherent to granting suspended declarations of invalidity.

PROPOSALS FOR REFORM

Despite an extensive literature criticizing the justifications for issuing suspended declarations of invalidity, the Supreme Court in *Bedford* chose not to engage with the problems identified and the solutions offered by legal scholars. As I explain below, it is possible to employ the justificatory test for rights infringements to determine whether a suspended declaration of invalidity is appropriate. It is also feasible to suspend declarations of invalidity while providing individual litigants with interim remedies. I nevertheless agree with recent scholarship contending that both of these positions are inconsistent with the text of the Constitution, which demands that the Supreme Court abandon its practice of suspending declarations of invalidity in cases in which such a remedy is not compelled by an unwritten constitutional principle. Even in those circumstances, however, I maintain that courts should suspend a declaration of invalidity only for as long as the legislature needs to pass a law achieving the same end.

Proportionality

Grant Hoole suggests that courts ought to employ the proportionality test under section 1 of the *Charter* in determining whether a suspended declaration of invalidity should be granted.[38] From the perspective of a constitutional litigant, Hoole maintains that "the effects of a declaration temporarily extending the operation of an unconstitutional law will often be equivalent to the outright limitation of a right,"[39] at least during the period in which the declaration operates.[40] As such, Hoole maintains, any judicial decision to issue a suspended declaration must further a pressing and substantial objective; be rationally connected to that objective; minimally impair the affected constitutional rights; and strike a proportionate balance between the purpose of suspending the declaration of invalidity and the impact on rights.[41] For Hoole, this approach provides a principled framework for determining when to grant a suspended declaration of invalidity since it need not rely on the rigid categories set out in *Schachter* or solely on institutional capacity arguments to justify a remedy.[42]

This approach avoids several of the problems that Hoole identifies with the Supreme Court's jurisprudence. First, as occurred in *Bedford,* the court tends to provide inadequate reasoning since it relies only on institutional considerations to justify suspending a declaration of invalidity.[43] Second, Hoole maintains that suspended declarations of invalidity are often premised on faulty assumptions that legislatures are willing and able to remedy a constitutional defect.[44] Whether the government intentionally uses the time that a law's unconstitutionality is suspended to do nothing or is simply incapable of acting because of some other constraint, Hoole maintains that legislatures often do little to respond to constitutional rulings.[45] Third, and most importantly, the Supreme Court's abandonment of the *Schachter* categories fails to account for the profound effects of a suspended declaration of invalidity on Charter rights.[46]

120 | *Attenuating Rights*

Hoole's approach alleviates these defects by including all of the *Schachter* factors and institutional considerations within section 1's analytical framework. Pursuant to that analysis, it is necessary to consider whether some public harm – based either on the *Schachter* categories or on other public harms – would follow from direct invalidation of a law. If so, then it is further necessary to ask whether a suspended declaration of invalidity would avert the public harm.[47] Next courts must consider whether there are multiple options to cure the constitutional defect and, if so, whether direct invalidation would effectively impose one option over others.[48] Finally, if the preceding factors favour a suspended declaration, then Hoole contends that courts should consider whether it is possible to provide exemptions to the litigants and similarly situated people during the suspended declaration of invalidity without causing unjustifiable public harm or undermining the legislature's ability to craft an effective reply law.[49]

As is evident from Hoole's framework, the institutional capacity of courts is a relevant consideration in the proportionality analysis. This factor, however, should trump constitutional rights only when "the pursuit of an optimal remedy will be frustrated" by any remedy other than a suspended declaration of invalidity.[50] In other words, institutional considerations ought not to be enough to override rights even for a minimal period.[51] In Hoole's view, suspended declarations are prudent only when there exists "a serious impediment to legislative discretion that will be produced by an immediate declaration, or a constitutionally intolerable harm consequent upon immediate invalidation."[52] This follows because "it is the interests of the public that suspended declarations are intended to service, not the interests of the legislature."[53]

Two Tracks

Kent Roach maintains that suspended declarations of invalidity ought to operate on a two-track basis.[54] Each track is designed to promote the objectives of either judicial or political constitutionalism.[55] As Roach explains, his model "attempts to provide successful litigants with a tangible remedy while deferring to the superior ability of the executive and legislature to craft systemic remedies in a more democratic and participatory manner."[56] Thus, the litigant in a successful constitutional challenge would be granted a remedy because their rights ought not to be overlooked by the courts.[57] At the same time, Roach's approach appeases political constitutionalists by allowing the party with more resources, time, and information to respond to rights issues.[58] His approach therefore allows courts to start the conversation by remedying an immediate rights violation but also allows legislatures to continue the dialogue by determining how to reply to judicial rulings.[59] For Roach, however, judicial deference is not absolute. If legislatures are unwilling to address a rights violation adequately, then courts should respond by ordering "more aggressive and prescriptive systemic remedies and/or more individual remedies."[60]

Notably, Roach does not claim that his remedial framework is justified based on its ability to increase the legislature's range of policy options. In a criticism of the Supreme Court's early jurisprudence, Bruce Ryder maintained that, "[b]y emphasizing the role of suspended declarations in fostering legislative choice, and dialogue with affected groups, the [Supreme] Court seems to be suggesting that suspensions have the effect of enlarging a legislature's range of choices and consultative possibilities."[61] Ryder is correct in observing that suspended declarations do not achieve these ends. As he observes, "[w]hether the operation of a declaration of invalidity is immediate or delayed, a legislature faces the exact same range of constitutional possibilities ... [and] is also free to consult as widely as it wishes in the design of a new *Charter*-compliant legal regime."[62] However, this criticism has no application to the two-track model because Roach justifies that model exclusively based on the increased legitimacy of judicial review when engaging in institutional dialogue.

Nor should Roach's model be understood as abandoning immediate declarations of invalidity. In his earlier writing, Roach suggested that the initial determination of whether to impose a suspended declaration of invalidity ought to be guided by core principles underlying judicial remedies.[63] In so concluding, he rejected both the "rule-based" approach to suspended declarations of invalidity in *Schachter* and the unfettered discretion permitted by the Supreme Court's subsequent jurisprudence.[64]

122 | *Attenuating Rights*

Instead, Roach maintained that remedial decisions ought to be based on a balancing of "the need to respect the role of the legislature and the purposes of the *Charter.*"[65] Although this approach serves only as a starting point – which Hoole developed by appealing to the proportionality principle under section 1 of the Charter[66] – Roach does not assume that suspended declarations of invalidity should always be granted.[67]

Roach nevertheless acknowledges a separate criticism of the two-track model: it allows for "queue jumping."[68] As Albie Sachs explains, providing a remedy only to the immediate parties of a constitutional challenge allows those with "the sharpest elbows" to receive remedies for constitutional violations, whereas others must wait for the legislature to provide systemic reform.[69] Robert Leckey similarly observes that providing remedies only to successful litigants creates "horizontal" inequality since similarly situated people are denied a constitutional right.[70] For Roach, however, "[q]ueue jumping by litigants is part and parcel of common law constitutionalism that stresses that successful litigants, as opposed to all who are similarly situated to litigants, have a right to a remedy."[71] Put differently, it is possible that the need to facilitate dialogue between courts and legislatures on the legitimate scope of rights outweighs the need to provide external parties with immediate remedies in at least some circumstances.

Roach nevertheless thinks that the two-track model should allow for litigants similarly affected by an unconstitutional law to apply for exemptions and receive orders similar to those granted to the applicants in limited circumstances.[72] He illustrates this point with the Supreme Court's decisions in *Carter v Canada (Attorney General).*[73] Roach suggests that the initial decision to suspend the declaration of invalidity with respect to a law prohibiting euthanasia was justified because it served to facilitate dialogue on a complex policy matter. However, because the federal government was unable to pass a reply law during the initial suspension, Roach also supports the Supreme Court's decision to extend the suspension of invalidity while allowing litigants to apply for exemptions during the interim period.[74] The Supreme Court's approach in *Carter* therefore struck a more nuanced balance between the legislature's interests in devising a reply law and the constitutional rights of those affected by the original law.

Roach's two-track model nevertheless might be problematic in some circumstances because of the incentives underlying granting remedies only to litigants. As the *Bedford* case illustrates, public interest litigation can involve selecting litigants to be representative parties for the purposes of the case. If Roach's two-track approach is adopted, then those organizing similar constitutional challenges might be pressured to bring more people under the umbrella of litigation to protect as many affected individuals as possible. As seen in *Bedford,* the government can slow down litigation by challenging each individual party for standing. This problem is also likely unavoidable. If each individual could receive a remedy, then appellate courts could not abstain from deciding issues of standing, as occurred in *Bedford.*

Such a circumstance could deter people from bringing public interest litigation given the greater time commitment needed to engage in rights litigation. It would also increase the costs to the justice system more broadly given the increased motions necessary for challenging each applicant's standing. Modifying the two-track response by automatically allowing third parties to apply for exemptions would alleviate this tension since it would be necessary to consider only other affected parties' applications after the constitutional challenge is complete. Such an approach nevertheless subsumes the dialogical benefits of Roach's two-track model and therefore is unlikely to strike his desired balance between the need to uphold rights and the need to increase the institutional dialogue between courts and legislatures.

The Notwithstanding Clause

Those who suggest that "proportionality" and "dialogue" offer justifications for suspended declarations of invalidity have yet to reconcile their position with section 33 of the Charter. Subsection 33(1) provides that a legislature may declare that a particular law "shall operate notwithstanding a provision included in section 2 or sections 7 to 15 of this *Charter.*" Subsection 33(3) nevertheless limits the operation of the notwithstanding clause to a five-year period, though subsections 33(4)

124 | *Attenuating Rights*

and 33(5) allow the legislature to renew any invocation of the notwithstanding clause after the initial five-year period elapses. The existence of the notwithstanding clause therefore raises a question: Is a suspended declaration of invalidity necessary to promote the dialogical ends that its supporters claim legitimize its use?

Sarah Burningham was the first to answer this question implicitly in the negative. In her view, if a legislature deemed a grace period necessary to craft an adequate response to a judicial decision striking down a law under sections 2 or 7–15 of the Charter, then it could temporarily invoke the notwithstanding clause.[75] During the extension application in *Carter*, Justice Brown similarly asked the Crown why it could not employ the notwithstanding clause.[76] Emmett Macfarlane subsequently endorsed this view, suggesting that it is "odd for the government to request that the [Supreme] Court extend a suspended declaration when Parliament is free to give itself more time by employing a readily available constitutional tool."[77] For Macfarlane, "when the notwithstanding clause is available, it is questionable whether courts should provide suspensions in contexts that fall outside of the *Schachter* guidelines."[78]

Brian Bird agrees with these criticisms but goes further by interpreting section 33 of the Charter alongside section 52 of the Constitution. As he observes, the Supreme Court originally concluded that the plain language of the latter section does not permit suspended declarations of invalidity.[79] Moreover, Bird reasonably maintains that no other aspect of the Constitution – the remedial provision in section 24(1) of the Charter, the inherent jurisdiction of superior courts, or the "internal architecture" of the Constitution – provides a legal means for judges to suspend a declaration of invalidity.[80] Thus, only those unwritten constitutional principles – such as the rule of law – can permit a court to impose such a remedy.[81]

Yet it is not clear that courts are the only institutional actor that can invoke an unwritten constitutional principle to justify suspending a law's invalidity.[82] For Bird, "[i]f a dimension of the rule of law justifies the use of suspended declarations, there is no apparent reason why these declarations should be in the judicial but not the legislative toolbox."[83] This position is sensible since both courts and legislatures are trusted with upholding the Constitution.[84] Although a court must necessarily make an initial finding of invalidity – otherwise it would be unclear whether there is a constitutional issue for the legislature to address – nothing stops a legislature from employing an unwritten constitutional principle to postpone the effect of a judicial decision.

Bird's position nevertheless assumes that legislatures are able to *immediately* pass a reply law. The legislative process in Parliament and the provincial legislatures is complex, with laws often taking significant time to pass through the relevant houses. Although the *Manitoba Language Reference* circumstance would likely garner unanimous support to pass a law expediently, perhaps not all laws that call for a suspended declaration of invalidity would garner the same support, especially when minority governments are in power. Enduring a state of affairs in which a law is inconsistent with an unwritten constitutional principle for even the short period of time necessary to pass a law suspending a declaration of invalidity risks serious consequences. For this reason, the Supreme Court is correct to suspend a declaration of invalidity for some period in cases in which an unwritten constitutional principle is implicated.

I nevertheless maintain that it is inappropriate for courts to grant an extension longer than is necessary for the legislature to pass an interim reply law setting out the required length of the extension.[85] Put differently, the fact that courts typically are the first to apply an unwritten constitutional principle to suspend a piece of legislation's invalidity does not mean that they must also be tasked with determining the *duration* of the suspension. If legislatures are equally competent to employ unwritten constitutional principles to address a constitutional emergency, then it is necessary to consider whether legislatures are better equipped than courts to determine the appropriate length of the extension.

As Leckey observes, the typical judicial suspension of one year is often far too short for legislatures to engage in meaningful consultation with the public, experts, and other stakeholders to ensure that their legislation carefully considers all the policy options and competing

126 | *Attenuating Rights*

interests inherent to responding to complex rights decisions.[86] It is possible that courts do not appreciate the difficulties inherent to passing legislation and therefore require a response much more quickly than is reasonable.[87] More likely, as Leckey maintains, the prospect of suspending a declaration of invalidity for longer periods – five years in some cases – is unlikely to meet with approval by the courts.[88] The current judicial practice will therefore either pressure a legislature into acting too quickly – risking ill-informed law making – or result in the legislature applying for a further extension. To avoid both of these scenarios, it is prudent to allow the party with the most experience and knowledge related to the complexities of passing legislation – the legislature – to determine the length of any suspended declaration of invalidity.

Requiring legislatures to reply to the Supreme Court's jurisprudence by temporarily overturning its ruling nevertheless can be opposed on more practical grounds. As various commentators have observed, employing the notwithstanding clause is controversial and has become largely dormant as a result.[89] Yet the Supreme Court could lift much of the weight from the legislatures' shoulders by explicitly recognizing that 1) suspended declarations of invalidity are an acceptable part of the dialogical function of the Constitution; 2) granting a suspended declaration of invalidity is nevertheless typically outside the authority of a court despite recent practice; and 3) such an approach constitutes a legitimate use of the notwithstanding clause if the legislature justified its decision by explaining to the public why its decision to temporarily override rights is a proportionate response to a judicial decision striking down a law. Hoole's proportionality proposal outlined earlier provides a workable framework for any such response.

Proponents of the two-track model might further object that litigants will go uncompensated for proving a rights violation. This problem is likely unavoidable given the structure of the Constitution. Because there is a textual and unwritten basis for legislatures to suspend rights violations, even successful applicants cannot complain that their rights are unduly infringed since the Constitution must be read as a whole. It is nevertheless possible for the legislature to devise a "two-track" response alongside its use of the notwithstanding clause to ensure fairness to litigants and similarly situated persons. Moreover, the legislature might include an application process for constitutional exemptions if its reply law is not passed within an initially promised time frame. The political tide might indeed favour these types of compromises in the aftermath of a Supreme Court decision striking down a law. As Leckey observes, an offence that has "succumb[ed] to constitutional attack likely no longer represents social consensus."[90]

The Supreme Court's Response

In *Ontario (Attorney General) v G*,[91] the Supreme Court recently provided a response to the literature criticizing its jurisprudence for granting suspended declarations of invalidity. Agreeably, the Supreme Court did not permit a broader appeal to facilitating "dialogue" between courts and legislatures to justify a suspension of Charter rights.[92] Only when failing to grant that a suspended declaration of invalidity would "significantly impair" the legislature's ability to legislate can any appeal to institutional considerations be employed to justify a suspended declaration of invalidity.[93] In essence, the majority adopted a proportionality-based approach, concluding that suspended declarations of invalidity should not be invoked "unless the government demonstrates that an immediately effective declaration would endanger a compelling public interest that outweighs the importance of immediate constitutional compliance and an immediately effective remedy for those whose *Charter* rights will be violated."[94] In so concluding, the majority also cautioned that declarations of invalidity should be "rare," noting that it had refused to suspend a declaration of invalidity in its past thirteen decisions.[95]

More controversially, a majority of the Supreme Court – despite a compelling dissent written by Justices Côté and Brown[96] – disagreed with the argument that the text of section 52 of the *Constitution Act, 1982* and the notwithstanding clause render judicial discretion to suspend declarations of invalidity impermissible. Citing a brief passage from a foreign authority, the majority asserted that a general power to suspend declarations of invalidity "arise[s] from accommodation of

128 | *Attenuating Rights*

broader constitutional considerations and is included in the power to declare legislation invalid."[97] As a result, it concluded that "[a] court cannot shirk its responsibility to remedy constitutional violations simply because [of] s. 33."[98]

The majority's brief retort was unpersuasive since it failed to engage with the text of section 52 of the Constitution. As explained earlier, there is simply no reasonable way of reading that section to allow for anything but an immediate declaration of invalidity. The ability of legislatures to suspend a declaration of invalidity using the notwithstanding clause bolsters this interpretation since it explicitly permits legislatures to achieve its aim without resorting to the courts. As Justices Côté and Brown concluded, this interpretation is also consistent with remedial approaches under foreign constitutions because several of the countries that allow courts to suspend declarations of invalidity explicitly include such a power in their constitutions.[99] If the power is so clearly "inherent" to declaring a law invalid, then such a provision is unnecessary. Finally, the majority did not explain why courts are better institutionally equipped than legislatures to provide such remedies. There is no reason to conclude that courts are more capable than legislatures of determining both when to suspend a declaration of invalidity and for how long a law's declaration of invalidity ought to be suspended. The combination of these criticisms ensures that the judicial practice of suspending declarations of invalidity will remain legally questionable.

APPLICATION TO *BEDFORD*

Applying each of the frameworks discussed in the preceding section would have required the Supreme Court in *Bedford* to abandon or at least modify its decision to suspend the sex work laws' declaration of invalidity. Beginning with Hoole's proportionality principle, sex workers' security of the person interest could not reasonably be sacrificed for the potential benefits deriving from a suspended declaration of invalidity. This follows for three main reasons. First, as outlined by Justice Himel, striking down the three sex work laws at issue would not have

Suspended Declarations of Invalidity | 129

created a legal vacuum. Instead, a plethora of other existing criminal laws could have substituted for the sex work laws to criminalize similar (though not identical) conduct.

Second, the Supreme Court acknowledged that the same harms to the security of the person interest of sex workers would be incurred as a result of suspending the declaration of invalidity. Approximately a decade after the Pickton murders, the court wrote those harms – which included the lives of many sex workers – ought to have weighed much more heavily on the scales of justice. Although it is important to ensure that the legislature is given adequate time to respond to rights decisions, it is difficult to conceive how this consideration could outweigh the security interests of some of Canada's most vulnerable and marginalized citizens.

Third, to the extent that facilitating dialogue is relevant to the proportionality analysis, the Supreme Court's judgment facilitated dialogue in other ways. As highlighted in Chapter 5, the court's development of the instrumental rationality principles placed few restrictions on Parliament and gave it a choice among numerous policy responses. Moreover, the Conservatives held a majority government at the time and therefore easily could have suspended the declaration of invalidity by invoking the notwithstanding clause. Since that clause is an integral feature of the dialogical framework underlying the Charter, suspending the declaration of invalidity was unnecessary to facilitate dialogue between courts and legislatures concerning the appropriate scope of sex workers' rights.

Even assuming that a suspended declaration of invalidity was appropriate, Roach's two-track model would have resulted in the applicants being exempted from the sex work laws. His focus on the values underlying judicial constitutionalism required that the litigant(s) be granted a remedy where feasible. This nevertheless would have led to an odd situation in which only a small number of people affected by the sex work laws would be allowed to engage fully in the practice of sex work. Even a model that allows sex workers to apply for exemptions would be unworkable. Sex workers are unlikely to tell the state that they wish to participate in sex work given the poor relationship between

130 | *Attenuating Rights*

the state and sex workers and the various privacy interests implicated by disclosing such information. Even if these hurdles could be overcome, the sheer number of exemptions that would need to be granted would significantly slow down the justice system.

Finally, and most preferably, the Supreme Court ought to have provided more weight to the plain text of section 52 of the Constitution and the role of the notwithstanding clause in determining whether a suspended declaration of invalidity should be granted. Since *Bedford* applied section 7 of the Charter, Parliament had the option of invoking the notwithstanding clause. Moreover, because there was no threat to an unwritten constitutional principle by immediately striking down the sex work laws, the Supreme Court had no lawful basis to suspend the declaration of invalidity. The only plausible reason that the Crown wanted the Supreme Court to suspend the declaration of invalidity was to avoid any political fallout from Parliament's invocation of the notwithstanding clause. Such a reason, however, should not be allowed to trump the plain meaning of constitutional text.

A better approach would require the Supreme Court to first admit that its current practice of suspending declarations of invalidity under section 52 of the Constitution is impermissible. It could then explain to the public that the notwithstanding clause could be used legitimately by legislatures to provide them with adequate time to respond to complex rights decisions. Whether unconstitutional legislation is suspended by courts or legislatures, it serves a similar dialogical function under the Charter. Requiring Parliament to invoke the notwithstanding clause nevertheless imposes an additional safeguard since it will need to ensure that its decision is amenable to the general population. Although sometimes this might be difficult, overriding rights for even a temporary period should not occur with ease. This approach is therefore likely to result in a more principled balancing between the need both to facilitate dialogue and to minimize state intrusions into constitutional rights.

PART 3

RETHINKING *BEDFORD*

7

The Case for Upholding the Sex Work Laws

THE CROWN'S PRIMARY argument in *Bedford* was that the impugned sex work laws did not violate section 7 of the Charter because an individual's choice to engage in sex work severed any causal connection between the harms suffered by sex workers and the sex work laws.[1] Although some sex workers choose to work in the trade, the Supreme Court rejected the Crown's choice-based argument because many sex workers are victims, not voluntary actors.[2] As Chief Justice McLachlin explained, "while [these sex workers] may retain some minimal power of choice ... these are not people who can be said to be truly 'choosing' a risky line of business."[3] It is therefore possible to conclude that the laws engaged these sex workers' security of the person interest by exacerbating the dangers inherent to their work.[4]

It is important to unpack the implications of the Supreme Court's reliance on an absence of choice to bolster its conclusion that the sex work laws caused harm to sex workers. The absence of choice that the court raised is not choice in the physical sense. Instead, it is what George Fletcher calls "normative" or "moral" involuntariness.[5] This conception of volition recognizes that external pressures can deprive a person of a "realistic choice" whether to perform an act.[6] The prohibition against convicting people for morally involuntary actions has been constitutionalized as a principle of fundamental justice under section 7 of the

134 | *Rethinking* Bedford

Charter. Anyone who commits a crime in a morally involuntary manner therefore has a constitutionally protected defence.[7]

The Supreme Court's acknowledgment that "survival sex workers"[8] have no realistic choice but to engage in their trade does not give rise by itself to a defence. Since sex work was legal when *Bedford* was decided, sex workers were not being compelled to commit a crime per se. The fact that survival sex workers cannot realistically be expected to leave their trade nevertheless provides important context for understanding why they break the law. The external pressures exerted on them leave them with no reasonable avenue of escape from the sex trade. Given the nature and frequency of the dangers posed to sex workers when engaging in their work, I further contend that the harm is sufficiently grave and temporally connected to their actions to give rise to a moral involuntariness defence. Survival sex workers are therefore entitled to an acquittal under section 7 of the Charter. It follows that the sex work laws need not cause any of the harms to survival sex workers alleged by the applicants.

It is nevertheless plausible that a survival sex worker's actions *become* morally voluntary the more safety precautions the worker is permitted to take. Based on the evidence in *Bedford,* the most rudimentary precaution is screening a sex worker's clientele. Similarly, the trial judge in *Bedford* found that it is difficult to alleviate the grave dangers faced by sex workers unless they are permitted to work in stable indoor locations. Because it is these actions that I think are subject to a moral involuntariness defence, I maintain that it is less necessary for survival sex workers to hire staff – which most are unable to afford – to protect themselves. Even if this law does have an illogical or harsh impact on some survival sex workers, I maintain that the pressing objective underlying the living on the avails offence – preventing sex workers from being exploited – ought to result in the law being upheld under section 1 of the Charter.

As for those who choose to engage in sex work, I agree with the Supreme Court that the sex work laws are causally connected to the harms faced by voluntarily acting sex workers. However, the fact remains that the sex work laws apply only to those who choose to engage in a dangerous field of work knowing that some of the rudimentary safety precautions are criminalized for legitimate criminal law purposes. The voluntarily acting sex worker's choice ought to weigh heavily on the scales of justice at the section 1 stage of the analysis. Relatedly, I contend that narrowly confining the objectives of the bawdy house and communication offences is unprincipled. In my view, each law must also be found to serve an implicit and broader objective: to deter people from choosing to enter the sex trade. The harm averted by this broader purpose combined with the ease with which a voluntarily acting sex worker can avoid the dangers inherent to sex work suggests that Parliament's choice to criminalize the impugned acts ought to constitute a proportionate response to a complex social problem.

Eschewing the idea that laws always promote single objectives is also a more honest approach to constitutional analysis. As the Supreme Court determined when interpreting laws outside the constitutional context, legislation often "does not simply further one goal but rather strikes a balance among several goals, some of which may be in tension."[9] In my view, the reason that the Supreme Court wishes to distill the law into a single objective is that it simplifies instrumental rationality analysis. Yet it is possible for this analysis to occur even though a law serves multiple objectives. Applying such an approach, I contend that the impugned sex work laws can be framed in a manner that violates the individualistic conception of the instrumental rationality principles. Each infringement is nevertheless justified under section 1 of the Charter given these sex workers' choice to engage in sex work and the ability of the laws to collectively deter some people from entering or remaining in an inherently dangerous trade.

BEDFORD AND VOLITION

The Supreme Court's basis for concluding that the sex work laws have unconstitutional effects with respect to survival sex workers derived from the fact that they do not freely engage in the sex work trade. To follow the law and forgo taking the basic precautions at issue in *Bedford* therefore can be expected to result in a dramatically increased risk that

136 | *Rethinking* Bedford

these sex workers will endure violence. In coming to this conclusion, however, the court neglected to ask a more basic question: Should a survival sex worker who screens clientele or works in a bawdy house actually be convicted of those offences?

In circumstances in which a defence uniformly applies to a category of persons, it is incorrect to conclude that the law "prohibits" their conduct since ultimately they will be acquitted. This point is bolstered by considering the relationship among offences, defences, and constitutional law more generally. It is unlikely that the constitutionality of any other offence would be determined without considering available defences. To conclude otherwise would allow all offences to be constitutionally challenged. This follows since defences such as duress, necessity, and self-defence are collectively applicable to all criminal offences. If these defences are not considered when assessing a law's constitutionality, then it is reasonable to conclude that every offence is drawn broadly enough to catch morally involuntary conduct or, worse yet, conduct that is "justified" and therefore considered "rightful."[10] It would follow that the Supreme Court's decision to constitutionalize the moral principle(s) underlying criminal defences rendered the scope of all offences violative of section 7 of the Charter.[11] To avoid this absurd result, it is necessary to consider the constitutionality of offences in light of available defences.

It is therefore important that the Supreme Court in *Bedford* used the language of moral involuntariness in describing the working conditions of survival sex workers.[12] As Justice LeBel explained in *R v Ruzic*,[13] "[a] person acts in a morally involuntary fashion when, faced with perilous circumstances, she is deprived of a realistic choice whether to break the law."[14] Thus, the moral involuntariness principle concedes that the act was physically voluntary but recognizes that those who commit a crime because of extreme pressure are not truly choosing their actions. In rejecting the Crown's choice-based argument, the Supreme Court in *Bedford* employed similar reasoning.[15] If survival sex workers are not meaningfully "choosing" their line of work, then it is necessary to consider whether these workers at times will have any more of a "realistic choice" than to take basic precautions to protect themselves from the dangers inherent to their work.

Answering this question requires a general review of the two defences that the Supreme Court maintains are encompassed by the moral involuntariness principle: duress and necessity.[16] Although the moral involuntariness principle was constitutionalized in the context of a duress claim, the principle was first adopted under the common law in the context of a necessity defence.[17] Generally speaking, these defences apply when some external force compels an accused person to commit a criminal act. In the case of duress, the external force is a threat from a third party. A necessity defence involves any other external threat that might compel an accused to commit a criminal act.[18] Both defences therefore share the common feature of an accused who has no realistic choice but to commit a crime to avoid some type of harm.[19]

It is prudent at the outset to consider which defence a survival sex worker might plead. Although pimps often threaten those under their control with physical harm, it is doubtful that they compel sex workers to break the law when conducting their work. A pimp simply desires to make as much profit from that work as possible. As such, a duress defence might not always be sustainable based on the pimp's threats alone. A sex worker who chooses to break the law when screening clients is compelled more by the potential dangers arising from violent clients. A violent act by a client gives the sex worker a right to fight back in self-defence when the threat becomes reasonably foreseeable. However, this right is of limited utility at the time that a sex worker screens her clientele and often will be useless when any violence begins since many sex workers will not be physical matches for their abusers.

Similarly, if a group of marginalized and vulnerable sex workers were to set up a bawdy house for protective purposes, then their choice is unlikely to be compelled by a third-party pimp. The pimp likely does not care where individual sex workers serve their clientele. A pimp's primary concern is that the sex workers under their control actually participate in and derive profit from their work. If a group of sex workers sets up a bawdy house for protective purposes, then again

138 | *Rethinking* Bedford

it is likely because they fear those johns who act violently toward them, not because of any foreseeable threat from a pimp. The threat posed by pimps relates primarily to whether sex workers have the ability to leave the trade.

The survival sex worker's defence therefore derives more immediately from the threat posed by clients, whereas the pimp's threats are relevant to why the sex worker is compelled to engage in sex work. Although these threats come from third parties, the survival sex worker's circumstances also bear a resemblance to the necessity defence since the social circumstances that sex workers operate within are what allow pimps to control and johns to abuse sex workers. Put differently, if sex workers were not historically marginalized people, then it is unlikely that they would face the threats inherent to their trade. To the extent that societal behaviours and attitudes have resulted in circumstances under which violence toward sex workers is pervasive, the sex worker's moral involuntariness claim bears some resemblance to a necessity defence.

Given this unique blend of considerations, it is prudent to focus less on the strict doctrinal requirements underlying each defence and more on the moral involuntariness principle itself.[20] As explained earlier, this principle requires that the accused had no realistic choice but to commit a criminal offence.[21] It is therefore sensible to require that the accused reasonably believed that she faced a threat of serious harm.[22] As the Supreme Court concluded in *Ruzic,* however, it is inconsistent with the moral involuntariness principle to require third-party threats to be imminent. The threat must only be temporally connected to the harm faced.[23] Moreover, the accused must take any reasonable avenue of escape available. Failure to do so results in the accused choosing to remain in her perilous circumstances.[24] Finally, the emotions underlying an accused's moral involuntariness plea must derive from legitimate fear for her safety.[25]

As I have argued in detail elsewhere, these factors – which do not include utilitarian proportionality between the harm caused and the harm averted – are sufficient to establish a moral involuntariness claim.[26] Various scholars agree that proportionality between the harms caused

The Case for Upholding the Sex Work Laws | 139

and the harms averted is irrelevant to whether an accused person's actions are morally involuntary.[27] Even if I am wrong and proportionality is inherent to the moral involuntariness principle, then surely survival sex workers' security interests when screening clientele or setting up a bawdy house are more important than any nuisance arising from conducting their work. As such, proportionality would be readily made out in the context under consideration.

Survival sex workers would also be capable of meeting the other elements of the moral involuntariness defence. The threat of harm that sex workers face is serious and, as the court observed in *Bedford*, can be fatal.[28] Although sex workers do not know exactly when the harm will arise, imminence is not a requirement for a moral involuntariness claim.[29] A temporal connection between the harm threatened and the sex worker's decision to break the law should exist given the Supreme Court's conclusion that survival sex workers endure violence with an "alarming" frequency.[30] Because it is unreasonable to expect survival sex workers to leave their work – given "financial desperation, drug addictions, mental illness, or compulsion from pimps"[31] – they also do not have any reasonable prospect of escaping from their circumstances. The only other means to avoid harm are precisely those prohibited by the sex work laws. Finally, the emotions underlying the survival sex worker's actions need not be unpalatable; instead, survival sex workers are likely to break the law out of legitimate fear for their personal safety.

It is nevertheless possible to contest the general availability of a moral involuntariness defence. For instance, it can be argued that state-funded programs provide "reasonable avenues of escape" for survival sex workers.[32] However, scholars have found that legislative frameworks at times do more to hinder than to help sex workers exit the sex trade, and in other circumstances they are too poorly funded to be effective.[33] Moreover, this barrier can be overcome by sex workers who show that their work is affected by a variety of circumstances related to financial need, addiction, abuse, and other contextual factors.[34] Although the use of state resources to extricate oneself from the sex work trade might be possible for some, the moral involuntariness principle requires that it be a reasonable option given the particular

140 | *Rethinking* Bedford

circumstances of each sex worker. For many sex workers, the Supreme Court in *Bedford* strongly implied that state programs would be insufficient to render their "choice" to engage in sex work "realistic."[35]

The utility of voluntariness as a means for governing sex work offences can also be questioned. Some scholars maintain that the distinction between voluntary and survival sex work "is not sustainable either at a theoretical or at a material level in the lives of girls and women."[36] For these scholars, "[b]inary positions of free and forced, voluntary and involuntary ... serve to disguise the commonality amongst trafficked and prostituted girls and women in both the process of entry into and entrapment within prostitution."[37] More commonly, scholars recognize that many sex workers are in the trade as a result of choice. It is thus "critical to conceptually and materially draw clear distinctions between trafficking, forced prostitution, and freely chosen sex work."[38] For these scholars, the experiences of sex workers are "strongly differentiated, and the presence of consent in entering prostitution and engaging in sexual acts within it ... becomes the defining concept in determining what is acceptable, permissible, and legal."[39]

It is important to recognize at the outset that any suggestion that individual sex workers fall permanently into a "voluntary" or "survival" category is undefendable. Sex work as a form of labour is too fluid to sustain such a conclusion. Some women regularly engage in sex work, whereas others participate sporadically or even on a single occasion.[40] Others simultaneously attend school or participate in traditional paid labour positions.[41] The latter category of sex worker generally views sex work as a lucrative profession when compared to unskilled labour[42] and as an easy means to earn money quickly.[43] These sex workers might also prefer to engage in sex work because of the independence and flexibility that it affords when practised outside the commercial context.[44] A sex worker's earnings therefore might be used at times to meet basic necessities but in other circumstances finance a preferred lifestyle.[45]

Other sex workers might participate in the trade because they are curious about sex work or find it sexually invigorating.[46] A general attraction to "eroticism and sex work" might represent "a natural extension of [a sex worker's] lifestyle."[47] For those who work in non-street-based environments, the "glamour of the industry" can also attract and keep them in the trade.[48] It is further possible that some sex workers view sex work as a means to forge human connections and thereby avoid isolation.[49] This might help to explain why some sex workers from nondisadvantaged backgrounds choose to enter the sex trade.[50]

The relationship between sex work and drug use is more germane to determining whether a sex worker's participation in the sex trade is morally involuntary. Although many sex workers are not drug dependent, some sex workers' drug use creates what is described as a "'work-score-use' cycle."[51] This in turn leaves the sex worker with few viable options for subsistence.[52] In circumstances in which drugs are scarce, sex workers are often left "at the mercy of customers, pimps and drug dealers," which in turn results in these workers engaging in risky (but legal) behaviour to sustain their livelihood.[53] As one scholar concludes, "[l]eaving sex work may be frustrated by the economic costs of substance dependence, and by the limited social and medical resources, as well as work opportunities, that are realistically available to women seeking to overcome addiction while emerging from a socially and legally impugned lifestyle."[54] Drug dependence can therefore play an important contextual role alongside other factors such as poverty and risk of violence in assessing the voluntariness of a sex worker's actions.

The fact that a moral involuntariness defence has never been applied to the sex work offences does not undermine my argument. There are several reasons that such a defence has not been developed. First, sex work offences are typically low stakes when they involve a sex worker who screens clientele or works in a bawdy house.[55] It is therefore unlikely that a sex worker would run a novel and lengthy trial to avoid a minimal punishment that many sex workers view as a "licensing fee."[56] Second, it is unlikely that a survival sex worker's counsel, in most instances Legal Aid, would devote scarce time and resources to developing such a defence. As explained earlier, the duress and necessity defences are morally complex and do not always provide a clear-cut defence.

Yet there is no explicit offence to which the duress and necessity defences cannot apply in theory.[57] Nor did Parliament exclude the sex work offences from the list of offences in section 17 of the *Criminal*

142 | *Rethinking* Bedford

Code that it maintains ought not to be afforded a duress defence. The fact that a link has not been drawn between the moral involuntariness principle and survival sex work is best explained by one of the driving motivations for the *Bedford* litigation: the relevant evidence of the harms caused by the sex work laws was not commonly cited in courts. With that information available, it is reasonable to develop a broader defence for survival sex workers. However, if survival sex workers have a defence, then it must follow that the harms that they face cannot be included in considering the constitutionality of the sex work laws.

Some scholars might raise further objections to relying on the moral involuntariness principle as the basis for a defence to sex work–related charges. For these scholars, a binary between voluntary and involuntary sex work provides an impoverished understanding of the agency of those who engage in sex work. As Angela Campbell explains, the history of sex work reveals that sex workers "are viewed either as passive victims or as offenders fully capable of choice."[58] Such an approach "imagine[s] sex workers as preyed upon by those who coerce and exploit them, or as calculating and maladjusted social threats that merit sanction and call for rehabilitation."[59] The limited findings of "guilty" and "not guilty" permitted by the Anglo-American structure of criminal law perpetuate this problem since they provide inadequate space for understanding a sex worker's reasons for engaging in sex work.

Although such concerns are legitimate, I think that it is preferable to allow other stages of the criminal law analysis to correct for any misunderstandings in cases in which a sex worker acts in a morally voluntary manner. Indeed, there is ample room at the sentencing stage to recognize the agency of sex workers who choose to engage in sex work but are not "calculating and maladjusted social threats." Judges might not only identify the illegality of their conduct but also recognize the rationale underpinning their choice in the particular sex worker's circumstances and then take this context into consideration when tailoring a sentence. The focus of the sentencing process on the individual offender would directly facilitate such an analysis. It is also possible to consider circumstances that do not give rise to a moral involuntariness defence at the sentencing stage, since any factors impeding (but not undermining) volition can mitigate the moral blameworthiness of the offender. Recognizing the unique circumstances of every sex worker would allow for better-informed sentences that in practice might reveal little public interest in severely punishing sex workers in most cases.

Finally, it can be contended that requiring sex workers to plead a defence is impractical. The evidence establishes that survival sex workers make up a significant proportion of sex workers and therefore would need to plead a defence in many cases. This arguably points to a broader problem with criminalizing sex work that is better addressed by striking down the offence despite the availability of a defence.[60] This is both an interesting and a unique suggestion because such an argument has not arisen when constitutionally challenging a criminal offence under the Charter. Yet this suggestion is also radical since it supports abandoning the Anglo-American structure of criminal law for a single category of offences. However, criminal defences such as self-defence also arise in everyday life. Criminal justice actors can deal with duress claims in the sex work context in a similar way that police deal with self-defence cases: screening the sex worker's reasons for engaging in what is otherwise a criminal offence. Where there is no reason to disbelieve the sex worker's explanation for screening clientele or working in a bawdy house, it would be an abuse of process to charge that person with a criminal offence given the now widely recognized fact that sex workers endure highly dangerous conditions.

In deciding whether to charge a sex worker, the officer would need to consider the factors emphasized earlier when reviewing the moral involuntariness jurisprudence. The most important of these factors would be readily apparent upon engaging a survival sex worker: her place of work (street) and/or the type of establishment where she is employed (a modest bawdy house). Other contextual factors such as drug addiction, poverty, and pimps are also important indicators that a sex worker engages in her work in a normatively involuntary manner. Barring a significant cultural shift rendering sex work a safe occupation, these factors ought to be sufficient to render criminal charges inappropriate. In summary, then, my approach would ensure that the courts are not flooded with duress defences, survival sex workers are not unduly

144 | *Rethinking* Bedford

accosted by police, and the Anglo-American structure of the criminal law remains the vehicle for determining which actions warrant criminal condemnation.

I suspect that some scholars still might not be fully satisfied with my approach given the fact that sex workers typically are marginalized people.[61] This fact alone might render it preferable to forgo requiring sex workers to plead a defence and instead simply strike down the sex work offences. In addition to the concerns expressed earlier, an approach that prefers striking down the sex work laws also pays inadequate attention to the impact of using a bill of rights to strike down a democratically enacted law. Although laws inconsistent with the Charter should be struck down, it is judicial overreach to declare a law unconstitutional when the common law can be developed in a manner that rids it of the effects that underpin the constitutional argument. If this position is forceful, then the law should accept that the restraint necessary when exercising the power of judicial review will result in some inconvenience to survival sex workers. Although this outcome is not perfect, it is hardly a reason to abandon the basic structure of criminal law and allow for judicial overreach when delineating the constitutional boundaries of the criminal law.

BEDFORD AND CAUSATION

Whether the sex work laws are unconstitutional as they apply to those who truly choose to engage in sex work raises other questions. The first relates to the law of causation. For a law to cause an unconstitutional effect and thereby engage the life, liberty, or security of the person interest protected under section 7 of the Charter, there must be a sufficient connection between the law's effect and the harm suffered by the complainant.[62] As the Supreme Court explained in *Bedford,* this standard does not demand that the impugned law is the only or even the dominant cause of the harm suffered.[63] The link simply must be "real" as opposed to "speculative."[64] Setting the standard at this lower level is reasonable because it allows courts to engage with often complex

The Case for Upholding the Sex Work Laws | 145

social science evidence explaining why legislation or state action might have unintended but constitutionally suspect consequences.[65]

The Crown maintained that there were two reasons that the sex work laws did not meet the causation standard. The first is because complainants "choose" to engage in an activity that they know endangers their section 7 interests.[66] Since the *Bedford* case assumed that the criminal law's ambit is broad enough to include regulation of sex work,[67] the Crown argued that Parliament's prohibitions were permissible and that those who choose to disobey them tacitly accept the risks associated with sex work.[68] To conclude otherwise would allow the claimants to assert "a constitutional right to engage in risky commercial activities" based on their preferred "lifestyle choice[s]."[69]

The Crown also maintained that causation ought to be severed if the relevant threat comes from a third party as opposed to a law or state action. In *Bedford,* the Crown maintained that it was not the impugned restrictions that endangered sex workers. Instead, it was "[t]he johns who use and abuse prostitutes and the pimps who exploit them" who cause the relevant harms.[70] Since it is these third parties who abuse sex workers, the Crown contended, sex workers' security of the person interest was inadequately affected by the sex work restrictions and therefore did not engage section 7 of the Charter.

The Supreme Court rejected both of these arguments. In dismissing the latter claim, it maintained that the applicants were not asserting a right to have the government put in place affirmative measures to ensure safe sex work.[71] Instead, the applicants were asking the courts to strike down laws that aggravated the serious and substantial risks that sex workers face when performing a legal form of work.[72] The fact that this danger frequently derived from pimps and johns made no difference since "[t]he impugned laws deprive people engaged in a risky, but legal, activity of the means to protect themselves against those risks."[73]

In rejecting the Crown's choice-based argument, the Supreme Court implicitly adopted the distinction between survival and voluntary sex work.[74] With respect to the latter category, the court again emphasized the fact that sex work was not illegal at the time that *Bedford*

146 | *Rethinking* Bedford

was decided.[75] To illustrate the significance of this point, Chief Justice McLachlin relied on an analogy to a fictional law prohibiting people from wearing a helmet while riding a bicycle. In her view, the fact that "the cyclist chooses to ride her bike does not diminish the causal role of the law in making that activity riskier. The challenged laws relating to prostitution are no different."[76]

There are two interrelated problems with this argument. First, a law that prohibits riding a bike while wearing a helmet is an inapt comparison. It is difficult to see what objective this hypothetical law could forward other than intentionally endangering human life. The law would therefore be void *ab initio* because a law with such a purpose violates any number of constitutional principles. The impugned sex work laws served lawful objectives: namely, avoiding the societal nuisances associated with sex work and preventing sex workers from being exploited. The constitutional question in relation to the sex work laws therefore can be properly framed since it is possible to weigh the effects caused by each law against lawful objectives.

Second, relying on the legality of sex work as the basis for striking down the sex work laws encourages Parliament to over-criminalize consensual actions. Put differently, Parliament could have responded to the *Bedford* decision by instating a broader prohibition against selling sex. Such a prohibition, combined with the recognition that survival sex workers must be permitted to take basic safety precautions, would address the constitutional issues. This follows because applicants cannot credibly plead that the sex work laws "caused" them harm if they were barred from performing the broader act of selling sex and *chose* to break the law. In such a circumstance, sex workers could only contend that Parliament does not have jurisdiction to criminalize the sale of sex, an argument unlikely to succeed based on the current jurisprudence.[77]

These critiques are not meant to undermine the Supreme Court's conclusion that the sex work laws at issue in *Bedford* "caused" harm to voluntary sex workers. As I maintain below, however, the fact that the choices made by voluntarily acting sex workers are largely what cause the harms that they incur, and the fact that Parliament could avoid the constitutional challenge by criminalizing sex work, should dramatically have affected the section 1 analysis. Before detailing those arguments further, it is necessary to consider one other critique of the Supreme Court's rationale for striking down the sex work laws.

DETERMINING OBJECTIVES

It is difficult to accept the Supreme Court's conclusion that the sex work laws served only the narrow purposes outlined in *Bedford*. Since elsewhere the court maintains that legislation often serves multiple purposes,[78] it is plainly incongruous to conclude that legislation must always serve a single purpose when it is constitutionally scrutinized. It is therefore necessary to consider why the Supreme Court maintains this legal fiction. In my view, the only plausible explanation is to facilitate cleaner constitutional analysis. Inserting multiple objectives when considering a law's logicality or harshness complicates the analysis because it requires courts to balance additional factors. Although courts frequently balance numerous factors when applying the law to individuals, constitutional cases often implicate legislative facts that are more complex and therefore more difficult to weigh.

To illustrate this point, consider the other objective of the communication and bawdy house offences adopted by Justice Lamer in the *Sex Work Reference:* deterring people from choosing to enter a dangerous trade.[79] Although illegitimate objectives partially underpinned sex work governance in Canada,[80] I explained in Chapter 1 why I agreed with Lamer that use of the criminal law when enacting the impugned offences also sought to render the practice of sex work difficult so as to deter people from engaging in sex work. Yet, if deterrence is an objective of the sex work laws, then it becomes difficult to conclude that the laws struck a disproportionate balance because the good achieved might balance any harm to those who voluntarily enter the sex trade. Accepting that a law can possess multiple objectives also complicates the overbreadth analysis. Although each law is overbroad compared with its narrower objective,[81] the sex work laws as a whole are capable of

148 | *Rethinking* Bedford

deterring some people from entering the trade by virtue of the deterrent effect inherent in criminalizing conduct.

It is nevertheless possible for an instrumental rationality challenge to succeed even though a law possesses multiple objectives. Applying the individualistic conception of the gross disproportionality principle, an applicant can devise a hypothetical scenario in which a sex worker would not be deterred by criminal prohibitions because she views the consequences as akin to a "licensing fee." Notably, the trial judge recognized this to be the case for many sex workers.[82] Although some prospective sex workers surely are deterred by the threat of criminal sanctions, deterrence inherently turns on the individual's processing of the costs and benefits of committing a crime. It is therefore not inconsistent to recognize a deterrent effect in some cases while maintaining that the effect will fail to accrue in other cases. The effect of the sex work laws on the undeterred sex worker would be grossly disproportionate when the impacts of those laws on their security interest are compared with the law's nuisance abatement objective.

The sex worker undeterred by the prospect of criminal prohibition might also contend that the sex work laws are overbroad since they are incapable of deterring sex work, preventing nuisances, or protecting sex workers from exploitation in some scenarios. As outlined in Chapter 5, the communication and bawdy house offences have overbroad effects because they apply in places and in ways that do not give rise to a nuisance. Similarly, the living on the avails provision is overbroad since it denies sex workers the ability to hire staff to protect them from being exploited. Sex workers therefore might contend that the law is not capable of achieving both of its objectives in some narrow scenarios.

This approach nevertheless sits uncomfortably with the Supreme Court's decision in *R v Malmo-Levine*.[83] In challenging the prior marijuana laws, the accused contended that the gross disproportionality analysis should take into account the relative ineffectiveness of those laws.[84] The Supreme Court did not rule out the unwillingness of citizens to follow a law as a relevant consideration in the section 7 analysis.[85] It did express, however, reasonable concern about relying on refusal to comply with the law as a means for questioning its constitutionality.

As the majority held, "[i]t is difficult to see how that refusal can be elevated to a constitutional argument ... [since] it would be inconsistent with the rule of law to allow compliance with a criminal prohibition to be determined by each individual's personal discretion and taste."[86]

The sex work laws differ in an important respect from other criminal laws: there is an objectively rational basis for disregarding these laws. The fact that sex workers viewed the fines that they typically received as a "licensing fee" suggests that criminal punishment was significantly outweighed by sex workers' ability to earn money selling sex.[87] This is not the case with other economically motivated offences since the amount received will typically inform the applicable punishment that the offender receives. This could not occur with the impugned offences because it is difficult to imagine a scenario in which a sex worker's earnings will be relevant to any offence since selling sex was legal under the old sex work laws. I therefore cannot see how acknowledging the sex work laws' unique incentive structure undermines "the rule of law." Instead, it creates a more accurate picture of each law's ability to achieve its objective of preventing people from choosing to engage in sex work. This perspective ought to imbue any consideration of each law's instrumental rationality. As I maintain below, such context is equally valuable when considering an aspect of the constitutional analysis largely overlooked in *Bedford:* whether any infringements of section 7 could be upheld under section 1 of the Charter.

SECTION 1 OF THE CHARTER

Prior to the *Bedford* decision, the Supreme Court all but refused to justify infringements of section 7 rights under section 1 of the Charter.[88] The exceedingly high standard imposed for justifying such infringements – exceptional conditions "such as natural disasters, the outbreak of war, [and] epidemics"[89] – likely deterred the Crown in *Bedford* from making any section 1 arguments.[90] The court in *Bedford* nevertheless softened its view and directly encouraged the Crown to raise section 1 arguments in future section 7 cases.[91] My conclusions above related to the availability of a moral involuntariness defence for survival sex workers, the

150 | *Rethinking* Bedford

weakened causal relationship between the sex work laws and the harms caused to voluntary sex workers, and the need to consider multiple objectives underlying the impugned laws provide a drastically different context for considering whether any of the sex work laws might qualify as justifiable infringements of Charter rights under section 1.

Communication and Bawdy House Offences

Both the communication and the bawdy house offences promoted the same objectives: abating nuisances and deterring people from choosing to enter or remain in the sex trade. Because criminalizing the impugned activity is capable of achieving each end separately, each law is rationally connected to its objectives.[92] Although there are narrow instances in which each objective might not be achievable, the rationale connection branch of the section 1 test does not demand a perfect connection between the law's means and ends. As long as the law is capable of forwarding its objectives in a broader sense, it will pass this stage of the section 1 test.[93]

A law is minimally impairing if it violates a right only as much as "reasonably possible."[94] Put differently, the courts ought not strike down a law simply "because they can conceive of an alternative which might better tailor objective to infringement."[95] Applying this standard to the sex work laws, it is important to reiterate the conclusion that the Supreme Court's causation analysis and the availability of a moral involuntariness defence together provide an alternative means for Parliament to uphold the sex work laws: criminalize sex work. Yet this approach does little to protect voluntarily acting sex workers from the harms inherent to their trade. Instead, it encourages Parliament to over-criminalize consensual conduct to avoid constitutional challenges. In a sense, then, Parliament's attempt to use the impugned sex work laws to deter sex work as opposed to abolishing it outright constitutes a measured response.

The fact that each law violated the gross disproportionality principle nevertheless strongly implies that the communication and bawdy house offences did not balance their salutary and deleterious effects. As the Supreme Court concluded in *R v Oakes*,[96] "[t]he more severe the deleterious effects of a measure, the more important the objective must be if the measure is to be reasonable and demonstrably justified in a free and democratic society."[97] Yet the opposite conclusion should apply with equal force. The less the law is responsible for unconstitutional effects, the more readily it should be found to strike a proper balance between its objective and effects. This observation is relevant for the reasons explained earlier: both sex workers and the sex work laws are responsible for the harms faced by voluntary sex workers. Although it is difficult to apportion blame to each cause, it is my view that these sex workers' choice to enter a dangerous trade is at least a substantial cause of the harm incurred by voluntary sex workers.

It is also important that the communication and bawdy house laws each served constitutionally acceptable purposes. Although avoiding the nuisances arising from an activity is among the criminal law's less important objectives, these objectives are nonetheless permissible under current law. More importantly, the law's ability to deter people from choosing to enter the sex work trade is likely capable of preventing many people from enduring any of the harms commonly associated with the sex trade. Because criminalizing an act is widely thought to deter conduct,[98] this effect might reasonably be thought to have accrued, though the extent of the effect is necessarily difficult to quantify. Notably, this position is not inconsistent with my argument above that the sex work laws created an incentive structure that encouraged at least some offenders to violate the law. The ability of the law to deter conduct is necessarily an individualized phenomenon. For most people, the prospect of a criminal record is enough to deter them. For those much less easily deterred, the sex work laws provide an irrational incentive structure.[99]

Although it might be retorted that decriminalizing or legalizing sex work would have better protected sex workers' safety, such an argument aggravates the tensions raised in Chapter 4. Should courts, with their limited ability to understand social science evidence, impose the model of sex work regulation that they think best balances the numerous competing interests inherent to sex work regulation? I do not think that courts are currently equipped to decide this question.

152 | *Rethinking* Bedford

The limited and contentious nature of the empirical evidence pertaining to whether decriminalizing, legalizing, or criminalizing only the purchase of sex constitutes the best balance between the various competing interests inherent to sex work regulation implicates a wider debate that remains highly contentious. The weighing of the evidence in *Bedford* is also of limited precedential value in resolving this debate since many of the harms counted against the sex work laws constituted legal actions given the availability of a defence for survival sex workers. Given the evidentiary lacunae on the effects of the sex work laws as applied in the novel legal context outlined above, I maintain that Parliament ought to have been shown deference in its policy decisions pertaining to which model of sex work to adopt.

Living On the Avails Offence
Since I maintain that survival sex workers were able to screen clientele and set up bawdy houses, it is not clear that the additional prohibition against living on the avails of sex work would engage the moral involuntariness principle. It is likely that the other safety precautions permitted for this group of sex workers would render the risk of harm too remote to give rise to a temporal connection between the harm and the threat. It is therefore necessary to consider whether the living on the avails prohibition as applied to all sex workers should have been upheld under section 1 of the Charter. Since the Supreme Court in *Bedford* did not suggest that the law failed the rationale connection test,[100] it is necessary to consider only whether this law was minimally impairing and struck a reasonable balance between its salutary and deleterious effects.

The fact that the sex work laws applied differently to survival and voluntary sex workers nevertheless provides important context for determining whether the living on the avails prohibition can be justified under section 1 of the Charter. Importantly, the Supreme Court in *Bedford* recognized that providing sex workers with some protections but not others might affect the constitutional analysis. As Chief Justice McLachlin explained, "[g]reater latitude in one measure – for example, permitting prostitutes to obtain the assistance of security personnel –

The Case for Upholding the Sex Work Laws | 153

might impact on the constitutionality of another measure – for example, forbidding the nuisances associated with keeping a bawdy-house."[101]

Applying this rationale to survival sex workers, it is first necessary to consider whether the living on the avails provision provides them with any safety benefits. As suggested earlier, these sex workers are the most marginalized and vulnerable in their trade. In my view, it is unlikely that this category of sex workers – typically impoverished and/or drug-addicted street workers – could make much use of this provision. Survival sex workers are unlikely to have the resources to hire protective staff, and their pimps are unlikely to give up some of their profits to protect their sex workers. If true, then the ability to hire protective staff is practically useless to the survival category of sex worker.

Assuming that some survival sex workers might benefit from the living on the avails provision, it is necessary to ask whether the broad application of the provision is minimally impairing of constitutional rights. The Crown argued in *Bedford* that living on the avails of sex work must be broadly prohibited in order to capture exploitive relationships otherwise difficult to identify.[102] In my view, it is reasonable to conclude that a bright-line prohibition against living on the avails of sex work will result in more prosecutions against those who exploit sex workers. This in turn should deter exploitive behaviours that would increase the safety of sex workers to some difficult to quantify extent. Because a similar rationale was adopted by the majority in *R v Downey*,[103] reviewed in Chapter 1, this fact ought to have weighed heavily in favour of the law being minimally impairing of section 7 rights in *Bedford*.

In its brief section 1 analysis, the Supreme Court in *Bedford* nevertheless concluded that the living on the avails offence failed the minimal impairment test. In its view, a pimp could not pretend to occupy positions such as receptionist or accountant as a means of avoiding detection by police.[104] Unfortunately, the court provided no rationale for this claim. It is simply unclear that a pimp could not camouflage their behaviour by occupying any role in a bawdy house to avoid detection by police. It is therefore difficult to give the court's reasons any weight at the minimal impairment stage of the analysis.

154 | *Rethinking* Bedford

The living on the avails provision also strikes a reasonable balance between its salutary and deleterious effects. First, it is relevant that survival sex workers must be permitted to screen clientele and work in bawdy houses with other such workers. Per the Supreme Court's reasons in *Bedford,* the greater latitude that the law provides these workers in some areas, the more readily a different restriction ought to be upheld.[105] The fact that survival sex workers might screen clientele in public and set up bawdy houses addresses many of the safety issues faced by this group of sex workers. Because it is unlikely that many of these workers can afford to hire protective staff, limiting the ability of this group of sex workers to hire protective staff will have a minimal impact on their security interest.

Second, it is necessary to consider other negative effects of striking down the living on the avails offence. As Janine Benedet observes, striking down this provision provided pimps with a "convenient shield" to avoid prosecution by claiming that they are legitimate employees.[106] The Supreme Court also did not consider whether encouraging profiteering based on sex work would cause other harms, such as making it more difficult for sex workers to leave the trade and requiring them to service more customers.[107] The ability of the living on the avails provisions to mitigate these harms also weighs in favour of upholding the law under section 1.

Finally, it is important to acknowledge that weighing the salutary and deleterious effects of the living on the avails provision presents evidentiary challenges. Although the Crown maintained that criminalizing living on the avails of sex work facilitated prosecutions, I am unaware of any empirical evidence bolstering such a claim. Similarly, though the Supreme Court in *Bedford* was provided with ample evidence demonstrating the harms resulting from the sex work laws, it is unlikely that the available evidence detailing those harms would have the same probative value in a substantially changed legal context in which survival sex workers are afforded the rights to work in bawdy houses and to communicate in public for the purposes of sex work but not to hire protective staff. The court's comments in *Bedford* nevertheless suggest that some deference should be shown to Parliament if such evidentiary lacunae were to arise since sex work regulation constitutes a "complex and delicate matter."[108]

Not all of these arguments apply to voluntary sex workers. As I concluded earlier, this category of sex workers cannot rely on the moral involuntariness defence when screening clients or setting up bawdy houses. Moreover, those who voluntarily perform sex work typically take up this work because of its financial benefits. As a result, they are likely able to hire staff to protect them while performing their work. The living on the avails prohibition therefore negatively affects this category of sex workers' security of the person interest in a manner that is at least overbroad per the Supreme Court's reasoning in *Bedford*. However, as with the section 1 analysis related to the bawdy house and communication offences, the fact remains that Parliament simply could criminalize sex work and that any effects on voluntary sex workers would become constitutional. Since there is little purpose in requiring Parliament to enact such a law, the living on the avails offence should be minimally impairing of constitutional rights.

As for the law's ability to balance its salutary and deleterious effects, the fact that voluntary sex workers choose to engage in a risky business strongly suggests that the fault for any effects that accrue to them is not solely attributable to the law. The salutary effects of denouncing and deterring exploitive practices also weighs in favour of the living on the avails offence being a proportionate means to pursue its objective. Although again it is difficult to prove the extent of these effects, it is unprincipled to ignore them at the final stage of the section 1 analysis. Given the heightened importance of the living on the avails provision's objective and the reduced responsibility of the law in harming voluntarily acting sex workers, I maintain that the living on the avails offence also ought to have been upheld under section 1 of the Charter since it applied to voluntary sex workers.

It is nevertheless concerning that upholding a set of laws that prohibits voluntary sex workers from working in bawdy houses, screening clients, or hiring protective workers would result in violence toward these workers. It is important to reiterate here that I take no position on whether Parliament's sex work laws were good criminal law policy.

I am concerned only with the constitutional rationale offered in *Bedford*. If my analysis is correct, then the harms endured by sex workers either were not attributable to the sex work laws because of the availability of a moral involuntariness defence or were a proportionate means of combatting the dangers inherent to sex work. Although Parliament's decision to adopt the Nordic model of sex work regulation rendered the old sex work laws' constitutionality a historical question, the choice-based framework will nevertheless prove to be useful in considering the constitutionality of the new sex work laws.

8

The Constitutionality
of the New Sex Work Laws

ON 6 DECEMBER 2014, Parliament adopted a variation of the "Nordic" or "end demand" model of sex work regulation by passing Bill C-36, also known as the *Protection of Communities and Exploited Persons Act (PCEPA).*[1] The date that the *PCEPA* was passed was no coincidence. As Conservative Member of Parliament Joy Smith stated in the House of Commons, the date is "Canada's national day of remembrance and action on violence against women that commemorates the 14 young women who were brutally murdered at École Polytechnique in 1989."[2] Smith continued, noting that "[w]omen and girls continue to face violence and harassment in their homes, schools, workplaces, online and on the streets" and that "[w]omen's equality advocates identify prostitution [as one] of the most serious forms of violence against women."[3] For Smith and the Conservatives, it was therefore necessary to end the practice of sex work.[4]

The federal government further justified its policy choice by appealing to a month-long public consultation on sex work regulation in Canada. The public narrowly supported the criminalization of purchasing sexual services.[5] Notably, this result was contrary to three then-recent studies conducted by the Angus Reid Institute on public sentiment about sex work. As John Lowman and Christine Louie explain, these three studies – conducted in 2009, 2010, and 2011 – found

158 | *Rethinking* Bedford

that "just 8%, 10%, and 7% of respondents supported 'punishing clients only.'"[6] The discrepancy between these studies and the federal government's 2014 study is glaring and worthy of closer scrutiny.[7] From a legal perspective, however, the important question arising from Parliament's decision to adopt a variant of the Nordic model concerned its impact on the safety interest of sex workers.

The applicants in *Bedford* expressed grave concerns about the new sex work laws. As Amy Lebovitch responded, "[w]e didn't expect it to be simply rewriting the laws in different language."[8] For Lebovitch and others, the *PCEPA* posed the same dangers to sex workers as the previous sex work laws.[9] Criminalizing purchasers would require street workers to jump into cars more quickly or conduct their work in remote areas where their ability to screen clientele is unlikely to prevent violence. The *PCEPA*'s narrower re-enactment of the prohibitions at issue in *Bedford* also fell far short in terms of security protections.[10] Various commentators further questioned the ability of the Nordic model to achieve its purported aim of ending the sex work trade and thereby protecting the dignity and equality interests of women.[11] Other commentators, however, strongly endorsed the Nordic model's ability to further those aims and supported Parliament's adoption of the *PCEPA* on that basis.[12]

The constitutionality of criminalizing the purchase of sex will likely turn on the existing empirical research investigating the efficacy of the Nordic model. If the new sex work laws are successful in removing people from the sex work trade, then the Crown will be able to claim that in fact these laws protect the interests of sex workers and women's equality more generally. Although some sex workers might endure violence as a result, any illogical or severe effects arising from the new sex work laws are arguably justifiable given the overall good that the new model claims to achieve. I maintain that this is precisely the sort of question that courts are ill equipped to determine given the inadequacies of the adversarial model of justice, the mixed international evidence of the Nordic model's efficacy, and the lack of experience with the Nordic model in Canada.[13] Deference therefore ought to be afforded to Parliament's policy choice.

The Constitutionality of the New Sex Work Laws | 159

Alongside criminalizing the purchase of sex, the *PCEPA* (re)created various restrictions on operating bawdy houses, living on the avails of sex work, and procuring, advertising, and communicating in public for the purposes of sex work. Each prohibition similarly aims to denounce and deter sex work in order to eradicate such work to the extent possible. In passing the *PCEPA,* however, Parliament was mindful of the Supreme Court's direction in *Bedford* that sex workers need to be able to take basic precautions during the interim period to satisfy the requirements of the Charter. This fact alone does not mean, however, that Parliament sought to protect sex workers as one of the law's objectives. Comparing the effects of each law with its sole objective of discouraging the sex work trade ought to result in each of these provisions being upheld under the Charter. Viewing these offences through the lens of choice developed in the previous chapter bolsters this argument.

THE *PCEPA*

The *PCEPA* modified the offences struck down in *Bedford* and added several other offences. Subsection 213(1.1) of the *Criminal Code of Canada*[14] replaced the prior communication prohibition. The new provision prohibits sex workers from communicating for the purpose of sex work in a public place, or any place open to public view, if the communication takes place next to a "school ground, playground, or daycare centre." Subsection 213(2) continues to define "public place" as including "any place to which the public have access as of right or by invitation, express or implied, and any motor vehicle located in a public place or in any place open to public view." Those who violate this provision can be subject to a fine of no more than $5,000, two years less a day of prison, or both.[15]

Section 286.1 of the *Criminal Code* now prohibits any purchase or sale of sex. The prohibition against selling sexual services nevertheless must be read in conjunction with the immunity provision found in section 286.5. Subsection 286.5(2) excludes anyone who sells their own sexual services from prosecution. The new sex work laws therefore

160 | *Rethinking* Bedford

make it illegal for an individual to purchase or sell sexual services even if the latter conduct will not be prosecuted. However, it remains a prosecutable offence to aid or abet a person to use another sex worker's services. Thus, a sex worker who refers a client to a co-worker would be a party to the co-worker's offence, even though the co-worker herself would not be prosecuted.[16] Various mandatory minimum fines are in place for violating this provision depending on the nature of the act committed and the Crown's election to proceed by way of summary conviction or indictment.[17]

Section 286.2 of the *Criminal Code* prohibits receiving a financial or other "material benefit" knowing that it was obtained from the direct or indirect sale or purchase of sex. Subsection 286.5(1)(a) nevertheless provides immunity to sex workers who sell their own sexual services. Subsection 286.2(3) further provides that proof a person "lives with or is habitually in the company of a person who offers or provides sexual services for consideration is, in the absence of evidence to the contrary, proof that the person received a financial or other material benefit from those services." However, subsection 286.2(4) carves out several exceptions for those who receive such a benefit because they are in a "legitimate living arrangement" with a sex worker; have a "legal or moral obligation [toward] the person from whose sexual services the benefit is derived"; receive the benefit "in consideration for a service or good that they offer, on the same terms and conditions, to the general public"; or, if the latter exception is inapplicable, the person who provided the good or service "did not counsel or encourage that person to provide sexual services and the benefit is proportionate to the value of the service or good."

Subsection 286.2(5) of the *Criminal Code* nevertheless narrows the exemptions provided in subsection 286.2(4). The first set of these exceptions to the exemptions is intuitive. It criminalizes those receiving a material benefit who use violence, intimidation, or coercion; abuse a position of trust, power, or authority; provide an intoxicant to aid or abet the sex worker to provide sexual services; or illegally procure the sex worker from whom the accused derives a benefit.[18] The controversial aspect of subsection 286.2(5) provides that the exemptions in section 286.4 are not available if the accused "received the benefit in the context of a commercial enterprise that offers sexual services for consideration."[19] As I explain below, the meaning of the term "commercial enterprise" is currently unclear and can dramatically limit the extent to which sex workers provide their services from bawdy houses. Those found guilty of this offence can be sentenced to ten years of imprisonment if prosecuted by way of indictment or two years less a day, a $5,000 fine, or both if prosecuted by way of summary conviction.[20]

Section 286.3 of the *Criminal Code* restates the prior procuring offence – not challenged in *Bedford* – and adds several restrictions related to setting up bawdy houses.[21] The new provision criminalizes "[e]veryone who procures a person to offer or provide sexual services for consideration" or, "for the purpose of facilitating an offence under section 286.1(1), recruits, holds, conceals or harbours a person who offers or provides sexual services for consideration, or exercises control, direction or influence over the movements of that person." The term "procure" means causing, inducing, or persuading a person to offer or provide sexual services.[22] The term "influence" connotes conduct less coercive than the term "direction" and can apply merely by proposing that a person engages in sex work followed by any attempt to persuade that person to follow through.[23] A person who violates this provision is guilty of an indictable offence and liable to a maximum penalty of fourteen years of imprisonment.

Finally, section 286.4 of the *Criminal Code* prohibits anyone who "knowingly advertises an offer to provide sexual services for consideration." Importantly, the exemption found in subsection 286.5(1)(b) excludes sex workers from liability for advertising their own sexual services. A sex worker might nevertheless be liable for helping others to advertise their services or advertising as a collective. Moreover, it is illegal for anyone to help a sex worker advertise their services. Depending on the business acumen of the individual sex worker, this restriction can severely hinder a sex worker from operating a sustainable business.[24]

THE OBJECTIVE OF THE *PCEPA*

Determining the purpose of the offences found in the *PCEPA* is critical to determining their constitutionality. Unfortunately, scholars currently disagree about the objective(s) underlying the new sex work laws. Hamish Stewart maintains that the *PCEPA* claims to further two objectives: "denouncing and deterring sex work" and "improving sex workers' safety."[25] Other scholars similarly have suggested that the new sex work laws serve "to ensure that Canadian criminal law no longer endangers sex workers' lives and security."[26] To the contrary, Debra Haak maintains that the *PCEPA* has one objective: reducing the demand for sex work so as to discourage entry into the profession, deter current sex workers from participating in the trade, and ultimately abolishing the practice to the extent possible.[27] I agree with Haak. Although laws ought to be able to forward multiple purposes pursuant to a constitutional analysis, the new sex work laws do not take this approach. Instead, their aim is to deter sex work to the greatest extent possible and ultimately abolish the practice itself.

Determining Objectives

The Supreme Court has provided several guiding principles for determining the objective of a law. As I explained in the previous chapter, requiring that a law promotes only one objective is often a legal fiction, and the legal test ought to be interpreted in a way that avoids this contradiction. The Supreme Court's analysis nevertheless is still useful for distilling a law's objectives for the purposes of constitutional analysis. First, a law's objectives must be distinct from the means used to achieve them. Put differently, the text of the provision is not necessarily determinative of legislative intent.[28] Second, a law's objectives must be characterized at the appropriate level of generality. A law's objectives must therefore avoid appealing to an "animating social value" or stating the objectives in terms synonymous with those of the text.[29] Third, a law's objectives must be described in a "precise and succinct" way that captures "the main thrust of the law."[30] Fourth, the appropriateness or

The *Constitutionality of the New Sex Work Laws* | 163

achievability of the law's aim is irrelevant to determining the law's objectives. Instead, courts take the objectives of a law "at face value."[31]

Distilling these principles into a legal test, the Supreme Court requires that courts interpret the purpose of legislation from sources derived from the legislative process. First, courts must give weight to any statutory statements of purpose in the legislation and its preamble.[32] Second, courts must consider "the text, context, and scheme of the legislation."[33] Third, courts can rely on any relevant extrinsic evidence pertaining to a law's "legislative history and evolution."[34] In considering evidence deriving from these sources, the aim is always to "articulate the legislative objective in a way that is firmly anchored in the legislative text, considered in its full context, and [to] ... avoid statements of purpose that effectively predetermine the outcome of the ... analysis without actually engaging in it."[35]

The *PCEPA*

The preamble to the *PCEPA* states that Parliament's objective in passing the new sex work laws was to prevent "the exploitation that is inherent in prostitution ... [and] the social harm caused by the objectification of the human body and the commodification of sexual activity." The preamble further purports that it is "important to protect human dignity and the equality of all Canadians by discouraging prostitution," "to denounce and prohibit the purchase of sexual services because it creates a demand for prostitution," and to denounce and prohibit "the procurement of persons for the purpose of prostitution and the development of economic interests in the exploitation of the prostitution of others as well as the commercialization and institutionalization of prostitution." Finally, the preamble expresses Parliament's intention "to encourage those who engage in prostitution to report incidents of violence and to leave prostitution."

Statements made in the legislature are consistent with the deterrence-based rationale espoused in the preamble to the *PCEPA*. Minister of Justice Peter McKay commenced the second reading of Bill C-36 by observing that it constitutes a "significant shift in prostitution-related

164 | *Rethinking* Bedford

criminal law policy from treatment of prostitution as a nuisance toward treatment of prostitution for what it is: a form of exploitation."[36] McKay also noted that Bill C-36 "is about protecting vulnerable Canadians, communities that sometimes are at risk, and in particular ... a specific group of Canadians to whom we do have a fiduciary duty to protect, and that is mainly our children."[37] McKay further noted during second reading that "we do not believe that other approaches, such as decriminalization or legalization, could make prostitution a safe activity."[38] Nowhere in his description of the purpose of the *PCEPA* did he explicitly state that the law's aim is to make sex work safer.[39]

A technical paper released alongside enactment of the *PCEPA* also endorsed the broader deterrence rationale of the new sex work laws. As the Department of Justice stated, the *PCEPA*'s "overall objective is to reduce demand for prostitution with a view to discouraging entry into it, deterring participation in it and ultimately abolishing it to the greatest extent possible."[40] As the authors of the technical paper explain, the purchasing offence found in section 286.1 of the *Criminal Code* most directly purports to achieve this objective by "reducing demand for sexual services."[41] Similarly, they explain that the material benefit offence is aimed at deterring "the development of economic interests in the exploitation of the prostitution of others, as well as the institutionalization and commercialization of prostitution."[42] Similar comments were made with respect to the procuring and advertising offences.[43]

The authors of the technical paper identified a similar objective with respect to the prohibition against communicating in public for the purposes of sex work. In their view, the objective of this provision is "to protect children from exposure to prostitution, which is viewed as a harm in and of itself, because such exposure risks normalizing a gendered and exploitive practice in the eyes of impressionable youth and could result in vulnerable children being drawn into a life of exploitation."[44] Endorsing this rationale, Haak maintains that "[d]iscouraging the normalization of prostitution can be understood as consistent with the objective of denouncing and deterring prostitution and its underlying understanding of the activity as exploitive, particularly of women and girls."[45] Put differently, by limiting the ability of children

The Constitutionality of the New Sex Work Laws | 165

to witness sex work, these highly impressionable citizens will be less likely to engage in such work.

The text and history of the *PCEPA* nevertheless provide some basis for concluding that Parliament's new sex work laws aim to increase the safety of sex workers. They do so by broadening the places where sex workers may communicate in public and allowing them to work from indoor places if certain conditions are met and to hire limited staff. However, these provisions must be read alongside the *Bedford* decision and Parliament's clear intention to end sex work to the extent possible. Parliament explicitly recognized that the latter objective would take time to achieve and took the view that the *Bedford* decision constitutionally required taking some safety measures during the interim period.[46]

Although Parliament could have avoided its laws "causing" harm by criminalizing sex work, as I explained in the previous chapter, this route was available only if Parliament was aware that survival sex workers have a moral involuntariness defence. Parliament therefore operated within a legal context in which it was reasonable to conclude that the *Bedford* decision required loosening some restrictions on sex work. Viewed in this light, the text of the provisions need not result in the safety of sex workers being an explicit objective of the legislation even if the laws have such an effect. As Haak explains, "[t]here is a difference between seeking to improve the overall safety of those who continue to exchange sexual services and taking steps to ensure that legislative acts do not preclude them from taking certain measures" that Parliament believes are compelled under the Charter.[47]

Appellate courts are currently divided on the purposes underlying the new sex work laws. In *R v Alcorn*,[48] Justice Mainella wrote for a unanimous Manitoba Court of Appeal that "[t]he *PCEPA* is designed to discourage, denounce and prohibit the demand for prostitution in order to protect communities, human dignity and equality, and to encourage victims to report violence and leave prostitution."[49] In *R v NS*,[50] a unanimous Ontario Court of Appeal agreed that the main objective of the law is to abolish sex work to the extent possible.[51] Interestingly, however, the court also concluded that the sex work laws

166 | *Rethinking* Bedford

purport "to mitigate *some* of the dangers associated with the continued, unlawful provision of sexual services for consideration."[52] In its view, "Parliament's latter objective is to ensure that, *as much as possible,* persons who continue to provide their sexual services for consideration, contrary to law, can avail themselves of the safety-enhancing measures identified in *Bedford.*"[53] Yet this position inadequately addresses the context of the *Bedford* case outlined earlier. Since allowing some safety precautions was practically compelled by *Bedford,* it seems to be disingenuous to interpret those concessions as part of the objective of the new sex work laws when no other evidence supports this explanation for why Parliament adopted the Nordic model.[54]

THE CONSTITUTIONALITY OF BILL C-36

Several courts and commentators have isolated some constitutionally questionable effects when applying the instrumental rationality principles to the new sex work laws. Although I concluded that these principles are fundamentally flawed,[55] courts have applied and are likely to continue applying the same principles used in *Bedford* to the new sex work laws. In so doing, courts should find those laws constitutional for two interrelated reasons. First, many of the questionable effects of the laws are irrelevant to the constitutional analysis when viewed through the lens of choice. Second, courts are ill equipped to determine the effects of the Nordic model, especially when it is transplanted into a new social context.

The Communication Provision

The revised communication provision in section 213 of the *Criminal Code* ought to be upheld for two reasons. First, if a sex worker is working near a place where children are likely to be present, then that worker can be expected to change locations. Second, sex work is illegal under the new sex work laws. Any argument that Parliament is making a legal practice more dangerous is therefore unavailable to sex workers. As expressed in the previous chapter, the fact that sex work was previously legal ought not to have resulted in the sex work laws being struck down.

The Constitutionality of the New Sex Work Laws | 167

If my reasons are unpersuasive, then the new sex work laws render such an argument moot because the sale of sex itself is now illegal.

In *R v NS*,[56] Justice Sutherland nevertheless expressed disagreement with the conclusion that sex work is now illegal. He contended that "substance" matters over "form," and the fact that no consequences arise from selling sex means that it cannot be considered illegal for the purposes of constitutional analysis.[57] Substance must nevertheless also be informed by context. Unfortunately, Sutherland ignores the fact that the legality of sex work drove the analysis in *Bedford*. To conclude that sex work is not illegal tells Parliament that, if it wants to uphold restrictions on the practice of sex work, then it must impose criminal consequences. This again results in a perverse incentive to over-criminalize consensual crimes. Read plainly, sex work was made illegal – even though it may not be prosecuted – and courts ought to respect that policy choice given the unique context of the *Bedford* case. For similar reasons, the Ontario Court of Appeal unanimously overturned Sutherland on this point, affirming that sex work is now illegal.[58]

Hamish Stewart nevertheless maintains that the new communication provision might be struck down because "some people have no realistic choice but to make their living through sex work, and the fact that this is now an unlawful choice ... [ought not to] stop the section 7 claim in its tracks."[59] However, in the unlikely scenario that a survival sex worker is specifically coerced into working in an area where children are likely to be present, that worker would be acting in a morally involuntary manner when screening potential clients for the reasons expressed in the previous chapter. Because the sex worker would have a criminal defence, such a scenario cannot be included in assessing whether the law violates the principles of fundamental justice.

James Gacek and Richard Jochelson go further and contend that the new communication provision is unconstitutional because it will continue to have harmful effects on all types of sex workers. As they observe, the provision will result in the displacement of those selling sex in areas where children are likely to be present, which can give rise to the same safety issues discussed in *Bedford*.[60] Respectfully, this argument plays down the fact that sex workers can conduct their business

168 | *Rethinking* Bedford

in places not near areas where children are expected to be present. Parliament's aim of limiting children's exposure to sex work is not unreasonable, and without evidence that sex workers cannot move to equally secure places, it is difficult to conclude that this provision practically endangers those who choose to engage in sex work.

A final argument impinging the new communication provision's constitutionality is that the provision is overbroad. Since the new offence applies at all times of day, Haak suggests that communicating in public for the purposes of sex work at nighttime would not further the objectives of the law since children are unlikely to be present.[61] It is nevertheless likely that some children – youth in particular – could be out at late hours of the night. Even if the communication offence is overbroad, it is likely that such a violation would be upheld under section 1 of the Charter. The minimal impairment analysis requires that rights be violated only as much as "necessary."[62] As the Supreme Court observes, "[t]he tailoring process seldom admits of perfection and the courts must accord some leeway to the legislator."[63] Courts should find that the law constitutes one of a range of reasonable alternatives for balancing the interests of sex workers and children. This follows because inserting a temporal aspect into the prohibition is unlikely to fully prevent the aims that Parliament sought to forward with its new communication provision.

The Criminalization of Purchasers

Section 286.1 and subsection 286.5(2) of the *Criminal Code* provide a novel prohibition. Unlike the previous sex work laws, these provisions criminalize purchasing sex but make the sale of one's own sexual services nonprosecutable. This law is arguably unconstitutional because of the dangers that it poses to sex workers. Social science evidence suggests that criminalizing purchasers drives the sale of sex to more remote, less visible areas.[64] Survival sex workers therefore will have to conduct their business in riskier areas since their clients will be wary of using fixed indoor places that are easy targets for police. This raises the question: What good is the ability to screen clients if there are fewer means available to seek help – because of the remote location – if something

The Constitutionality of the New Sex Work Laws | 169

goes wrong? Although it is possible to hire a bodyguard under the new law, it is unlikely that all sex workers could afford such services. Thus, the prohibition against purchasing sex might violate the gross disproportionality principle by forcing some sex workers to the margins, where any safety benefits provided to them by the remaining sex work laws will be diminished.

Critics also maintain that the Nordic model results in other detrimental effects to the safety interests of sex workers. For instance, street sex workers in Sweden – the first country to implement the Nordic model – reported increased frequency of violence largely because the clients who "remain are more likely to be drunk, violent, and to request unprotected sex."[65] The decline in clients "on the stroll" also resulted in greater competition for those clients, which in turn eroded sex workers' bargaining power with respect to fees and safety precautions. These conditions therefore require street workers to service more clients, increasing exposure to violence and sexually transmitted diseases.[66] Sex workers have also reported increased stigma as a result of their line of work, resulting in various social consequences, including increased difficulty accessing health care, acquiring social aid, and maintaining housing.[67]

Although the Nordic model undoubtedly has some negative effects on sex workers,[68] Parliament's overall objective in passing the *PCEPA* – ending the practice of sex work – arguably will save lives by preventing people from engaging in sex work. This argument has at least surface-level appeal since the current approach to conducting an instrumental rationality analysis requires courts to assume that the law achieves its objective.[69] Yet, as I explained in Chapter 5, this rule is flawed because it allows the legislature to shield its laws from more searching constitutional scrutiny.[70] If Parliament's objectives are presumed to be achieved, then the Crown can maintain that attaining an important objective – such as protecting the "human dignity and the equality of all Canadians by discouraging prostitution"[71] – strikes a reasonable balance compared with any risks posed to sex workers. To avoid granting the Crown such an undue advantage, it is necessary to scrutinize the ability of the law to achieve its objective at the section 7 stage of the analysis.

170 | *Rethinking* Bedford

As the Nordic model was adopted by Sweden, Norway, and Iceland at the time of the *Bedford* litigation,[72] the trial judge reviewed evidence of the model's efficacy from these jurisdictions. It is notable that France, Northern Ireland, Ireland, and Israel also adopted the Nordic model post-*Bedford*.[73] In reviewing the available evidence, Justice Himel observed that Sweden's switch from decriminalization to criminalization of purchasers resulted in "the number of women involved in sex work decreasing from 2,500 in 1999 to less than 1,500 in 2002 ... [and] [t]he number of women in street prostitution [decreasing] from 650 in 1999 to less than 500 in 2002."[74] Himel further observed that "[g]overnment reports suggest that there are almost no foreign women remaining in street prostitution, and there is some suggestion that human traffickers may now find Sweden to be an unattractive destination for trafficked women."[75] A study conducted after the trial decision in *Bedford* further found that the model "disrupted organized crime, deterred sex act purchasers, changed public attitudes, and cut street-level prostitution in half."[76] The study also "found nothing whatsoever to suggest that Sweden's abolitionist model had negatively affected those being exploited."[77] The Swedish model, however, has not been a panacea. Despite a 300 percent increase in arrests, convictions remain relatively rare.[78]

The merits of the Nordic model must also be compared with those of decriminalizing sex work. Relying primarily on Justice Himel's findings of fact, Benjamin Perrin observes that in jurisdictions where decriminalization has been adopted – the Netherlands, New Zealand, Germany, Queensland, and Nevada[79] – the policy often results in "the most vulnerable prostitutes (street-level) [remaining] in [their] precarious situation[s]."[80] After decriminalization in the Netherlands, almost half of sex work occurred illegally and typically involved "foreign prostitutes providing out-calls set up by telephone and over the internet."[81] A Queensland government report similarly found that 75 percent of sex work continued to operate illegally despite aggressive policing of street workers.[82] In New Zealand, the number of street workers remained constant after decriminalization despite proponents of decriminalization maintaining that the number would decrease.[83] A three-year post-decriminalization review in Germany similarly found that "no measurable improvements are detectable in achieving social protection for prostitutes, improving working conditions, encouraging prostitutes to exit the industry, or reducing crime."[84]

In Perrin's view, the available research favours adoption of the Nordic model "because much of what has driven the *Bedford* case is the need to ensure that street-level prostitutes are given protection since they are considered to be most at risk of violence."[85] In his reading of the international evidence, Perrin concludes that street workers "would not receive materially enhanced protection under a legalized or decriminalized approach to prostitution."[86] To the contrary, the Nordic model might serve to reduce sex work and thereby protect the interests of the most vulnerable sex workers in the long term, even if some of them will incur harms in the interim similar to those described in the *Bedford* case.

How a court resolves the constitutionality of section 286.1 and subsection 286.5(2) of the *Criminal Code* will therefore turn on the available social science evidence. The complexity of answering that question – the evidence reviewed above providing only a snapshot of the debate[87] – strongly suggests that the courts should show deference to Parliament when assessing the constitutionality of Bill C-36. Although Justice Himel was capable of making findings of fact with respect to the prior sex work laws, there is no guarantee that the next trial judge will be as deft at navigating this complex area of study.[88] Equally important, the debate concerning whether to adopt the Nordic model or to decriminalize/legalize sex work is ongoing and operates with limited data.[89] More concerning, little empirical literature has arisen in Canada with respect to the Nordic model. As comparative methodologists observe, it is dangerous to take conclusions from different contexts and apply them to another jurisdiction.[90] Without better evidence and improved capacity of courts to assess social science evidence, I maintain that courts should show deference to Parliament on the question of whether the adoption of the key feature of the Nordic model – the criminalization of purchasers – is consistent with the Charter.

172 | *Rethinking* Bedford

The Material Benefit Offence

The material benefit offence effectively provides a narrower version of the previous living on the avails provision. Potential problems nevertheless arise from the fact that liability follows if the person "received the benefit in the context of a *commercial enterprise* that offers sexual services for consideration."[91] In Hamish Stewart's view, "[t]his limit makes the exemptions nearly meaningless in the context of sex work from a fixed, indoor location."[92] As Stewart explains, "although the landlord might appear to fall under the exemption in section 286.2(4)(c) for a service or good offered to the general public, they would lose that exemption under section 286.2(5)(e) because they would receive the rent 'in the context of a commercial enterprise.'"[93] He further maintains that "the sex worker would not be able to lawfully hire a receptionist, bookkeeper, driver, or bouncer, as [the 'commercial enterprise' clause] would deny these employees any exemption from the material benefit offence."[94] Given the potential party liability for aiding or abetting the sale of another's sexual services, Stewart further maintains that it will be difficult for sex workers to sell sex in groups.[95] He therefore contends that "the only lawful way for a sex worker to maintain a permanent location in which to do this work is to buy a suitable building or apartment and operate the business entirely on their own."[96]

The first court to seriously consider the constitutionality of these provisions did not read the provision so narrowly.[97] In *R v Anwar*,[98] Justice McKay found that the term "commercial enterprise" under subsection 286.2(5)(e) allowed sex workers to be "immune from prosecution if they sold sexual services cooperatively with another individual or individuals ... by sharing space."[99] Although sex workers cannot aid or abet other sex workers, they can still take defensive actions if a co-worker finds herself in perilous circumstances. McKay further found that the term need not exclude sex workers who sell only their own sexual services from retaining "the services of third parties such as drivers, receptionists, assistants or security personnel."[100] However, he also concluded that "a third-party manager who is not engaged in coercion and simply fulfils the same sorts of roles that they would in another industry clearly commits an offence under section 286.2."[101] As the Ontario Court of Appeal later observed, it is third-party profiteering – for example, economic exploitation by a third party – that animates the prohibition against receiving a material benefit while working in an establishment that offers sexual services for consideration.[102]

Justice McKay nevertheless concluded that the material benefit provision violates section 7 of the Charter. His reasoning was heavily influenced by the view that the new laws are too complex for sex workers to navigate and therefore will expose them to criminal liability.[103] This rationale is difficult to accept since a law's complexity has never been used to undermine its constitutionality under section 7 of the Charter. Courts can instead explain the impact of the law in as simple terms as possible. If sex workers follow that interpretation, then they are able to set up bawdy houses, work in groups, and hire protective staff, with some restrictions, but must do so without the aid of a third-party manager.[104]

Parliament's concern about pimps masquerading as legitimate managers is likely why the provision does not apply to third-party managers. Given this laudable purpose, combined with the broader rights of sex workers to set up bawdy houses, screen clients, and hire nonmanagerial staff, it is not clear how this provision would have unconstitutional effects. As I maintained in the previous chapter, a similar argument ought to have been accepted as a basis for upholding the prior living on the avails provision. In light of the other safety options available to sex workers, any detrimental effects caused by prohibiting managers from working with sex workers are likely balanced by the good done by making it more difficult for pimps to exploit sex workers.

Justice Sutherland nevertheless offered a narrower interpretation of the impugned law in *NS*. In his view, the phrase "their own sexual services" in subsection 286.5(1)(a) and the term "commercial enterprise" in subsection 286.2(5)(e) of the *Criminal Code* prohibit sex workers from working cooperatively.[105] This in turn makes it difficult for many sex workers to raise the necessary funds to hire protective staff or sustain their business more generally.[106] Although the Ontario Court of Appeal overturned this interpretation,[107] the possibility that another

174 | *Rethinking* Bedford

appellate court might adopt it renders Sutherland's interpretation worth addressing.

In my view, the distinction between voluntary and involuntary sex work again mitigates any constitutional concerns. As I maintained in the previous chapter, survival sex workers are constitutionally permitted to operate a bawdy house together to protect their security interests. Voluntary sex workers, however, must rely on a "right" to conduct what is now an illegal act. Their choice to break the law cannot be saved by the fact that, when they break the law, they wish to do so safely. As a result, the only legally relevant motivation behind their actions is economic. I cannot agree that such a right is protected under section 7 of the Charter since the Supreme Court has repeatedly excluded economic interests from its purview.[108]

The Procuring Provision

In *Anwar*, Justice McKay provided two scenarios to illustrate the constitutional issues with the procuring provision.[109] Justice Sutherland in *NS* relied on similar scenarios in his analysis.[110] The first scenario involves a couple who run an escort agency that provides consensual sexual services to their clientele. After recruitment ads have been posted, prospective escorts go through a rigorous interview process during which the owners of the agency outline the nature of the work, fee arrangements, employment benefits, and protection provided by the agency for the escort. The latter items involve the agency providing a detailed description of the permissible conduct before an escort meets with a client and ensuring that the escort is accompanied by a driver who could intervene quickly should something go wrong. In sum, the escort agency would treat the escort humanely and provide her with benefits similar to those in other employment contexts. The applicant is then asked to rate her desire to work as an escort. Only those who continue to express a strong desire to do so are hired by the agency.[111]

The second scenario involves a pair of university students who want to enter the sex trade to help pay for their tuition and book fees. To do so, they approach an experienced sex worker to obtain advice about starting up their business since they know little about the sex trade.

The sex worker helps the students find a rental place in which to operate, hire security personnel and a receptionist, and arrange for a photographer and website designer to aid in advertising their services online. The students follow the sex worker's advice and begin selling sexual services.[112]

The couple in the first scenario violated the "procuring" prohibition in section 286.3. This follows given the plain definition of that term: "to cause, or to induce, or to have a persuasive effect upon the conduct that is alleged."[113] Justice McKay was troubled by the fact that a couple in a nonexploitive relationship with a sex worker would commit the procuring offence.[114] However, the constitutionality of the offence must be viewed in light of two facts. First, the sex worker is not a survival sex worker given her employment arrangement. Second, sex work is now illegal, even if it cannot be prosecuted. As a result, any finding that the procuring prohibition in section 286.3 is unconstitutional based on the first hypothetical scenario would effectively provide a right to profit from another person's voluntary and illegal sex work. Such economic rights are not protected under section 7 of the Charter.[115]

The second scenario also ought not lead to a constitutional violation. Each student's security interest is arguably engaged as a result of the law rendering the students incapable of receiving advice from an experienced sex worker about how to practise sex work safely. The sex worker might run afoul of either "recruiting" or "influencing" the students. Although the need to pay tuition and book fees is important, it is highly unlikely that such a predicament leaves a person with no "realistic choice" but to enter the sex trade. There are various other options for such students, such as taking up other employment, acquiring loans, deferring their studies, or enrolling in fewer classes. As such, the student sex workers would be *voluntary* sex workers. This again renders their argument akin to an economic right to participate in sex work using their preferred means despite that conduct now being illegal. For the reasons expressed earlier, section 7 of the Charter cannot be read broadly enough to provide pure economic rights.[116]

The second mode of liability in the procuring provision can also be interpreted narrowly to avoid catching the hypothetical sex worker's

176 | *Rethinking* Bedford

conduct. As Justice Hoy concluded in *NS,* even though this mode requires a high degree of *mens rea* – any influence must be done "for the purpose" of committing the offence[117] – the influence must be directed at more than "facilitating" commercial sex work. Instead, section 286.3 requires that the influence be directed at "obtaining" sexual services. Put differently, the secondary mode of liability criminalizes providing any advice to a person who seeks to *obtain* the hypothetical students' sexual services, not to facilitate their ability to *sell* those services.[118] For this reason, any concern about the sex worker in the second hypothetical scenario "recruiting" or "influencing" the students is moot since the new sex work laws do not prohibit such conduct.

The Advertising Provision
Finally, section 286.4 of the *Criminal Code* regulates the advertisement of sexual services. Whereas sex workers are not liable for advertising their individual services, those who assist sex workers in advertising their services are liable. As the Ontario Court of Appeal observed in *R v Gallone,*[119] section 286.4 captures "those who assist sellers in advertising their sexual services even if there [was] no exploitative relationship between them."[120] In *Anwar,* the Crown rightly conceded that the prohibition on advertising sexual services violated the right to freedom of expression protected under section 2(b) of the Charter. Such an admission was prudent since one's choice to aid another person in advertising a particular service surely constitutes an attempt to "convey meaning."[121]

Given the violation of section 2(b) of the Charter, Justice McKay proceeded to consider whether the infringement was justifiable under section 1 without determining if the law also violated section 7. He nevertheless invoked language suggesting that section 7 of the Charter was engaged. As he wrote, "[g]iven the practical necessity for the vast majority of sex workers of involving third parties in the creation of advertising, [the laws have] the practical effect of depriving sex workers of critical tools which enhance the safety of sex workers."[122] McKay continued, observing that "[l]imiting the ability of sex workers to clearly communicate terms and conditions for their services and to

The Constitutionality of the New Sex Work Laws | 177

effectively screen potential clientele will result in a significantly increased risk of serious injury or death."[123]

The distinction between voluntary and survival sex workers should again influence the application of the Charter. If a sex worker enters the trade voluntarily, such as the students in Justice McKay's second hypothetical scenario, then it is not clear that the advertising prohibition does anything more than thwart economic promotion of what is now illegal activity. By restricting the best means for promoting sex work – advertising services – to only those who advertise their own services, voluntarily acting sex workers can be expected to leave the trade because of increased difficulty in marketing their services. There might nevertheless be scenarios in which a survival sex worker must seek assistance to conduct advertising and would prefer to make screening clientele part of that advertising. In such a scenario, it is arguable that preventing the sex worker from obtaining assistance in screening her clientele risks her personal safety.

Yet it is not clear that any deficiency in screening clients by prohibiting advertising cannot be addressed by sex workers who screen them in the manner currently permitted under section 213(1.1) of the *Criminal Code*. Such an argument would effectively serve as a section 1 justification for the law's infringement of the right to freedom of expression protected under section 2(b) of the Charter. If the ability to screen clientele using the means permitted under section 213(1.1) is equally effective from a safety standpoint, then the limit on freedom of expression would be readily justified. If screening within the context of advertising services is better able to protect sex workers – which might be true given that the screening under section 213(1.1) is now likely to occur in remote areas because of the criminalization of purchasers – then the section 1 analysis would need to consider whether these effects are outweighed by the law's ability to achieve its overall objective.

Because eliminating advertising is an important component of Parliament's legislative scheme, it is reasonable to show Parliament deference with respect to the ability of its new laws to achieve their overall objective at such an early stage of their implementation. This follows for two interrelated reasons that have animated my argument thus far. First, the judiciary possesses limited institutional capacity to understand complex social science evidence. Since the new sex work laws require courts to delve into the empirical literature with respect to a novel means of sex work regulation, courts should be cognizant of their institutional limitations. Second, there is currently a dearth of evidence of the efficacy of the Nordic model in Canada. Until at least the latter deficit is alleviated, it is imprudent to use the limited international evidence as a basis for striking down the new sex work laws. As explained earlier, scholars are deeply divided in their consideration of which regulatory model constitutes better social policy. As the broader debate about the efficacy of these models is unlikely to be resolved any time soon, courts should be reluctant to decide that debate based on their current sex work policy preferences.

9

Sex Work and the Criminal Law

THE ARGUMENT PUT forward in this part of the book might strike some readers as "cold" or "unworkable."[1] I do not think that these responses can reasonably be directed at the doctrinal analyses in the preceding two chapters. In all other areas of criminal law, an accused person is required to provide reasons for committing anything that constitutes a criminal offence. If the sex work offences are truly crimes, then I can see no reason why those who commit these offences ought not to be required to do the same. Although the sex workers who plead such a defence are vulnerable actors, so are many of those who plead other criminal defences. As with these other accused persons, those who communicate in public for the purposes of sex work or work in a bawdy house therefore ought to be required to provide reasons why their conduct is morally involuntary or otherwise be found guilty of the offence.

If this requirement strikes the reader as objectionable, I suspect it is not because there is a serious objection to accused persons being required to provide reasons for committing offences. This is a basic and sensible feature of the Anglo-American criminal law. It would be surprising if it were discarded for a small subset of criminal offences. Instead, I suggest that the actual site of contestation concerns whether the sex work offences are proper objects of criminal law at all. The *Bedford* case, however, did not consider whether sex work comes within

180 | *Rethinking* Bedford

the legitimate scope of the criminal law. The reason that the constitutional challenge was not framed this way derives from then-recent Supreme Court jurisprudence and, in particular, the person running the constitutional challenge: Alan Young.[2]

A decade before his challenge to the sex work laws was decided, the Supreme Court released its reasons in *R v Malmo-Levine*.[3] Another landmark section 7 case, Young was heavily involved in challenging the marijuana possession and possession for the purposes of trafficking laws in the now repealed *Narcotic Control Act*.[4] Central to the constitutional challenge was the claim that the principles of fundamental justice require the state to adhere to John Stuart Mill's "harm principle." According to Mill, the harm principle ensures that only conduct that harms another person can be subject to criminal sanction.[5] For the applicant, personal use of marijuana would not harm anyone else. Although there is a small chance that marijuana use would harm some users, the fact remains that only the person who chooses to use marijuana would incur that harm and therefore would not cause harm to others.[6]

The Supreme Court in *Malmo-Levine* ultimately rejected the applicant's argument.[7] The rationale underlying why the harm principle was not adopted as a principle of fundamental justice is tied to a famous debate between H.L.A. Hart and Lord Patrick Devlin.[8] In addition to advocating the traditional legal moralism thesis – the idea that the criminal law may be used to express society's disapproval of a practice that it deems morally objectionable[9] – Devlin suggested that immoral acts cause *social* harms that may justify the use of criminal sanctions.[10] In response, criminologists began investigating whether such harms arise from any conduct possibly classified as immoral. This history is complex, but Devlin and his progeny claimed that numerous acts often considered a "nuisance" would cause "societal disintegration" and therefore the type of harm that the criminal law is invested in prohibiting.[11]

Devlin's inclusion of public harms within the harm principle was central to the Supreme Court's rejection of the constitutional challenge in *Malmo-Levine*. In its view, the harm principle failed to meet the two most important criteria to qualify as a principle of fundamental justice.[12] The first requires that the proposed principle be adequately precise. This requirement ensures that "vague generalizations about what our society considers to be ethical or moral" do not form the basis for declaring democratically enacted laws unconstitutional.[13] The sheer breadth of the public harm thesis sealed the fate of the harm principle's ability to provide an adequately precise principle for delineating the scope of the criminal law. Since "disorderly conduct" such as loitering, panhandling, and squeegeeing were now linked to social disintegration, harm could be seen in almost any activity.[14] Implicitly relying on such arguments, the Supreme Court in *Malmo-Levine* found that "[c]laims of harm have become so pervasive that the harm principle has become meaningless."[15] The debate about whether harm existed instead became a debate about how to balance competing harms. On that question, however, the harm principle is silent.[16]

The Supreme Court in *Malmo-Levine* also confirmed that a principle of fundamental justice must attract sufficient "societal consensus."[17] This requirement turns on whether the proposed principle is founded on "shared assumptions upon which our system of justice is grounded."[18] As the court observed, these assumptions "find their meaning in the cases and traditions that have long detailed the basic norms for how the state deals with its citizens" and are principles that "[s]ociety views ... as essential to the administration of justice."[19] Despite Mill's understanding of harm as typically providing the basis for criminal censure,[20] the court found that harm itself is not capable of explaining a small number of criminal offences such as cannibalism,[21] bestiality,[22] and incest.[23] In the court's view, these exceptions to the general rule are adequate to result in a lack of societal consensus that the harm principle is fundamental to justice despite most offences causing harm in the Millian sense.[24]

As I have argued elsewhere, the Supreme Court's analysis in *Malmo-Levine* did not consider whether the problems that the court identified with Mill's harm principle could be rectified by incorporating another popular delimiting principle of criminal law: the offence principle.[25] As Joel Feinberg explains, "offensive" conduct is also the proper object of criminal prohibition regardless of whether harm is caused in the

182 | *Rethinking* Bedford

Millian sense.[26] Compared with any other reason for criminalizing conduct, Feinberg concludes in his treatises, "harm and offense prevention are far and away the best reasons that can be produced in support of criminal prohibitions, and the only ones that frequently outweigh the case for liberty."[27]

His development of the offence principle is nevertheless distinct from the legal moralism thesis. As Feinberg explains, "[p]rovided that very real and intense offense is taken predictably by virtually everyone, and the offending conduct has hardly any countervailing personal or social value of its own, prohibition seems reasonable even when the protected sensibilities are not."[28] Put differently, if people generally are disgusted by one's activity, then that will render the conduct a candidate for criminalization. To be criminalized, however, the degree of offence in the community must further be weighed against whether the offence can be readily avoided and whether any risk is voluntarily assumed by members of the public.[29] In other words, the easier it is for the public to avoid settings in which the conduct occurs, the less serious the offence is considered.[30] Pornography is illustrative since it can cause affront to many people when it is viewed, but the seriousness of that affront is diminished dramatically because of the general ability of the public to avoid pornography.

In addition, the importance of the offensive conduct must be examined from the perspective of the offender.[31] The more important the conduct is to an accused's way of life, the greater the strength of the claim not to have the conduct prohibited. As part of this examination, restrictions on the conduct become more acceptable if there are satisfactory alternative times when and places where the individual can perform the conduct with less offence.[32] This "alternative opportunities" factor is nevertheless only one among several factors to consider, including the degree of offensiveness that the conduct raises in the community.[33] Importantly, there is also a requirement in Feinberg's offence principle that the offensiveness weigh clearly in favour of criminal prohibition. Put differently, there must be a convincing case for prohibition that outweighs any good arising from the impugned act.[34]

Sex Work and the Criminal Law | 183

Feinberg's offence principle obviously is not beyond criticism.[35] The role played by offence in the criminal law that Feinberg advocates does provide, however, a feasible alternative rationale for why actions that do not cause harm in the Millian sense might be criminalized. Using the examples listed by the Supreme Court in *Malmo-Levine,* an offence such as cannibalism does not necessarily involve harm to another living person. It is nevertheless a crime because many cultures find that the activity runs contrary to deeply held beliefs about the sanctity of the human body.[36] Bestiality runs contrary to a deeply held tenet that individuals must show a base measure of respect for other sentient beings. Any act that qualifies as cruelty to animals therefore comes within the legitimate scope of the criminal law.[37] And incest – to the extent that it ought to be a criminal offence – raises a significant measure of offence because of its inversion of basic and long-accepted familial roles.[38]

If it is reasonable to adopt harm and offence as the twin rationales underlying the criminal law, then several questions necessarily arise in the context of sex work regulation. How would this more robust understanding of the principles delineating the scope of the criminal law affect the constitutionality of the sex work laws at issue in *Bedford?* Could these twin principles be adopted as a combined principle of fundamental justice under section 7 of the Charter? If so, then would the harm and offence principles provide a firmer basis for challenging restrictions under the new sex work laws? Alternatively, are the harm and offence principles better infused into the definition of "criminal law" under section 91(27) of the 1867 *Constitution Act?*[39]

These are complex questions that require more discussion of the harm and offence principles than is possible here. The argument does not strike me, however, as unfeasible in principle. It nevertheless faces an important doctrinal barrier. As Hamish Stewart correctly observes, "[t]here is no support in the case law for the proposition that a moral purpose of [the] kind [underlying the sex work laws] is constitutionally improper: indeed, the Supreme Court of Canada has stated the opposite."[40] It is certainly understandable, then, that those who sought legal reform litigated the issue using other constitutional means such as the

184 | *Rethinking* Bedford

instrumental rationality principles. The constitutional analysis in *Bedford* nevertheless remains unsatisfactory for the reasons that I explained in the preceding chapters: it ignores the role of defences within the criminal law.

With this context in mind, it is prudent to consider whether the aim of decriminalizing sex work can be achieved by challenging whether acts such as communicating in public for the purposes of sex work or working in bawdy houses cause harm or offence in the required sense. This seems to be at least plausible. These offences impose no proven "harm" to any other person as Mill understood that term. It is also doubtful whether deterring individuals from entering a dangerous trade falls within the scope of the harm or offence principle. If the criminal law cannot tell people how to exercise their liberty vis-à-vis themselves, then criminalizing sex work–related conduct for the sake of protecting people from themselves – in the sense of making such conduct a "true crime"[41] – is a nonstarter. Although this rationale proved to be forceful under my section 1 analysis, that analysis occurred within a context that assumed the criminal law was properly in use. Ascribing the self-protection factor any weight when considering whether a law qualifies as harmful or offensive relies on the faulty assumption that this is a legitimate reason for criminalization. While self-protection is a legitimate reason for regulating an activity, it is much less clear that it ought to be sufficient to make conduct criminal.

In addition, the "nuisance" rationale underlying the sex work offences is of minimal weight when considering whether the laws are adequately offensive. This follows from the growing acceptance of sex work as a legitimate form of labour and questions about whether criminalizing it forwards gender equality in any meaningful sense. Also, any case for criminalization would require that the offensiveness of sex work be weighed against the importance of such work as a form of labour to many people and the importance of taking basic safety measures to ensure that the work is safe. I have difficulty rationalizing how criminal prohibition of these aspects of sex work can "clearly" result in "offence" in the sense described by Feinberg.

I include these final thoughts in light of one of my motivations for writing this book: improving the relationship between Canadian constitutional law and criminal law. The Supreme Court's decision in *Reference re Section 94(2) of the Motor Vehicle Act*[42] allowing courts to constitutionalize substantive principles of criminal law was prudent given the language of section 7 of the Charter and the lack of legislative desire to provide wholesale criminal law reform in Canada.[43] Yet, as I explain elsewhere, there are also significant risks in allowing courts to constitutionalize substantive criminal law.[44] One is that the courts might render the criminal law less coherent. In my view, this does not just happen as a result of judicial misunderstanding of the relevant legal philosophy. At other times, courts understandably get cold feet when asked to strike down laws by constitutionalizing their favourite principles of moral philosophy under section 7 of the Charter. This rationale will prove to be especially forceful when the principle constitutionalized has vast implications for the permissible scope of the criminal law.

In my view, the latter consideration best explains the Supreme Court's decision in *Malmo-Levine*. Constitutionalizing the harm principle threatened the viability of an offence such as possession of marijuana and would constitutionally impugn many other criminal offences. Its refusal to constitutionalize the harm principle, however, also had implications for future constitutional challenges such as *Bedford*. Without delineating a constitutional boundary for what can be criminalized, the courts were left to consider any effects of a law on individual sex workers and weigh them against the purpose of the law. Yet this resulted in a second fundamental error of criminal law theory: it read out the law of defences from constitutional analysis. In my view, the best approach moving forward is for the Supreme Court to clarify – in a case such as the criminalization of sex work that directly turns on the issue – the constraints on what may be criminalized by Parliament. That approach will require careful reconstructive surgery, but that is what is required given the fallout of the Supreme Court's decisions in *Malmo-Levine* and *Bedford*.

Finally, I want to be clear on one last point: the misguided develop-

186 | *Rethinking* Bedford

ment of the relationship between criminal law and constitutional law is no fault of Young's. His tireless work for the disadvantaged and his numerous attempts to render the relationship between criminal law and constitutional law coherent deserve nothing but praise. In my view, the Supreme Court's decision in *Malmo-Levine* handcuffed future constitutional challenges to offences of questionable criminal law substance in such a way that future litigants could be expected to employ only the instrumental rationality principles of fundamental justice. The problem that I wish to highlight, then, is an institutional one that casts doubt on whether courts are living up to (or are capable of living up to) the promises made by the Supreme Court in the *Motor Vehicle Act Reference* when it imbued the term "fundamental justice" with substantive content. That question, however, requires telling another complex story about the ability of courts to develop a deep theory of criminal law under a provision such as section 7 of the Charter. Since I have already written that story elsewhere, I need not repeat it here.[45]

CONCLUSION

T HE SUPREME COURT'S judgment in *Bedford* was initially counted among the historic "wins" for social justice activists litigating rights issues under the Charter. That conclusion belies the legal rationale underpinning the decision. Although the sex work laws were declared unconstitutional, the *Bedford* case attenuated rights in several ways. First, it subjected the constitutionality of laws to the capacity of individual judges to understand social scientific evidence by requiring that appellate courts defer to a trial judge's findings of legislative fact. Although the judiciary as a whole possesses limited capacity to determine legislative facts, allowing a greater number of justices to assess empirical evidence increases the likelihood that errors will be spotted. In the absence of broader reforms aimed at helping judges to understand expert evidence, the *Bedford* decision left courts with even fewer means to ensure that constitutional decisions are not decided based on faulty understandings of empirical evidence.

Second, the Supreme Court's overhaul of the instrumental rationality principles of fundamental justice was flawed in multiple ways. In addition to the confusing overlap among these principles, it is unclear that all of the principles underlying the court's new framework qualify as "principles of fundamental justice." The new framework is also problematic because it requires courts to assume that an impugned law achieves its objective. This rule can shield problematic laws from constitutional scrutiny. Although it is possible to address the latter issue by sharing the burden of proof at the section 7 stage, this approach effectively readopts the Supreme Court's "holistic" conception of the

187

188 | *Conclusion*

instrumental rationality principles that rightly was abandoned for its redundancy. Most importantly, the instrumental rationality principles make it simple for legislatures to sidestep judicial rulings by slightly modifying a law's objectives or effects. These principles therefore allow legislatures to pass constitutionally questionable reply laws without providing justificatory reasons or invoking the notwithstanding clause.

Third, the Supreme Court's decision to suspend the declaration of invalidity ensured that sex workers would continue to face the same dangers that drove the court to strike down the old sex work laws. The existing scholarship weighs in favour of abandoning the court's approach of automatically suspending declarations of invalidity solely to facilitate dialogue with the legislatures. Yet the law requires further refinement since the Supreme Court does not have any textual basis for granting a suspended declaration of invalidity. Legislatures, conversely, possess the requisite legal powers to suspend a declaration of invalidity by invoking either the notwithstanding clause or unwritten constitutional principles. Although courts also maintain a limited power to invoke unwritten constitutional principles to justify suspending a declaration of invalidity, institutional considerations suggest that legislatures are better equipped to determine the duration of such a remedy.

Although these aspects of the *Bedford* decision have implications for future litigation, the case is most problematic because of its limited engagement with the legal principles relevant to the constitutional challenge. The Supreme Court planted the seeds of a criminal defence for survival sex workers, but it did not consider whether they act in a morally involuntary manner when screening clients or setting up bawdy houses. Nor did the court consider how the limited causal connection between these laws and the harms faced by voluntary sex workers ought to affect the constitutional analysis. The court's narrow conception of the objectives underlying the communication and bawdy house offences also did not consider the main benefit deriving from these laws: deterring people from entering the sex work trade. These facts provide a drastically different context for considering the constitutionality of the sex work laws and ought to have resulted in the communication and bawdy house offences being upheld under section 1 of the Charter.

Conclusion | 189

These distinctions also animated the constitutionality of the living on the avails offence. This law is much less relevant to survival sex workers since it is unlikely that they can hire protective staff. As for voluntarily acting sex workers, the living on the avails provision ought to have been upheld for reasons similar to those relating to the bawdy house and communication provisions. First, these sex workers choose to enter the sex trade and therefore in part are responsible for the harms that they endure. Second, the objective of the living on the avails provision is much weightier than the nuisance abatement objective that the courts maintained bolstered the other provisions. Although it is difficult to prove the extent to which this law protected sex workers from exploitation, it is also likely that striking down the law would result in other harms, such as providing pimps with greater cover to exploit sex workers, making it more difficult for sex workers to leave their trade, and requiring them to service more clients. Given this broader context, the Supreme Court should have upheld the living on the avails offence under section 1 of the Charter.

The choice-based lens that I developed to reconsider the constitutionality of the old sex work laws is also relevant to Parliament's response to the *Bedford* decision: the *PCEPA*. If anything, my choice-based arguments should apply with greater force since the new sex work laws make selling sex illegal and narrow several of the restrictions challenged under the old sex work laws. However, Parliament's decision to adopt a variant of the Nordic model of sex work regulation by criminalizing the purchase of sex provides an entirely new offence for the courts to consider. The courts will be asked to determine the effects of this law, which will prove to be challenging given Canada's limited experience with that model. Although several countries either endorse or reject the Nordic model, I suggest that courts should be wary of invoking the still developing empirical debates to strike down the new sex work laws.

To the extent that one finds this constitutional analysis objectionable, I think that what drives such a response is a question that received no mention in the litigation of the sex work laws: Are these laws the proper object of criminal law? Because a person who breaches these laws causes no demonstrable harm to anyone else, the conduct is inconsistent with

190 | *Conclusion*

the most common basis for criminalizing an act. The harm principle further neutralizes one of the main factors given weight in the section 1 analysis: any utility derived from "deterring" sex work. This is simply not a legitimate object of the criminal law given the lack of tangible harm to others caused by engaging in sex work. Moreover, the offence principle requires legislatures to demonstrate that any nuisance-based law *clearly* weighs in favour of criminal prohibition based on the degree of offensiveness taken to the action by society. In addition to waning opposition to sex work, the offence principle demands that the importance of the labour to sex workers and the need for them to perform certain actions to conduct their work safely weigh heavily in favour of decriminalization. It follows that there is at least a prima facie case that the sex work laws are not proper objects of criminal law if the courts are inclined to reform their understanding of which acts can be criminalized.

Before concluding, I want to comment briefly on a final aspect of the *Bedford* decision that has received sparse mention thus far: it was unanimous. This fact should surprise readers for two reasons. First, some scholars believe that judges' political backgrounds are likely to influence their decision-making.[1] Since five of the nine justices in *Bedford* were appointed by a Conservative government, one might expect at least some disagreement on a question as politically divisive as the constitutionality of the sex work laws. The fact that the judges did not allow their political backgrounds to affect their decision bolsters Chief Justice McLachlin's observation that "[t]he evidence that judges in Canada pursue private political agendas is lacking."[2] In her view, "[a]n objective review of the thousands of judicial decisions reported each year reveals that judicial concern is focused not on plans to change society, but on interpreting and applying the law in a way that reflects legislative purpose."[3]

Second, and more importantly, the Supreme Court's decision in *Bedford* was unanimous despite various controversial legal issues being decided. As I have endeavoured to show throughout this book, commentators have extensively criticized the *Bedford* decision. I have also used this book to build on those criticisms. Given the ease with which

Conclusion | 191

commentators have criticized the *Bedford* case, it is necessary to ask: Did none of the justices see any of the problems with their reasoning in the case subsequently raised by legal scholars?

Given the high regard in which the vast majority of Canadians rightly hold the Supreme Court,[4] it is unlikely that the individual justices were oblivious of all of these criticisms. The court is composed of some of Canada's finest legal minds, and it stretches rationality to conclude that its nine justices would fail to problematize a decision that they knew would be crucial to Charter jurisprudence. As such, it is necessary to look elsewhere to explain why the *Bedford* decision was unanimous. In particular, I think that it is necessary to consider the leadership style of Beverley McLachlin, Canada's longest-standing chief justice and one of the most prolific judges in Canadian history.

In her first press conference as chief justice, McLachlin identified "consensus building" as one of her primary aims.[5] Her desire for consensus building is understandable given her judicial background. As Jamie Cameron observes, McLachlin "is a veteran of the Lamer years, which were punctuated by activist and divisive decisions that generated profound disagreement – in and outside the [Supreme] Court – about the scope of *Charter* rights and judicial powers."[6] In stark contrast, McLachlin explained that all of the Supreme Court justices under her tenure "try to eliminate unnecessary concurrences, unnecessary voices, and we talk a lot," and this discussion "leads us often to eliminate some of the differences" found in past decisions.[7]

Yet it is questionable whether dissent ought to be discouraged in constitutional cases of significant import. Judicial dissent has been justified for a variety of reasons, including justices' right to freedom of expression and the ability of dissent to promote the values underlying judicial independence.[8] Others argue that dissenting opinions result in better judgments. As John Alder observes, dissenting opinions narrow and clarify the issues at stake and set out a series of arguments to which the majority must respond.[9] Carissima Mathen makes a similar point in the context of the Supreme Court's equality rights jurisprudence, noting that, "by providing the space to fully flesh out points of disagreement, dissent has contributed to richer accounts of equality."[10]

192 | *Conclusion*

More fundamentally, dissenting Supreme Court opinions constitute an expression of judicial innovation that promotes the evolution of law.[11] As Chief Justice Hughes of the US Supreme Court observed, "[a] dissent in a court of last resort is an appeal to the brooding spirit of the law, to the intelligence of a future day, when a later decision may possibly correct the error into which the dissenting judge believes the court to have been portrayed."[12] Similarly, Justice L'Heureux-Dubé maintains that encouraging dissenting opinions ensures "that the seeds of innovation are not crushed under the weight of majority opinion, even before they are able to take root in the spirit of the law."[13] In the constitutional context especially, dissent encourages the growth of the Constitution, consistent with the metaphor that it is a "living tree" capable of change and expansion as society evolves.[14]

Even if dissenting positions are adopted infrequently by future courts, I agree with David Vitale that the "existence of dissenting opinions in those rare-but-important cases where the court later reconsidered to side with the dissent help to preserve the legitimacy of the court after the majority renders a morally reprehensible decision."[15] As he explains, such an opinion "demonstrates to the public that at least one of the judges had the wisdom and good sense to interpret the Constitution in the way we know it to be today."[16] Although *Bedford* does not rise to the category of a "morally reprehensible" decision, a similar logic applies to an apex court's judgment that is poorly reasoned or tersely decided. If I am correct that the *Bedford* decision requires revisiting, then the public will not be comforted by the fact that none of the judges on the Supreme Court raised the various problems with the judgment.

Others nevertheless maintain that judicial dissent can shake the public's confidence in the courts and thereby undermine their institutional legitimacy.[17] As Judge Learned Hand concludes, dissent "cancels the impact of monolithic solidarity on which the authority of a bench of judges so largely depends."[18] Put differently, the dissenting opinion calls into question the persuasiveness of the majority opinion. Yet other scholars put forward the reverse proposition: dissenting opinions increase judicial legitimacy by showing the public that the courts take all arguments made before them seriously.[19] As William Douglas puts it, "[a] judiciary that discloses what it is doing and why it does it will breed understanding. And confidence based on understanding is more enduring than confidence based on awe."[20]

Even if dissent detracts from institutional legitimacy, it is likely unavoidable if judges are to maintain fidelity to the law in the constitutional context. As Mathen contends, "[t]he nature of *Charter* adjudication, in which courts must weigh the importance of a particular legislative objective against the right at stake and the severity of the right's deprivation, seems almost to invite dissent."[21] As a result, Mathen agreeably suggests, "[i]t is unrealistic to expect judges to be of a single mind on such issues."[22] Although there are likely better and worse ways to dissent – strictly dissenting based on disagreement of interpretation is often preferable to questioning the legitimacy of the majority's decision[23] – the need to dissent in constitutional cases is arguably inherent to the field.[24]

To deter dissent is problematic in a landmark case such as *Bedford* because of the multiple legal rules deriving from that case. If it is erroneous to believe that the judges perfectly concurred on all issues, then it is also doubtful that each of the judges would have expressed the same disagreement. Did one group of judges care most about the amount of deference to be shown to lower court judges on legislative facts and negotiate consensus by conceding to the other judges' views on the instrumental rationality principles? Or did another group of judges think that it was of the utmost importance to suspend the declaration of invalidity and therefore put away their dissenting reasons related to whether deference ought to be shown to legislative facts? Perhaps another group felt so strongly about individualizing the instrumental rationality principles that they abandoned their dissenting reasons on one or more of the other major issues. The possibilities are numerous. In my view, this prospect is highly problematic since it turns constitutional decision-making into behind-closed-doors dealing. Unfortunately, I can see no other way for nine highly educated, critical-thinking justices to have come to a unanimous decision on all the complex and controversial points of law at issue in *Bedford*.

194 | *Conclusion*

This form of rulemaking is also problematic in a case such as *Bedford* given the high likelihood that Parliament would pass a law with similar effects on the security interests of sex workers. Notably, the constitutionality of the new sex work laws was raised before Bill C-36 was passed, with commentators expressing divergent views.[25] A critical judicial perspective on the *Bedford* case would have been useful to guide these authors and future litigants in considering the constitutionality of the new laws. Similarly, the development of a deeper understanding of section 7 would aid legislatures in crafting reply laws to judicial decisions more generally. Placing less value on cooperation makes it more likely that justices will record their concurring or dissenting reasons in controversial decisions. *Bedford,* then, casts doubt on the high value that the former chief justice placed on cooperation and exemplifies the need to encourage more robust concurring and dissenting reasons on the bench.

Notes

INTRODUCTION

1 2010 ONSC 4264, 102 OR (3d) 321.

2 See *Criminal Code of Canada*, RSC 1985, c C-46, s 210.

3 *Ibid*, s 213(1)(c).

4 *Ibid*, s 212(1)(j).

5 See *Bedford, supra* note 1 at paras 361–62.

6 *Ibid* at para 441.

7 See *Canada (Attorney General) v Bedford*, 2013 SCC 72, [2013] 3 SCR 1101, distinguishing *Reference re ss 193 and 195.1(1)(C) of the Criminal Code (Man.)*, [1990] 1 SCR 1123, 56 CCC (3d) 65 [*Sex Work Reference*]; *R v Downey*, [1992] 2 SCR 10, 90 DLR (4th) 449.

8 See *Bedford, supra* note 7 at paras 15, 41–42.

9 *Ibid* at paras 41–42.

10 See *Downey, supra* note 7.

11 See *Sex Work Reference, supra* note 7; *R v Skinner*, [1990] 1 SCR 1235, 56 CCC (3d) 1.

12 See *Sex Work Reference, supra* note 7.

13 These principles were constitutionalized in *R v Heywood*, [1994] 3 SCR 761, 120 DLR (4th) 348 (overbreadth), and *R v Malmo-Levine*, 2003 SCC 74, [2003] 3 SCR 571 (gross disproportionality).

14 Being Schedule B to the *Canada Act 1982* (UK), 1982, c 11 [Charter].

15 It is notable that commentators have elaborated the contours of this conception of *stare decisis*. See Michael Adams, "Escaping the 'Straitjacket': *Canada (Attorney General) v. Bedford* and the Doctrine of *Stare Decisis*" (2015) 78 Saskatchewan Law Review 325; Janelle Souter, "Clearly the Arc Bends: *Stare Decisis* and *Saskatchewan Federation of Labour v. Saskatchewan*" (2015) 78 Saskatchewan Law Review 397; Debra Parkes, "Precedent Revisited: *Carter v Canada (AG)* and the Contemporary Practice of Precedent" (2016) 10 McGill Journal of Law and Health S123; and Adil Abdulla, "The Circumstances of Change: Understanding

196 | *Notes to pages 2–6*

the *Bedford/Carter* Exceptions to Vertical *Stare Decisis*" (2020) 78 University of Toronto Faculty of Law Review 1. For criticism of the Supreme Court's ruling, see Dwight Newman, "Judicial Method and Three Gaps in the Supreme Court of Canada's Assisted Suicide Judgment in *Carter*" (2015) 78 Saskatchewan Law Review 217; and Brian Bird and Michael Bookman, "*Stare Decisis* and the *Charter*" (2019) 92 Supreme Court Law Review (2d) 125.

16 See *Bedford, supra* note 7 at para 56.

17 See, e.g., *R v Spence,* 2005 SCC 71 at para 64, [2005] 3 SCR 458.

18 See *Bedford, supra* note 7 at para 111.

19 *Ibid* at paras 112–13, 127.

20 *Ibid* at paras 120–22, 127.

21 *Ibid* at paras 124–29. S 1 of the Charter states that "[t]he Canadian Charter of Rights and Freedoms guarantees the rights and freedoms set out in it subject only to such reasonable limits prescribed by law as can be demonstrably justified in a free and democratic society." I will discuss this text in greater detail in later chapters.

22 *Ibid* at para 127.

23 See, e.g., Hart Schwartz, "Circularity, Tautology and Gamesmanship: 'Purpose' Based Proportionality-Correspondence Analysis in Sections 15 and 7 of the *Charter*" (2016) 35 National Journal of Constitutional Law 105 at 108–9.

24 See Charter, *supra* note 14, s 33.

25 See Colton Fehr, *Constitutionalizing Criminal Law* (Vancouver: UBC Press, 2022) at 118–27.

26 See *Bedford, supra* note 7 at para 169.

27 See *Protection of Communities and Exploited Persons Act,* SC 2014, c 25.

28 *Ibid*, Preamble.

29 See Lyne Casavant and Dominique Valiquet, "Legislative Summary of Bill C-36: An Act to Amend the *Criminal Code* in Response to the Supreme Court of Canada Decision in *Attorney General of Canada v. Bedford* and to Make Consequential Amendments to Other Acts" (18 July 2014), online: <https://lop.parl.ca/staticfiles/PublicWebsite/Home/ResearchPublications/LegislativeSummaries/PDF/41–2/c36-e.pdf>.

30 See *R v Boodhoo,* 2018 ONSC 7205, 51 CR (7th) 207; *R v Anwar,* 2020 ONCJ 103, 62 CR (7th) 402; *R v NS,* 2021 ONSC 1628; and *R v NS,* 2022 ONCA 160.

31 See *Bedford, supra* note 7 at para 86.

32 *Ibid* at para 66.

33 See *Perka v The Queen,* [1984] 2 SCR 232, 13 DLR (4th) 1; and *R v Hibbert,* [1995] 2 SCR 973, 99 CCC (3d) 193.

34 See *R v Ruzic,* 2001 SCC 24, [2001] 1 SCR 687.

35 See *M v H,* [1999] 2 SCR 3 at 70, 171 DLR (4th) 577.

Notes to pages 6–16 | 197

36 Although the constitutional challenge was decided by the Supreme Court in 2013, it was filed with the Ontario Superior Court of Justice six years earlier in 2007.

37 I will discuss this literature in detail in Chapter 4.

38 See *Spence, supra* note 17 at para 64.

39 I will discuss this literature in Chapter 6.

40 See Robert Leckey, "Assisted Dying, Suspended Declarations, and Dialogue's Time" (2019) 69 University of Toronto Law Journal 64.

41 See Jamie Cameron, "Law, Politics, and Legacy Building at the McLachlin Court in 2014" (2015) 71 Supreme Court Law Review (2d) 3.

42 See *Bedford, supra* note 1 at footnote 4. For a review of the sex workers' rights movement, see Valerie Jenness, "From Sex as Sin to Sex as Work: COYOTE and the Reorganization of Prostitution as a Social Problem" (1990) 37 Social Problems 403.

43 See Debra Haak, "Re(de)fining Prostitution and Sex Work: Conceptual Clarity for Legal Thinking" (2019) 40 Windsor Review of Legal and Social Issues 67 at 70.

44 *Ibid* at 92.

45 *Ibid.*

46 See, e.g., Erica Kunimoto, "A Critical Analysis of Canada's Sex Work Legislation: Exploring Gendered and Racialized Consequences" (2018) 10 Stream 27 at 28, citing Shawna Ferris, "Working from the Violent Centre: Survival Sex Work and Urban Aboriginality in Maria Campbell's *Halfbreed*" (2008) 34 English Studies in Canada 123 at 127.

47 See, e.g., Angela Campbell, *Sister Wives, Surrogates, and Sex Workers: Outlaws by Choice?* (London: Ashgate, 2013); Monica O'Connor, "Choice, Agency, Consent and Coercion: Complex Issues in the Lives of Prostituted and Trafficked Women" (2017) 62 Women's Studies International Forum 8 at 9; and Maddy Coy, "This Body Which Is Not Mine: The Notion of the Habit Body, Prostitution and (Dis)Embodiment" (2009) 10 Feminist Theory 61. I engage with these and other authors' perspectives on choice in Chapter 7.

CHAPTER 1: SETTING THE STAGE

1 See Constance Backhouse, "Nineteenth-Century Canadian Prostitution Law: Reflection of a Discriminatory Society" (1985) 18 Social History 387 at 388.

2 The Charter was adopted in 1982, and the relevant cases were decided in the early 1990s. See *Canadian Charter of Rights and Freedoms* being Schedule B to the *Canada Act 1982* (UK), 1982, c 11 [Charter].

3 *An Act for the Prevention of Contagious Diseases at Certain Military and Naval Stations in This Province,* 29 Vict (1865), c 8 [*CDA*].

198 | *Notes to pages 16–18*

4 *Ibid,* ss 2, 11–16.

5 *Supra* note 3.

6 See Constance Backhouse, "Canadian Prostitution Law 1839–1972" in *Prostitution in Canada* (Ottawa: Canadian Advisory Council on the Status of Women, 1984) 7 at 8.

7 *Ibid* at 8–9.

8 See, e.g., Eugenia Palmegiano, *Women and British Periodicals 1832–1867: A Bibliography* (New York: Garland, 1976) at xxxviii–xxxix.

9 See Judith Walkowitz, *Prostitution and Victorian Society: Women, Class and the State* (Cambridge, MA: Cambridge University Press, 1980) at 70.

10 See Backhouse, "Prostitution Law," *supra* note 6 at 9.

11 See, e.g., Jesse Smith, "Social Purity" in Ramsey Cook and Wendy Mitchinson, eds, *The Proper Sphere: Women's Place in Canadian Society* (Toronto: Oxford University Press, 1976) 234; and Lucy Brooking, "Conditions in Toronto" in Ernest Albert Bell, ed, *Canada's War on the White Slave Trade* (London: n.p., 1911) 364.

12 See John McLaren, "Chasing the Social Evil: Moral Fervour and the Evolution of Canada's Prostitution Laws, 1867–1917" (1986) 1 Canadian Journal of Law and Society 125 at 129.

13 See, e.g., Carol Bacchi, *Liberation Deferred: The Ideas of English Canadian Suffragists 1877–1915* (Toronto: University of Toronto Press, 1983) at 112–14.

14 This concern was often exaggerated, but many accounts show that white slavery persisted in North America. For a detailed review, see Backhouse, "Reflection," *supra* note 1 at 393, footnote 28; and McLaren, "Social Evil," *supra* note 12 at 136–38.

15 See Edward Bristow, *Vice and Vigilantes: Purity Movements in Britain since 1700* (Dublin: Gill and MacMillan, 1977) at 86.

16 See Ruth Rosen, *The Lost Sisterhood: Prostitution in America 1900–1918* (Baltimore: Johns Hopkins University Press, 1982) at 125.

17 See McLaren, "Social Evil," *supra* note 12 at 137 ("In their concern to apply middle class morality to working class problems, they failed to understand that if this was a moral problem it was one of the social immorality of consigning working class families, and females in particular, to the type of living conditions and lack of economic opportunity in which prostitution was seen as an attractive option").

18 32 & 33 Vict (1869), c 28.

19 *Ibid,* s 1.

20 32 & 33 Vict (1869), c 20.

21 *Ibid,* s 50.

22 See, e.g., Backhouse, "Reflection," *supra* note 1 at 395.

23 *Ibid.*

Notes to pages 18–21 | 199

24 *Ibid.*

25 *Ibid.*

26 *Ibid* at 415, footnote 81, citing Caroll Smith-Rosenberg, "Beauty, the Beast and the Militant Women: Study in Sex Roles and Social Stress" in Nancy Cott and Elizabeth Pleck, eds, *A Heritage of Her Own: Towards a New Social History of American Women* (New York: Simon and Schuster, 1979) 197 at 204.

27 See Backhouse, "Reflection," *supra* note 1 at 415–16. As Backhouse notes, it is questionable whether many of these women truly volunteered to stay at these institutions.

28 *Ibid.*

29 See, e.g., *An Act to Make Provision for the Detention of Female Convicts in Reformatory Prisons in the Province of Quebec,* 34 Vict (1871), c 30, s 2.

30 See *An Act Respecting the Andrew Mercer Ontario Reformatory for Females,* RSO 1887, c 239.

31 See Backhouse, "Reflection," *supra* note 1 at 417.

32 *Ibid* at 418.

33 *Ibid.*

34 For a detailed review, see McLaren, "Social Evil," *supra* note 12 at 142–50.

35 See *Criminal Code Amendment Act* (1913), 3 & 4 Geo V, c 13, s 9.

36 *Ibid,* s 23.

37 *Ibid,* s 9.

38 *Ibid,* ss 1, 11.

39 *Ibid.*

40 SC 1960, c 44, s 2(d).

41 For an excellent review, see Emily van der Meulen and Elya Durisin, "Sex Work Policy: Tracing Historical and Contemporary Developments" in Elya M. Durisin, Emily van der Meulen, and Chris Bruckert, eds, *Red Light Labour: Sex Work Regulation, Agency, and Resistance* (Vancouver: UBC Press, 2018) 27.

42 See, e.g., Backhouse, "Reflection," *supra* note 1 at 403–7. Backhouse gives several examples of common criminal records and their punishment in the late nineteenth century.

43 See Harvey Graff, "'Pauperism, Misery and Vice': Illiteracy and Criminality in the Nineteenth Century" (1977) 11 Journal of Social History 245 at 262.

44 See, e.g., EGALE, "Sex Work in Canada: Research Brief" (April 2021), online: <https://adobeindd.com/view/publications/b04e7320-d7b9–418f-b32b -14bdce281ca0/1/publication-web-resources/pdf/Sex_Work_Brief_Updated.pdf>.

45 See Backhouse, "Reflection," *supra* note 1 at 420.

46 *Ibid,* citing among other works Sylvia van Kirk, *"Many Tender Ties": Women in Fur-Trade Society 1670–1870* (Winnipeg: Watson and Dwyer, 1980).

47 See, e.g., Native Women's Association of Canada (NWAC), *Sexual Exploitation and Trafficking of Aboriginal Women and Girls: Literature Review and*

200 | *Notes to pages 21–22*

Key Informant Interviews, final report (Ottawa: NWAC, 2014) at 8, 11; Melissa Farley, Jacqueline Lynne, and Ann Cotton, "Prostitution in Vancouver: Violence and the Colonization of First Nations Women" (2005) 42 Transcultural Psychiatry 242 at 245; and Cherry Smiley, "A Long Road behind Us, a Long Road Ahead: Towards an Indigenous Feminist National Inquiry" (2016) 28 Canadian Journal of Women and the Law 308 at 311.

48 I am indebted to Backhouse for this review of the early appellate case law. See Backhouse, "Reflection," *supra* note 1 at 409–15.

49 See *ibid* at 409.

50 (1870) 30 UCQBR 509.

51 *Ibid* at 513–16. It was questionable whether a barrack yard met this definition. As the court observed, it "may have been, for anything that is shewn, in the most deserted, unfrequented part of the city."

52 *Ibid.*

53 (1883) 2 OR 523 (ONQB).

54 *Ibid* at 524.

55 (1888) 16 OR 560 (ONQB).

56 *Ibid* at 561.

57 As I explain in the next section, the Supreme Court eventually interpreted the term more broadly.

58 (1891) 1 CCC 66 (QBCA).

59 *Ibid.*

60 (1897) 1 CCC 63 (QBQB).

61 *Ibid* at 65.

62 *Ibid.*

63 *Ibid.*

64 For further cases, see Backhouse, "Reflection," *supra* note 1 at 411–15.

65 The courts often referred to sex workers as "unfortunate creatures" or similar phrases emphasizing pity. See, e.g., *Clark v Hagar* (1894), 22 SCR 510 at 541.

66 See Backhouse, "Reflection," *supra* note 1 at 413–14.

67 The history of obscenity and indecency offences is also relevant. For a review of the relevant Supreme Court jurisprudence, see *R v Hicklin* (1868), LR 3 QB 360; *R v Brodie,* [1962] SCR 681, 32 DLR (2d) 507; *R v Dominion News and Gifts (1962) Ltd,* [1964] SCR 251, [1964] 3 CCC 1; *R v Towne Cinema Theatres Ltd,* [1985] 1 SCR 494, 18 DLR (4th) 1; *R v Butler,* [1992] 1 SCR 452, 89 DLR (4th) 449; and *R v Labaye,* 2005 SCC 80, [2005] 3 SCR 728. Numerous academics criticized this area of law for undermining gender and other equality interests. See, e.g., Richard Jochelson, "After *Labaye:* The Harm Test of Obscenity, the New Judicial Vacuum, and the Relevance of Familiar Voices" (2009) 46 Alberta Law Review 741 at 750–57; Brenda Cossman, "Disciplining the Unruly: Sexual Outlaws, *Little Sisters* and the Legacy of *Butler*" (2003) 36 University of British

Notes to pages 22–24 | 201

Columbia Law Review 77 at 78–83; Brenda Cossman, "Feminist Fashion or Morality in Drag? The Sexual Subtext of the *Butler* Decision" in Brenda Cossman et al, eds, *Bad Attitude/s on Trial: Pornography, Feminism and the* Butler *Decision* (Toronto: University of Toronto Press, 1997) 107; Richard Moon, "*R. v. Butler:* The Limits of the Supreme Court's Feminist Re-Interpretation of Section 163" (1993) 25 Ottawa Law Review 361; Jamie Cameron, "Abstract Principle v. Contextual Conceptions of Harm: A Comment on *R. v. Butler*" (1992) 37 McGill Law Journal 1135; Leslie Green, "Pornographies" (2000) 8 Journal of Political Philosophy 27; Carl Stychin, *Law's Desire: Sexuality and the Limits of Law* (London: Routledge, 1995); Lisa Gotell, "Shaping *Butler:* The New Politics of Anti-Pornography" in Brenda Cossman et al, eds, *Bad Attitude/s on Trial: Pornography, Feminism and the Butler Decision* (Toronto: University of Toronto Press, 1997) 48; John Fisher, "Outlaws or In-Laws? Successes and Challenges in the Struggle for LGBT Equality" (2004) 49 McGill Law Journal 1183; Mariana Valverde, "The Harms of Sex and the Risks of Breasts: Obscenity and Indecency in Canadian Law" (1999) 8 Social and Legal Studies 181; and Kathleen Mahoney, "Obscenity, Morals and the Law: A Feminist Critique" (1984) 17 Ottawa Law Review 33.

68   See Backhouse, "Reflection," *supra* note 1 at 413.

69   Although this should be evident from the above review, it is notable that the leading account of the history of the sex work laws recognizes Parliament's divided motivations for governing sex work. See Backhouse, "Reflections," *supra* note 1 at 387–88, 393–96, 408–9, 413.

70   See *Reference re ss 193 and 195.1(1)(C) of the Criminal Code (Man.),* [1990] 1 SCR 1123, 56 CCC (3d) 65 [*Sex Work Reference*].

71   [1992] 2 SCR 10, 90 DLR (4th) 449.

72   The provisions initially challenged were included in the *Criminal Code of Canada,* RSC 1970, c C34. The provisions at issue in *Bedford* were from the *Criminal Code of Canada,* RSC 1985, c C-46.

73   See *R v Patterson,* [1968] SCR 157 at 162–63, 67 DLR (2d) 82.

74   See *R v Corbeil,* [1991] 1 SCR 830 at 834, 64 CCC (3d) 272.

75   *Ibid.* For various examples of this standard, see *Sex Work Reference, supra* note 70 at para 44.

76   See *Sex Work Reference, supra* note 70 at para 45.

77   See *Canada v Bedford,* 2010 ONSC 4264 at para 251, 102 OR (3d) 321, citing *Martin's Annual Criminal Code 2010* (Aurora, ON: Canada Law Book, 2009) at 417.

78   See *R c Lemieux* (1991), 70 CCC (3d) 434, 11 CR (4th) 224 (QBCA).

79   See *R v Wong* (1977), 33 CCC (2d) 6 at 10, 2 Alta LR (2d) 90 (ABCA).

80   See *Criminal Code (1970), supra* note 72, s 195(1)(c).

81   [1978] 2 SCR 476, 82 DLR (3d) 95.

82   *Ibid* at 477–78, 482.

83 See Sheilagh O'Connell, "The Impact of Bill C-49 on Street Prostitution: 'What's Law Got to Do with It?'" (1988) 4 Journal of Law and Social Policy 109 at 110, citing *Maclean's* 98 (1985) at 40–41.

84 See *An Act to Amend the Criminal Code (Prostitution)*, RSC 1985, c 51.

85 See *R v Lawrence*, 2002 ABPC 189 at para 19, 332 AR 188. See also *R v Searle* (1994), 163 NBR (2d) 123 (NBPC).

86 See *R v Head* (1987), 36 CCC (3d) 562, 59 CR (3d) 80 (BCCA).

87 See *Canada (Attorney General) v Bedford*, 2013 SCC 72 at para 141, [2013] 3 SCR 1101, citing *Shaw v Director of Public Prosecutions*, [1962] AC 220 (HL).

88 See *R v Barrow* (2001), 54 OR (3d) 417 at 421, 155 CCC (3d) 362 (ONCA), leave to appeal refused [2001] SCCA No 431.

89 (1991) 64 CCC (3d) 53, 2 OR (3d) 514 (ONCA).

90 *Ibid* at 521.

91 See, generally, *Downey, supra* note 71.

92 *Ibid*.

93 See *R v Grilo* (1991), 2 OR (3d) 514 (per Justice Arbour: "The true parasite whom s. 212(1)(j) seeks to punish is someone the prostitute is not otherwise legally or morally obligated to support").

94 See *Criminal Code (1970), supra* note 72, s 195(1).

95 CCSM, c C180.

96 See *R v Cunningham* (1986), 31 CCC (3d) 223 (MBPC).

97 See *Reference re ss 193 and 195.1(1)(C) of the Criminal Code* (1987), 38 CCC (3d) 408, 49 Man R (2d) 1; and *Sex Work Reference, supra* note 72.

98 [1990] 1 SCR 1235, 56 CCC (3d) 1.

99 *Ibid* ("[t]he arguments put forward to challenge s. 195.1(1)(*c*) under s. 2(d) were largely secondary to and dependent on those challenging the provision under the 2(b) guarantee of freedom of expression"). As a result, the Supreme Court in *Bedford, supra* note 87, did not even reference *Skinner* in its decision.

100 See *Irwin Toy Ltd v Quebec (Attorney General)*, [1989] 1 SCR 927 at 976, 58 DLR (4th) 577.

101 See *Sex Work Reference, supra* note 70 at 1187.

102 See *R v Keegstra*, [1990] 3 SCR 697 at 731, 61 CCC (3d) 1, citing *Irwin Toy, supra* note 100.

103 See *Sex Work Reference (MBCA), supra* note 97 at 411, 413, 421, 433 (reasons of Justice Huband with the rest of the Court of Appeal concurring).

104 *Ibid*.

105 See *Sex Work Reference, supra* note 70 at paras 1, 88–89.

106 See *Gosselin v Quebec (Attorney General)*, 2002 SCC 84, [2002] 4 SCR 429.

107 See, generally, *Bedford, supra* note 87.

108 The court previously came to this conclusion in *Re BC Motor Vehicle Act*, [1985] 2 SCR 486 at 515, 24 DLR (4th) 536 [*Motor Vehicle Act Reference*].

Notes to pages 28–31 | 203

109 See *Sex Work Reference, supra* note 70 at paras 14–15.

110 *Ibid* at para 48.

111 *Ibid.*

112 *Ibid* at para 49, citing Julian Symons, "Orwell's Prophecies: The Limits of Liberty and the Limits of Law" (1984) 9 Dalhousie Law Journal 115 at 116.

113 198 US 45 (1905).

114 For a review of the American case law, see *Sex Work Reference, supra* note 70 at paras 50–52.

115 *Ibid* at paras 53–54, citing *R v Edwards Books & Arts Ltd,* [1986] 2 SCR 713 at 785–86, 35 DLR (4th) 1.

116 See *Sex Work Reference, supra* note 70 at para 58, citing Charter, *supra* note 8, s 2.

117 *Ibid* at para 61, citing *Motor Vehicle Act Reference, supra* note 108 at 502–3; Eric Colvin, "Section Seven of the *Canadian Charter of Rights and Freedoms*" (1989) 68 Canadian Bar Review 560 at 573–74. I say "primarily" because Justice Lamer recognized at para 65 that security of the person could extend outside the criminal law context where the state caused serious physical or mental distress for a person.

118 See *Sex Work Reference, supra* note 70 at para 17. For Justice Lamer's concurrence, see para 38.

119 *Ibid* at para 34.

120 *Ibid* at paras 17, 42–46.

121 *Ibid* at para 18.

122 *Ibid.*

123 *Ibid* at paras 18–19.

124 *Ibid* at para 19.

125 *Ibid.*

126 See *Downey, supra* note 71 at paras 36–42, 69, 72.

127 *Ibid* at 18–19.

128 [1988] 2 SCR 3, 51 DLR (4th) 481.

129 *Ibid* at 19.

130 *Ibid.*

131 See *Downey, supra* note 71 at para 44.

132 *Ibid.*

133 *Ibid.*

134 [1986] 1 SCR 103, 26 DLR (4th) 200.

135 *Ibid* at 135–42.

136 *Ibid.*

137 *Ibid.*

138 *Ibid.*

139 *Ibid.*

204 | *Notes to pages 31–35*

140 *Ibid.*

141 *Ibid* at 140.

142 See *Sex Work Reference, supra* note 70 at para 2.

143 *Ibid* at para 3.

144 *Ibid* at paras 6, 8.

145 *Ibid.*

146 *Ibid* at para 4.

147 *Ibid* at para 5.

148 *Ibid.*

149 *Ibid* at para 6.

150 *Ibid.*

151 *Ibid* at para 7.

152 *Ibid* at para 8.

153 *Ibid* at para 9.

154 *Ibid* at para 121.

155 *Ibid* at para 11.

156 *Ibid* at paras 92, 96.

157 *Ibid* at para 92.

158 *Ibid.*

159 See McLaren, "Social Evil," *supra* note 12 at 139. Although Justice Lamer does not cite McLaren's work, the tone of his judgment is supportive of this view.

160 See *Sex Work Reference, supra* note 70 at paras 96–97.

161 *Ibid.*

162 *Ibid* at para 98.

163 *Ibid* at para 102.

164 *Ibid* at paras 103–5.

165 *Ibid* at paras 126–28.

166 *Ibid* at para 126.

167 *Ibid* at paras 130–31.

168 *Ibid* at paras 131–37.

169 *Ibid.*

170 *Ibid.*

171 See Special Committee on Pornography and Prostitution, *Pornography and Prostitution in Canada,* vol 2 (Ottawa: Minister of Supply and Services Canada, 1985) [Fraser Report]; and Committee on Sexual Offences against Children and Youths, *Sexual Offences against Children,* vol 2 (Ottawa: Minister of Supply and Services Canada, 1984) [Badgley Report].

172 See Fraser Report, *supra* note 171 at 379.

173 *Ibid.*

174 *Ibid.*

175 See Badgley Report, *supra* note 171 at 1057–58.

176 *Ibid.*

177 See *Downey, supra* note 71 at para 60.

178 *Ibid* at para 61.

179 *Ibid.*

180 *Ibid* at para 64.

181 *Ibid.*

182 *Ibid.*

183 *Ibid* at para 66.

184 *Ibid* at para 70.

185 *Ibid.*

186 *Ibid* at para 77.

187 *Ibid* at paras 78–80, 84.

188 *Ibid* at para 86.

189 *Ibid* at para 89.

190 *Ibid.*

191 *Ibid.*

192 See Maria Powell, "Moving beyond the Prostitution Reference: *Bedford v. Canada*" (2013) 64 University of New Brunswick Law Journal 187 at 189. See also Michelle Bloodworth, "A Fact Is a Fact Is a Fact: *Stare Decisis* and the Distinction between Adjudicative and Social Facts in *Bedford* and *Carter*" (2014) 32 National Journal of Constitutional Law 193 at 200–1; and Michael Da Silva, "Trial Level References: In Defence of a New Presumption" (2002) 2 Western Journal of Legal Studies 1 at 1.

193 See Powell, "Moving Beyond," *supra* note 192 at 194.

194 See Alan Young, "Proving a Violation: Rhetoric, Research, and Remedy" (2014) 67 Supreme Court Law Review (2d) 617 at 625, footnote 25, citing various sources.

195 *Ibid.*

196 *Ibid.* I discuss this point further below.

197 *Ibid* at 625–26, 635.

198 This is my reading of Powell, "Moving Beyond," *supra* note 192 at 194.

199 See Young, "Proving a Violation," *supra* note 194 at 625.

200 Only one law has been struck down for violating the vagueness principle. See *R v Morales,* [1992] 3 SCR 711, 77 CCC (3d) 91.

201 See *R v Heywood,* [1994] 3 SCR 761, 120 DLR (4th) 348 (overbreadth); *R v Malmo-Levine,* 2003 SCC 74, [2003] 3 SCR 571 (gross disproportionality). The arbitrariness principle had been recognized, but its content was still relatively unclear. See *R v Morgentaler,* [1988] 1 SCR 30, 44 DLR (4th) 385.

202 See Janice McGinnis, "Whores and Worthies: Feminism and Prostitution" (1994) 9 Canadian Journal of Law and Society 105 at 118.

203 *Ibid.*

206 | *Notes to pages 38–40*

204 *Ibid* at 118–19, citing *Keegstra, supra* note 102; *Butler, supra* note 67.
205 See McGinnis, "Feminism and Prostitution," *supra* note 202 at 125.

CHAPTER 2: THE ROAD TO *BEDFORD*

1 Tracey Tyler, "Prostitution Law Struck Down" *Toronto Star* (28 September 2010), online: <https://www.thestar.com/news/canada/2010/09/28/prostitution_laws_struck_down.html>.

2 These interviews were conducted on 7 and 30 July 2021. For Young's public discussion of the *Bedford* case, see Avnish Nanda, "Oral Arguments: Professor Alan Young on *Bedford*" *TheCourt.ca* (29 January 2014), online: <http://www.thecourt.ca/oral-arguments-professor-alan-young-on-bedford/>; Alan Young, *The Costs of Charter Litigation* (Ottawa: Department of Justice Canada, Research and Statistics Division, 2016), online: <https://www.justice.gc.ca/eng/rp-pr/jr/ccl-clc/ccl-clc.pdf>; and Teresa MacInnes and Kent Nasan, *Buying Sex* (2013), online: <https://www.nfb.ca/film/buying_sex/>.

3 See John Lowman, "Identifying Research Gaps in the Prostitution Literature" *Department of Justice* (March 2001), online: <https://www.justice.gc.ca/eng/rp-pr/csj-sjc/jsp-sjp/rr02_9/p1.html> at 1, citing D.H. Williams, "The Suppression of Commercial Prostitution in the City of Vancouver" (1941) 27 Journal of Social Hygiene 364 at 364–72.

4 See Lowman, "Research Gaps," *supra* note 3 at 1, citing James Gray, *Red Lights on the Prairies* (New York: Signet, 1971); Lori Rotenberg, "The Wayward Worker: Toronto's Prostitute at the Turn of the Century," in Janice Acton, Penny Goldsmith, and Bonnie Shepard, eds, *Women at Work: Ontario, 1850–1930* (Toronto: Canadian Women's Educational Press, 1974) 57.

5 See Lowman, "Research Gaps," *supra* note 3 at 1.

6 *Ibid* at 1–2, citing John Lowman, "Street Prostitution in Vancouver: Notes on the Genesis of a Social Problem" (1986) 28 Canadian Journal of Criminology 1; Deborah Brock, *Making Work, Making Trouble: Prostitution as a Social Problem* (Toronto: University of Toronto Press, 1998).

7 [1978] 2 SCR 476, 82 DLR (3d) 95.

8 See Sheilagh O'Connell, "The Impact of Bill C-49 on Street Prostitution: 'What's Law Got to Do with It?'" (1988) 4 Journal of Law and Social Policy 109 at 110, citing *Maclean's* 98 (1985) at 40–41.

9 See Committee on Sexual Offences against Children and Youths, *Sexual Offences against Children,* vol 2 (Ottawa: Minister of Supply and Services Canada, 1984) [Badgley Report]; and Special Committee on Pornography and Prostitution, *Pornography and Prostitution in Canada,* vol 2 (Ottawa: Minister of Supply and Services Canada, 1985) [Fraser Report].

Notes to pages 40–42 | 207

10 See Lowman, "Research Gaps," *supra* note 3 at 2, citing various sources.

11 *Ibid.*

12 *Ibid.*

13 *Ibid* at 2–4. Lowman cites other familial factors that cause youth to run away from home. For male sex workers, conflicts over their homosexuality or gender identity were more common catalysts for leaving home.

14 *Ibid.*

15 For a complete account of the Pickton murders, see Stevie Cameron, *On the Farm: Robert William Pickton and the Tragic Story of Vancouver's Missing Women* (Toronto: Vintage Canada, 2011).

16 See *R v Pickton,* 2006 BCSC 1090 at para 1, 260 CCC (3d) 185.

17 See Joanna Jolly, "Why I Failed to Catch Canada's Worst Serial Killer" *BBC News* (1 June 2017), online: <https://www.bbc.com/news/magazine-38796464>.

18 See Deborah Jones, "The Case of the Serial Killer" *Time* (26 January 2007), online: <http://content.time.com/time/world/article/0,8599,1582656,00.html>.

19 *Ibid.*

20 See Ethan Baron, "Horrors of Pickton Farm Revealed in Graphic Detail" *National Post* (20 February 2007), online: <https://web.archive.org/web/2007 1123065221/http://www.canada.com/nationalpost/story.html?id=20941e5e -aae7-4c73-87bb-fbbb484e08d5&k=0>.

21 *Ibid.* See also Jones, "Serial Killer," *supra* note 18; and "Pickton Described How He Killed Women, Former Friend Says" *CBC News* (16 July 2007), online: <https://www.cbc.ca/news/canada/pickton-described-how-he-killed-women -former-friend-says-1.635605>.

22 See *R v Pickton,* 2007 BCSC 2039, [2007] BCJ No 3109.

23 See Jones, "Serial Killer," *supra* note 18, noting that Pickton disclosed that he killed forty-nine sex workers.

24 See *Bedford v Canada,* 2010 ONSC 4264 at para 123, 102 OR (3d) 321.

25 *Ibid.*

26 *Ibid.*

27 See, e.g., Wally Oppal, *Forsaken: The Report of the Missing Women Commission of Inquiry,* vol 3 (15 November 2012) at 116, estimating that between eighteen and forty-three known victims died along this stretch of highway. For a more recent and detailed account of these tragedies, see Jessica McDiarmid, *Highway of Tears: A True Story of Racism, Indifference and the Pursuit of Justice for Missing and Murdered Indigenous Women and Girls* (Toronto: Random House, 2019). As with the Pickton murders, the number of victims is almost certainly much higher.

28 See, e.g., "Man Charged with Murder of Alberta Sex-Trade Worker" *CBC News* (10 May 2006), online: <https://www.cbc.ca/news/canada/man-charged

208 | *Notes to pages 42–45*

-with-murder-of-alberta-sex-trade-worker-1.580752>; and Clare Clancy, "RCMP KARE Team Broadens Mandate to Prevent Murders of At-Risk Individuals" *Edmonton Journal* (14 August 2017), online: <https://edmontonjournal.com/news/local-news/rcmp-kare-team-broadens-mandate-to-prevent-murders-of-at-risk-individuals>.

29 See, e.g., Darren Bernhardt, "Winnipeg Police Pull Out of Project Devote, Create New Model for Investigating MMIWG Cases" *CBC News* (6 March 2020), online: <https://www.cbc.ca/news/canada/manitoba/winnipeg-police-project-devote-1.5488266>.

30 See *Canada (Attorney General) v Bedford,* 2013 SCC 72 at para 158, [2013] 3 SCR 1101.

31 2003 SCC 74, [2003] 3 SCR 571.

32 *Ibid* at para 90, citing John Stuart Mill, *On Liberty and Considerations of Representative Government* (Oxford: Basil Blackwell, 1946).

33 [1994] 3 SCR 761, 120 DLR (4th) 348.

34 *Ibid* at para 51. It is notable that the Supreme Court was building on its previous decision in *Canada v Pharmaceutical Society (Nova Scotia),* [1992] 2 SCR 606, 93 DLR (4th) 36. It was not yet clear if overbreadth constituted its own principle of fundamental justice in the latter case.

35 See *Malmo-Levine, supra* note 31 at paras 141–45, expanding on the "per se" disproportionality principle first mentioned in *United States v Burns,* 2001 SCC 7 at para 78, [2001] 1 SCR 283; and *Suresh v Canada (Minister of Citizenship and Immigration),* 2002 SCC 1 at para 47, [2002] 1 SCR 3.

36 The text of section 12 prohibits "cruel and unusual punishment" but has been distilled into a prohibition against grossly disproportionate punishment. See *R v Boudreault,* 2018 SCC 58 at paras 45–46, [2018] 3 SCR 599.

37 See *Malmo-Levine, supra* note 31 at para 172.

38 See Nanda, "Young on *Bedford," supra* note 2. Young was clearly referring to the Pickton case in making these remarks.

39 *Ibid.*

40 For a more general review of this history and argument, see Colton Fehr, *Constitutionalizing Criminal Law* (Vancouver: UBC Press, 2022).

41 For a more detailed review of this history, see Colton Fehr, "The 'Individualistic' Approach to Arbitrariness, Overbreadth, and Gross Disproportionality" (2018) 51 University of British Columbia Law Review 55.

42 See *Bedford, supra* note 30 at para 15.

43 Benjamin Berger, "Putting a Price on Dignity: The Problem of Costs in *Charter* Litigation" (2002) 26 Advocates' Quarterly 235 at 236.

44 See Kent Roach, "Enforcement of the *Charter* – Subsections 24(1) and 52(1)" (2013) 62 Supreme Court Law Review (2d) 473 at 486.

45 See Robert Sharpe, "Access to *Charter* Justice" (2013) 63 Supreme Court Law Review (2d) 1 at 3.

46 See Andrew Petter, *The Politics of the Charter: The Illusive Promise of Constitutional Rights* (Toronto: University of Toronto Press, 2010) at 104–5. See also Larissa Kloegman, "A Democratic Defence of the Court Challenges Program" (2007) 16 Constitutional Forum 107 at 107; and Joseph Arvay and Alison Latimer, "Cost Strategies for Litigants: The Significance of *R. v. Caron*" (2011) 54 Supreme Court Law Review (2d) 427 at 427, 448–49.

47 See Young, *Charter Litigation, supra* note 2 at 3.

48 *Ibid* at 6. Notably, Young also applied to the recently reinstated Court Challenges Program but was denied because his Charter challenge did not implicate the equality rights provisions.

49 *Ibid*.

50 *Ibid*. When asked, Young stated that the additional counsel was necessary since he was not comfortable running the appeal alone given the complexities of a Supreme Court appeal.

51 *Ibid* at 7–8.

52 *Ibid*.

53 *Ibid*.

54 *Ibid* at 6–7.

55 *Ibid* at 19–20.

56 *Ibid* at 8.

57 *Ibid*.

58 2012 SCC 45, [2012] 2 SCR 524 [*Downtown Eastside*].

59 *Ibid* at para 67.

60 See *Bedford, supra* note 24 at para 152. Notably, the penalties for sex work offences have become much more lenient over time. See Chapter 1 in this volume.

61 See *Downtown Eastside, supra* note 58 at para 69, citing *R v Blais*, 2008 BCCA 389, 85 BCLR (4th) 1. There was also a post–*Sex Work Reference* constitutional challenge under section 7 of the Charter maintaining that the meaning of "acts of indecency" and "prostitution" in the bawdy house provision were unduly vague. This challenge failed but notably did not require empirical evidence to argue the case since a vagueness challenge questions only whether the law itself is understandable. See *R v DiGiuseppe* (2002), 161 CCC (3d) 424, 155 OAC 62 (ONCA).

62 See *Downtown Eastside, supra* note 58 at para 69, citing *R v Hamilton* (unreported).

63 *Ibid*.

64 *Ibid* at para 71.

65 *Ibid*.

66 *Ibid.* The latter rationale was not spelled out by the Supreme Court but seems to be reasonable.

67 See *Rules of Civil Procedure,* RRO 1990, Reg 194, rule 14.05(3).

68 See *R v Bedford* (2000), 184 DLR (4th) 727, 143 CCC (3d) 311 (ONCA).

69 See Terri-Jean Bedford, *Dominatrix on Trial: Bedford vs. Canada* (Bloomington, IN: iUniverse, 2011) at 178–81, 239. Young held a similar opinion.

70 See Chris Young, "Pressed on Prostitution Law, PM Jokes about Dominatrix" *Globe and Mail* (2 December 2010), online: <https://www.theglobeandmail.com/news/politics/ottawa-notebook/pressed-on-prostitution-law-pm-jokes-about-dominatrix/article613244/>.

71 *Ibid.*

72 See Michael Posner, "Meet the Dominatrix" *Globe and Mail* (16 September 2011), online: <https://www.theglobeandmail.com/news/national/meet-the-dominatrix/article594599/>.

73 See Heather Loney, "Who Is Terri-Jean Bedford, the Dominatrix Fighting Canada's Prostitution Laws" *Global News* (20 December 2013), online: <https://globalnews.ca/news/1043102/who-is-terri-jean-bedford-the-dominatrix-fighting-canadas-prostitution-laws/>.

74 It is also possible to establish public interest standing, as occurred in *Downtown Eastside, supra* note 58. However, in *Bedford,* the application for public interest standing was denied because at least one of the applicants had private interest standing. See *Bedford, supra* note 24 at para 61. As I explain below, however, all three litigants in *Bedford* were granted private interest standing.

75 See *Bedford, supra* note 24 at para 44.

76 *Ibid* at para 51.

77 *Ibid* at para 44.

78 *Ibid.*

79 *Ibid* at para 55.

80 See *Canada (Attorney General) v Bedford,* 2012 ONCA 186 at para 50, 109 OR (3d) 1.

CHAPTER 3: THE *BEDFORD* DECISION

1 The majority of the Ontario Court of Appeal upheld the communication provision. See *Canada (Attorney General) v Bedford,* 2012 ONCA 186 at para 328, 109 OR (3d) 1.

2 I discuss the relevant case law below.

3 See *Bedford v Canada,* 2010 ONSC 4264 at para 84, 102 OR (3d) 321. The trial court record was approximately 25,000 pages.

4 *Ibid* at para 27.

5 *Ibid* at para 26.
6 *Ibid* at para 28.
7 *Ibid.*
8 *Ibid.*
9 *Ibid* at para 29.
10 *Ibid* at para 30, citing *R v Bedford* (2000), 184 DLR (4th) 727, 143 CCC (3d) 311 (ONCA). As documented in the previous chapter, Alan Young was Bedford's counsel in this case.
11 See *Bedford, supra* note 3 at para 31.
12 *Ibid* at paras 32–33.
13 *Ibid* at para 34.
14 *Ibid* at para 35.
15 *Ibid* at para 32.
16 *Ibid.*
17 *Ibid* at para 32, note 6.
18 *Ibid* at para 38.
19 *Ibid* at para 37.
20 *Ibid* at para 38.
21 *Ibid* at para 39.
22 *Ibid* at para 37.
23 [1978] 2 SCR 476, 82 DLR (3d) 95.
24 See *Bedford, supra* note 3 at para 40.
25 *Ibid.*
26 *Ibid* at paras 41–42.
27 *Ibid* at para 84.
28 *Ibid* at paras 85–86.
29 *Ibid* at paras 87–88.
30 *Ibid* at paras 95–96.
31 *Ibid* at para 89.
32 *Ibid* at para 93.
33 *Ibid* at para 90.
34 *Ibid* at para 94.
35 *Ibid* at para 84.
36 *Ibid* at para 97.
37 *Ibid.*
38 *Ibid.*
39 *Ibid* at para 99.
40 *Ibid* at para 116.
41 *Ibid* at para 117.
42 *Ibid* at para 120.

43 *Ibid.*
44 *Ibid* at para 121.
45 *Ibid* at para 122.
46 *Ibid.*
47 *Ibid* at paras 127–28.
48 *Ibid* at para 125.
49 *Ibid* at para 131.
50 *Ibid* at para 133.
51 *Ibid.*
52 *Ibid.*
53 Special Committee on Pornography and Prostitution, *Pornography and Prostitution in Canada,* vol 2 (Ottawa: Minister of Supply and Services Canada, 1985) [*Fraser Report*].
54 See *Bedford, supra* note 3 at para 144, citing *Fraser Report, supra* note 53 at 383.
55 See *Bedford, supra* note 3 at para 142, citing *Fraser Report, supra* note 53 at 378.
56 See *ibid.*
57 See *Bedford, supra* note 3 at paras 147, 149, citing *Fraser Report, supra* note 53 at 531 ff.
58 See *Street Prostitution: Assessing the Impact of the Law Synthesis Report* (Ottawa: Department of Justice Canada, 1989) [*Synthesis Report*].
59 See *Bedford, supra* note 3 at paras 151, 154, citing *Synthesis Report, supra* note 58.
60 See *ibid.*
61 See *Victimization of Prostitutes in Calgary and Winnipeg* (Ottawa: Department of Justice Canada, 1994) [*Victimization Study*].
62 See *Bedford, supra* note 3 at para 157, citing *Victimization Study, supra* note 61.
63 See *Bedford, supra* note 3 at para 159, citing *Victimization Study, supra* note 61 at 36.
64 *The Challenge of Change: A Study of Canada's Criminal Prostitution Laws* (Ottawa: Communication Canada, 2006) [*Subcommittee Report*].
65 See *Bedford, supra* note 3 at para 165, citing *Subcommittee Report, supra* note 64.
66 See *ibid.* Since bawdy houses operate indoors, typically it is necessary to obtain a warrant before entering them, thus requiring devotion of police resources to the investigation.
67 See *Bedford, supra* note 3 at para 167, citing *Subcommittee Report, supra* note 64.

68 See *Bedford, supra* note 3 at para 169, citing *Subcommittee Report, supra* note 64 at 19.

69 *Ibid.*

70 See *Bedford, supra* note 3 at para 170, citing *Subcommittee Report, supra* note 64 at 61–66.

71 *Ibid.*

72 *Ibid.*

73 See *Bedford, supra* note 3 at paras 173–76, citing *Subcommittee Report, supra* note 64.

74 *Ibid.*

75 *Ibid.*

76 See *Bedford, supra* note 3 at para 177.

77 *Ibid* at para 182.

78 *Ibid.*

79 *Ibid* at paras 100–3.

80 *Ibid* at para 182.

81 The jurisdictions cited were the Netherlands, New Zealand, Germany, Australia, Sweden, and Nevada.

82 See *Bedford, supra* note 3 at para 186.

83 *Ibid* at para 187.

84 *Ibid.*

85 *Ibid* at para 189.

86 *Ibid* at para 187.

87 *Ibid* at para 188.

88 *Ibid.*

89 *Ibid.*

90 *Ibid* at para 206.

91 *Ibid*, citing *Fact Sheet on Prostitution and Trafficking in Human Beings* (Stockholm: Ministry of Industry, Employment and Communications, Division for Gender Equality, 2005).

92 See *Bedford, supra* note 3 at para 207.

93 *Ibid.*

94 *Ibid.*

95 *Ibid* at para 208.

96 *Ibid.*

97 *Ibid* at para 421.

98 See *Canada (Attorney General) v Bedford*, 2013 SCC 72 at paras 48–56, [2013] 3 SCR 1101.

99 See *Bedford, supra* note 3 at paras 165, 174, 315.

100 See *Bedford, supra* note 1 at footnote 3.

101 See, generally, *Bedford, supra* note 98.

102 This point is perhaps best illustrated by the fact that the *Canadian Bill of Rights*, SC 1960, c 44, was amended only in 2017 to prohibit discrimination based on gender expression or identity. Similarly, the *Criminal Code of Canada*, RSC 1985, c C-36, was amended only in the same year to allow for offences committed based on discrimination against transgender people to qualify as hate crimes. See Bill C-16, *An Act to Amend the Canadian Human Rights Act and the Criminal Code*, SC 2017, c 13. For a more general review of how transgender people have been subject to erasure in social science research and society more broadly, see Viviane K. Namaste, *Invisible Lives: The Erasure of Transsexual and Transgendered People* (Chicago: University of Chicago Press, 2000).

103 See, e.g., Leon Laidlaw, "Challenging Dominant Portrayals of the Trans Sex Worker: On Gender, Violence, and Protection" (2018) 41 Manitoba Law Journal 351 at 357–58.

104 *Ibid* at 358.

105 *Ibid*. See also Tara Lyons et al, "Negotiating Violence in the Context of Transphobia and Criminalization: The Experiences of Trans Sex Workers in Vancouver, Canada" (2017) 27 Qualitative Health Research 182; and Tor Fletcher, "Trans Sex Workers: Negotiating Sex, Gender, and Non-Normative Desire" in Elya M. Durisin, Emily van der Meulen, and Chris Bruckert, eds, *Selling Sex: Experience, Advocacy, and Research on Sex Work in Canada* (Vancouver: UBC Press, 2013) 98–113.

106 See Laidlaw, "Dominant Portrayals," *supra* note 103 at 364–65, reporting the author's qualitative research on transgender sex worker experiences with violence.

107 *Ibid* at 368–69.

108 The only mention of the impacts of the laws on the gay community was at the Ontario Court of Appeal, and it was exceedingly brief. See *Bedford, supra* note 1 at para 356.

109 See Supreme Court of Canada, case no 34788, factums on appeal, online: <https://www.scc-csc.ca/case-dossier/info/af-ma-eng.aspx?cas=34788>. Notably, there are significant limits on submissions at appellate courts that might account for the parties' narrowly written submissions.

110 See Justin Trudeau, "Remarks by Prime Minister Justin Trudeau to Apologize to LGBTQ2 Canadians" (28 November 2017), online: <https://pm.gc.ca/en/news/speeches/2017/11/28/remarks-prime-minister-justin-trudeau-apologize-lgbtq2-canadians>.

111 See Patrizia Gentile et al, "Another Limited Bill: Gay and Lesbian Historians on C-75" (11 June 2018), online: <https://www.ourcommons.ca/Content/Committee/421/JUST/Brief/BR10002313/br-external/HooperTom-e.pdf> at 2;

and Stuart Russell, "The Offence of Keeping a Common Bawdy-House in Canadian Criminal Law" (1982) 14 Ottawa Law Review 270 at 296.

112 See Gentile, "Limited Bill," *supra* note 111, appendix A.

113 See, e.g., Thomas Crofts, "Regulation of the Male Sex Industry" in Victor Minichiello and John Scott, eds, *Male Sex Work and Society* (New York: Harrington Park Press, 2014) 178.

114 See, e.g., John Scott, "A Prostitute's Progress: Male Prostitution in Scientific Discourse" (2003) 13 Social Semiotics 179 at 179–80.

115 *Ibid* at 181–82. For a brief review of the relevant history in Canada, see Trudeau, "Remarks," *supra* note 110.

116 See Joanna Jamel, "An Investigation of the Incidence of Client-Perpetrated Sexual Violence against Male Sex Workers" (2011) 23 International Journal of Sexual Health 63 at 74; and Melissa Farley and Howard Barkan, "Prostitution, Violence, and Posttraumatic Stress Disorder" (1998) 27 Women and Health 37.

117 See, e.g., Judith Connell and Graham Hart, *An Overview of Male Sex Work in Edinburgh and Glasgow: The Male Sex Worker Perspective* (Glasgow: MRC, University of Glasgow, 2003); and D.J. West and Buz de Villiers, *Male Prostitution: Gay Sex Services in London* (Binghampton, UK: Harrington Park Press, 1993).

118 See *Bedford*, *supra* note 3 at para 67, citing *David Polowin Real Estate Ltd v Dominion of Canada General Insurance Co* (2005), 255 DLR (4th) 633 at paras 119–20, 76 OR (3d) 161 (ONCA) [*General Insurance*].

119 See *Bedford*, *supra* note 98 at para 68, citing *General Insurance*, *supra* note 118 at para 121.

120 See *Bedford*, *supra* note 98 at para 45, citing *R v Morgentaler*, [1988] 1 SCR 30 at 52, 44 DLR (4th) 385.

121 See *Bedford*, *supra* note 1 at paras 64–68; and *Bedford*, *supra* note 98 at para 45.

122 *Ibid*.

123 See *Bedford*, *supra* note 98 at para 46.

124 See *Bedford*, *supra* note 1 at para 82.

125 *Ibid*. Notably, the Supreme Court decided not to reconsider this issue in light of other findings. See *Bedford*, *supra* note 98 at para 47.

126 See *Bedford*, *supra* note 1 at paras 83–84.

127 See *Bedford*, *supra* note 98 at para 42.

128 *Ibid* at para 43.

129 *Ibid*.

130 *Ibid* at para 47.

131 See *Bedford*, *supra* note 1 at paras 127–29, citing *Harper v Canada*, 2004 SCC 33 at paras 93–99, [2004] 1 SCR 827, citing *RJR-Macdonald Inc v Canada (Attorney General)*, [1995] 3 SCR 199 at 285–89, 127 DLR (4th) 1.

132 *Ibid* at para 48.

133 *Ibid*. I explain the terms "adjudicative" and "legislative" facts in more detail in the next chapter.

134 *Ibid* at para 51.

135 *Ibid* at para 52.

136 *Ibid*.

137 See *Re BC Motor Vehicle Act*, [1985] 2 SCR 486 at 515, 24 DLR (4th) 536 [*Motor Vehicle Act Reference*].

138 See, e.g., *Morgentaler, supra* note 120 at 56, 173; *Rodriguez v British Columbia (Attorney General)*, [1993] 3 SCR 519 at 587–88, 107 DLR (4th) 342; *Reference re ss 193 and 195.1(1)(C) of the Criminal Code (Man)*, [1990] 1 SCR 1123 at 1174, 56 CCC (3d) 65 [*Sex Work Reference*].

139 See *Bedford, supra* note 98 at para 76.

140 See *Bedford, supra* note 3 at paras 300–1.

141 *Ibid* at para 300.

142 *Ibid* at para 361.

143 *Ibid* at para 359; *Bedford, supra* note 1 at para 142; *Bedford, supra* note 98 at paras 58–72.

144 See *Bedford, supra* note 3 at para 242.

145 *Ibid* at para 274; *Sex Work Reference, supra* note 138 at 1134–35.

146 See *Bedford, supra* note 3 at para 242; and *R v Downey*, [1992] 2 SCR 10 at 32, 90 DLR (4th) 449.

147 It is notable that the applicants also maintained that the impugned laws violated a principle of fundamental justice requiring the state to legislate in accordance with the rule of law. See *Bedford, supra* note 3 at para 368. Since this principle was not argued at the Supreme Court, I leave it out of the analysis.

148 Elsewhere I describe the term using this language. See Colton Fehr, "The 'Individualistic' Approach to the Arbitrariness, Overbreadth, and Gross Disproportionality Principles" (2018) 51 University of British Columbia Law Review 55.

149 See *Chaoulli v Quebec (Attorney General)*, 2005 SCC 35 at para 130, [2005] 1 SCR 791.

150 See *R v Heywood*, [1994] 3 SCR 761 at 792–94, 120 DLR (4th) 348.

151 See *R v Malmo-Levine*, 2003 SCC 74 at para 169, [2003] 3 SCR 571, expanding the "per se" disproportionality principle first mentioned in *United States v Burns*, 2001 SCC 7, [2001] 1 SCR 283; and *Suresh v Canada (Minister of Citizenship and Immigration)*, 2002 SCC 1, [2002] 1 SCR 3.

152 See *Bedford, supra* note 98 at paras 123, 127.

153 *Ibid*.

154 *Ibid* at para 127.

155 See *Bedford*, *supra* note 98 at para 134, citing *Bedford*, *supra* note 3 at para 427. It is not clear why the Supreme Court included security staff in this list since such workers were prohibited by the living on the avails provision.
156 *Ibid*.
157 See *Bedford*, *supra* note 98 at paras 148–59.
158 *Ibid* at paras 139–44.
159 See *Motor Vehicle Act Reference*, *supra* note 137.
160 *Ibid* at 518.
161 *Ibid* at 531.
162 See *Bedford*, *supra* note 98 at para 161.
163 *Ibid*.
164 *Ibid* at para 162.
165 *Ibid*.
166 *Ibid*.
167 *Ibid* at paras 124–29.
168 *Ibid* at para 127.
169 *Ibid*.
170 Being Schedule B to the *Canada Act 1982* (UK), 1982, c 11.
171 See *Schachter v Canada*, [1992] 2 SCR 679 at 700–2, 93 DLR (4th) 1.
172 See *Bedford*, *supra* note 98 at para 164.
173 See *Bedford*, *supra* note 3 at para 509.
174 *Supra* note 171.
175 *Ibid* at 716.
176 *Ibid* at 719. In Chapter 6, I will explain in greater detail each ground for granting a suspended declaration of invalidity.
177 See, e.g., *R v Hayes*, [1998] BC No 2752, 115 BCAC 22 (BCCA).
178 See, e.g., *R v Yu*, 2002 ABCA 305, 171 CCC (3d) 90.
179 For a review of relevant case law, see *Bedford*, *supra* note 3 at paras 524–35.
180 *Ibid*.
181 *Ibid* at para 536.
182 *Ibid* at paras 537–38, citing Kent Roach, *Constitutional Remedies in Canada*, loose-leaf (Aurora, ON: Canada Law Book, 2009) at 14–97.
183 See *Bedford*, *supra* note 98 at para 167.
184 *Ibid* at paras 168–69.

CHAPTER 4: LEGISLATIVE FACTS AND THE CHARTER

1 See Kenneth Culp Davis, "An Approach to Problems of Evidence in the Administrative Process" (1942) 55 Harvard Law Review 364 at 402–3.

2   *Ibid* at 402. Scholars also refer to these facts as "case-specific" or "historical" facts. See, e.g., Donald Horowitz, *The Courts and Social Policy* (Washington, DC: Brookings Institution, 1977) at 45; and David Faigman, *Constitutional Fictions: A Unified Theory of Constitutional Facts* (Oxford: Oxford University Press, 2008) at 46.

3   See Davis, "Problems of Evidence," *supra* note 1 at 404. Courts also identify legislative facts as "social" facts to avoid implying that such facts are found only by legislatures. For brevity's sake, I will refer to this broader category of facts collectively as legislative facts.

4   See *R v Spence*, 2005 SCC 71 at para 57, [2005] 3 SCR 458.

5   See *Housen v Nikolaisen*, 2002 SCC 33 at para 10, [2002] 2 SCR 235.

6   See, e.g., *Harper v Canada*, 2004 SCC 33 at para 99, [2004] 1 SCR 827, citing *RJR-Macdonald Inc v Canada (Attorney General)*, [1995] 3 SCR 199 at 285–89, 127 DLR (4th) 1.

7   See *Canada (Attorney General) v Bedford*, 2013 SCC 72 at para 51, [2013] 3 SCR 1101.

8   *Ibid.*

9   *Ibid* at para 52.

10   See Jodi Lazare, "When Disciplines Collide: Polygamy and the Social Sciences on Trial" (2015) 32 Windsor Yearbook of Access to Justice 103 at 105.

11   See *Spence, supra* note 4 at para 64; and Peter Hogg, *Constitutional Law of Canada*, 5th ed, vol 2, loose-leaf (Scarborough, ON: Thomson Carswell, 2014) at 38-8, 38-9.

12   See *R v Buhay*, 2003 SCC 30 at para 46, [2003] 1 SCR 631, citing *R v Belnavis*, [1997] 3 SCR 341 at para 76, 151 DLR (4th) 443.

13   *Supra* note 12.

14   *Ibid* at para 46.

15   [1996] 1 SCR 254, 133 DLR (4th) 289.

16   *Ibid* at para 32.

17   See *Bedford, supra* note 7 at paras 51–52.

18   *Supra* note 5.

19   *Ibid* at para 16.

20   The concern that only the wealthy can consistently afford to have their Charter rights adjudicated has been noted by many of Canada's leading constitutional law scholars. See, e.g., Benjamin Berger, "Putting a Price on Dignity: The Problem of Costs in *Charter* Litigation" (2002) 26 Advocates' Quarterly 235 at 235; Kent Roach, "Enforcement of the *Charter* – Subsections 24(1) and 52(1)" (2013) 62 Supreme Court Law Review (2d) 473 at 486; Robert Sharpe, "Access to *Charter* Justice" (2013) 63 Supreme Court Law Review (2d) 3 at 3; and Andrew Petter, *The Politics of the Charter: The Illusive Promise of Constitutional Rights* (Toronto: University of Toronto Press, 2010) at 104–5.

Notes to pages 83–86 | 219

21 See *Housen, supra* note 5 at para 17.
22 See John Monahan and Laurens Walker, "Social Authority: Obtaining, Evaluating, and Establishing Social Science in Law" (1986) 134 University of Pennsylvania Law Review 477 at 497. See also Alan Young, "Proving a Violation: Rhetoric, Research, and Remedy" (2014) 67 Supreme Court Law Review (2d) 617 at 629 ("with respect to expert evidence, it is less critical for the judge to assess the demeanour of the witness in discharging the gatekeeper function").
23 Alan Young, personal interview (30 July 2021).
24 See *Canada (Attorney General) v Bedford*, 2012 ONCA 186 at paras 130–42, 109 OR (3d) 1.
25 See *Bedford, supra* note 7 at para 55.
26 *Ibid.*
27 See Benjamin Perryman, "Adducing Social Science Evidence in Constitutional Cases" (2018) 44 Queen's Law Journal 121 at 124. See also David Paciocco, "Taking a 'Goudge' Out of Bluster and Blarney: An 'Evidence-Based Approach' to Expert Testimony" (2009) 13 Canadian Criminal Law Review 135 at 146; and *R v Abbey*, 2009 ONCA 624 at para 72, 97 OR (3d) 330 (per Justice Doherty, "a deluge of experts has descended on the criminal courts ready to offer definitive opinions to explain almost anything," particularly where human behaviour is concerned).
28 See Ian Binnie, "Science in the Courtroom: The Mouse That Roared" (2007) 56 University of New Brunswick Law Journal 307 at 309. See also Justice Robert Sharpe and Vincent-Joël Proulx, "The Use of Academic Writing in Appellate Judicial Decision-Making" (2011) 50 Canadian Business Law Journal 550 at 569.
29 *Ibid.*
30 See David Paciocco, "Unplugging Jukebox Testimony in an Adversarial System: Strategies for Changing the Tune on Partial Experts" (2009) 34 Queen's Law Journal 565 at 567.
31 2000 SCC 43, [2000] 2 SCR 275.
32 *Ibid* at para 52.
33 See Paciocco, "Jukebox," *supra* note 30 at 575–77.
34 *Ibid* at 577.
35 *Ibid.*
36 *Ibid* at 581–82.
37 *Ibid* at 582–84.
38 *Ibid* at 583.
39 See, e.g., Peter Sperlich, "Social Science Evidence and the Courts: Reading beyond the Adversary Process" (1980) 63 Judicature 280 at 282; James Acker, "Social Science in Supreme Court Criminal Cases and Briefs: The Actual and Potential Contribution of Social Scientists as Amici Curiae" (1990) 14 Law and Human Behaviour 25 at 40; John Wesley, "Scientific Evidence and the Question

of Judicial Capacity" (1984) 25 William and Mary Law Review 675 at 685; David Caudill and Lewis LaRue, "Why Judges Applying the *Daubert* Trilogy Need to Know about the Social, Institutional, and Rhetorical – and Not Just the Methodological – Aspects of Science" (2003) 45 Boston College Law Review 1; Shirley Dobbin et al, "Applying *Daubert:* How Well Do Judges Understand Science and Scientific Method?" (2002) 85 Judicature 244; Honourable Stephen Goudge, *Report of the Inquiry into Pediatric Forensic Pathology in Ontario: Policy and Recommendations,* vol 3 (Toronto: Ontario Ministry of the Attorney General, 2008) at 500–2 [*Goudge Report*]; John Lee, Tess Sheldon, and Roberto Lattanzio, "Law and Ordered C.H.A.O.S.: Social Science Methodology, and the *Charter* Claims of Persons with Disabilities" (2013) 32 National Journal of Constitutional Law 61 at 68–69; and Glenn Anderson, *Expert Evidence,* 2nd ed (Toronto: LexisNexis, 2009) at 328.

40 See Jodi Lazare, "Judging the Social Sciences in *Carter v Canada (AG)*" (2016) 10 McGill Journal of Law and Health S35 at S48–49. See also Young, "Proving a Violation," *supra* note 22 at 641–42 ("[w]hen operating within the current legal framework of an adversarial approach to proof, there is greater risk that the legislative fact evidence could lead to a badly informed decision despite the appearance of being fully informed"). Elsewhere Lazare uses *Reference re: Section 293 of the Criminal Code of Canada,* 2011 BCSC 1588, 279 CCC (3d) 1 [*Polygamy Reference*] to illustrate the problems that judges have understanding and applying social science evidence. See, generally, Lazare, "Disciplines Collide," *supra* note 10.

41 See Lazare, "Judging," *supra* note 40 at S45.

42 *Ibid.*

43 *Ibid.*

44 See Peter Schuck, "Why Don't Law Professors Do More Empirical Research?" (1989) 39 Journal of Legal Education 323 at 325. More recently, see Geoffrey Conrad and Jodi Lazare, "The Lawyer in Context: Toward an Integrated Approach to Legal Education" in Ruth Sefton-Green, ed, *Démoulages: Du carcan de l'enseignement du droit vers une éducation juridique* (Paris: Société de Législation Comparée, 2015) 45 (discussing the deficiencies of legal education concerning training in nonlegal subjects).

45 See Binnie, "Mouse That Roared," *supra* note 28 at 307 ("the task of making courts more science friendly is important to sustaining the legitimacy of courts as dispute resolution institutions").

46 See Alan Young, "Proving a Violation," *supra* note 22 at 622. Similarly, see Jula Hughes and Vanessa MacDonnell, "Social Science Evidence in Constitutional Rights Cases in Germany and Canada: Some Comparative Observations" (2013) 32 National Journal of Constitutional Law 23 at 36–37. Referring to *Canada (Attorney General) v PHS Community Services Society,* 2011 SCC 44, [2011] 3 SCR 134; *Polygamy Reference, supra* note 40; *Bedford, supra* note 7; and *Carter v*

Canada (Attorney General), 2015 SCC 5, [2015] 1 SCR 331, the authors observe that "[e]ach of the cases was brought with the support of advocacy groups ... and the legal arguments were supported on both sides by sophisticated and substantial social science evidence."

47 See Perryman, "Social Science Evidence," *supra* note 27 at 172–73. For Perryman's summary with respect to further best practices, see 173–75.

48 See Alan Young, *The Costs of Charter Litigation* (Ottawa: Department of Justice Canada, Research and Statistics Division, 2016), online: <https://www.justice.gc.ca/eng/rp-pr/jr/ccl-clc/ccl-clc.pdf> at 9. These grants frequently fund Indigenous issues given their complexity and broader public importance but can also be issued for other cases of public importance.

49 *Ibid* at 9–10, citing *Carter v Canada (Attorney General)*, 2015 SCC 5 at para 134, [2015] 1 SCR 331.

50 *Ibid* at 10.

51 See Edward Purcell, *Brandeis and the Progressive Constitution: Erie, the Judicial Power, and the Politics of the Federal Courts in Twentieth-Century America* (New Haven, CT: Yale University Press, 2000) at 166–67.

52 208 US 412 (1908).

53 See *Polygamy Reference*, *supra* note 40 at paras 109–10, citing *Reference re: Anti-Inflation Act*, [1976] 2 SCR 373, 68 DLR (3d) 452 [*Anti-Inflation Act Reference*]; and *Reference re: Residential Tenancies Act (Ontario)*, [1981] 1 SCR 714, 123 DLR (3d) 554 [*Tenancies Act Reference*].

54 See *Tenancies Act Reference*, *supra* note 53 at 723.

55 See Hogg, *Constitutional Law*, *supra* note 11 at 60–14; and Monahan and Walker, "Social Authority," *supra* note 22 at 497.

56 *Ibid*.

57 *Ibid*.

58 See Allison Orr Larsen, "The Trouble with Amicus Facts" (2014) 100 Virginia Law Review 1757 at 1757.

59 See Young, "Proving a Violation," *supra* note 22 at 646–47.

60 See Binnie, "Mouse That Roared," *supra* note 28 at 322–23.

61 See Perryman, "Social Science Evidence," *supra* note 27 at 175.

62 *Ibid*.

63 See Hughes and MacDonnell, "Social Science Evidence," *supra* note 46 at 39.

64 *Ibid*.

65 *Ibid*.

66 *Ibid*.

67 *Basic Law for the Federal Republic of Germany* (1949).

68 See Hughes and MacDonnell, "Social Science Evidence," *supra* note 46 at 40.

69 Ibid.
70 Ibid at 41.
71 Ibid at 46.
72 See Binnie, "Mouse That Roared," *supra* note 28 at 323.
73 See *Federal Courts Rules* (SOR/98–106), Rule 69.
74 Alan Young, personal interview (30 July 2021).
75 See, e.g., Joëlle Vuille, "Admissibility and Appraisal of Scientific Evidence in Continental European Criminal Justice Systems: Past, Present and Future" (2013) 45 Australian Journal of Forensic Sciences 389.
76 See Eva Friss and Karsten Åström, "The Use of Court- and Party-Appointed Experts in Legal Proceedings in Sweden: Judges' Experiences and Attitudes" (2017) 3 Oslo Law Review 63 at 64, citing Anthony Champagne et al, "Are Court-Appointed Experts the Solution to the Problems of Expert Testimony?" (2001) 84 Judicature 178; Anthony Champagne, Daniel Shuman, and Elisabeth Whitaker, "An Empirical Examination of the Use of Expert Witnesses in American Courts" (1991) 31 Jurimetrics 375; Jennifer Mnookin, "Idealizing Science and Demonizing Experts: An Intellectual History of Expert Evidence" (2007) 52 Villanova Law Review 763; Jennifer Mnookin, "Expert Evidence, Partisanship, and Epistemic Competence" (2008) 73 Brooklyn Law Review 1009; Daniel Shuman, Elisabeth Whitaker, and Anthony Champagne, "An Empirical Examination of the Use of Expert Witnesses in the Courts – Part II: A Three City Study" (1994) 34 Jurimetrics 193; Ulf Stridbeck, Pål Grøndahl, and Cato Grønnerød, "Expert for Whom? Court-Appointed versus Party-Appointed Experts" (2015) 23 Psychiatry, Psychology and Law 246.
77 See Friss and Åström, "Experts," *supra* note 76 at 64, citing Peter Alldridge, "Forensic Science and Expert Evidence" (1994) 21 Journal of Law and Society 136; Elizabeth Butler-Sloss and Ananda Hall, "Expert Witnesses, Courts and the Law" (2002) 95 Journal of the Royal Society of Medicine 431; Champagne et al, "Solution," *supra* note 76; Stridbeck et al, "Expert for Whom?," *supra* note 76; and Catherine Williams, "Expert Evidence in Cases of Child Abuse" (1993) 68 Archives of Disease in Childhood 712.
78 See Alexandra Derwin, "The Judicial Admission of Faulty Scientific Expert Evidence Informing Wrongful Convictions" (2018) 8 Western Journal of Legal Studies 1 at 13.
79 *Ibid* at 14, citing *Civil Procedure Rules* (UK), 2017, s 35, online: <www.justice.gov.uk/courts/procedure- rules/civil/rules/part35#IDAJH0HC>.
80 SOR/98–106.
81 *Ibid,* s 52.1.
82 Even though expert evidence with respect to the natural sciences might seem to be more concrete, it is notable that there are many instances in which such evidence has led to wrongful convictions. See, generally, *Goudge Report, supra* note 39.

83 See *Canada v Bedford*, 2010 ONSC 4264 at para 182, 102 OR (3d) 321.

84 This is commonly referred to as "hot tubbing." See Derwin, "Judicial Admission," *supra* note 76 at 15.

85 See, e.g., Ken Anderson and Tracy Ayodele, "Hot-Tubbing in Canadian Patent Litigation: A Preliminary Assessment" (2012) 24 Intellectual Property Journal 201. For a critique of this type of testimony, see Freya Kristjanson, "Hot-Tubs and Concurrent Evidence: Improving Administrative Proceedings" (2012) 25 Canadian Journal of Administrative Law and Practice 79 at 86–89.

86 *Ibid*.

87 *Ibid*.

88 See Binnie, "Mouse That Roared," *supra* note 28 at 326.

89 See *Federal Court Rules*, *supra* note 80, ss 282.1, 282.2.

90 See Jennifer Roberts, "Why Experts Like 'Hot-Tubbing,'" *Globe and Mail* (19 April 2011), online: <www.theglobeandmail.com/report-on-business/industry-news/the-law-page/why-judges-like-hot-tubbing/article577733/>.

91 These are the courts to which the *Federal Court Rules*, *supra* note 80, apply. It is notable that Derwin, "Judicial Admission," *supra* note 78 at 16, implies that the *Canada Evidence Act*, RSC 1985, c C-5, s 7, permits concurrent testimony. However, that section concerns the number of expert witnesses that may be called, not the procedure by which experts may be called.

92 See *Spence*, *supra* note 4 at para 64.

CHAPTER 5:
THE PRINCIPLES OF INSTRUMENTAL RATIONALITY

1 See *Canada (Attorney General) v Bedford*, 2013 SCC 72 at para 107, [2013] 3 SCR 1101, citing Hamish Stewart, *Fundamental Justice: Section 7 of the Canadian Charter of Rights and Freedoms* (Toronto: Irwin Law, 2012) at 151.

2 See, e.g., *Canada (Attorney General) v PHS Community Services Society*, 2011 SCC 44, [2011] 3 SCR 134.

3 See *Bedford*, *supra* note 1 at para 127.

4 See, e.g., Lisa Dufraimont, "*Canada (Attorney General) v. Bedford* and the Limits on Substantive Criminal Law under Section 7" (2014) 67 Supreme Court Law Review (2d) 483 at 496–98; and Hamish Stewart, "*Bedford* and the Structure of Section 7" (2015) 60 McGill Law Journal 576 at 588–89.

5 See Don Stuart, "*Bedford*: Striking Down Prostitution Laws and Revising Section 7 Standards to Focus on Arbitrariness" (2014) 7 Criminal Reports (7th) 52; Colton Fehr, "The 'Individualistic' Approach to Arbitrariness, Overbreadth, and Gross Disproportionality" (2018) 51 University of British Columbia Law Review 55; and Colton Fehr, "Instrumental Rationality and General Deterrence" (2019) 57 Alberta Law Review 53.

6 See Colton Fehr, "Rethinking the Instrumental Rationality Principles of Fundamental Justice" (2020) 58 Alberta Law Review 133.

7 See Stewart, "*Bedford,*" *supra* note 4 at 587.

8 See Hamish Stewart, "The Constitutionality of the New Sex Work Law" (2016) 54 Alberta Law Review 69 at 82–83.

9 See Colton Fehr, *Constitutionalizing Criminal Law* (Vancouver: UBC Press, 2022) at 79–141.

10 See Stuart, "Revising," *supra* note 5; and Fehr, "Individualistic," *supra* note 5 at 64–65.

11 See *Bedford, supra* note 1 at para 111.

12 *Ibid* at para 119.

13 See Fehr, "General Deterrence," *supra* note 5 at 61.

14 *Ibid* at 64–65. As I observe in footnote 104, the Supreme Court's overbreadth cases exclusively apply the logical conception of overbreadth.

15 *Ibid.*

16 *Ibid.*

17 *Ibid.*

18 RSC 1985, c C-46.

19 For a detailed review of the literature, see Fehr, "General Deterrence," *supra* note 5 at 56–60.

20 *Ibid* at 59.

21 *Ibid* at 62.

22 *Ibid* at 62, 64.

23 See also Mark Carter, "Section 7 and 1 of the *Charter* after *Bedford, Carter,* and *Smith:* Different Questions, Same Answers?" (2017) 64 Criminal Law Quarterly 108 at 119. Carter does not identify exactly, however, which function the arbitrariness principle serves post-*Bedford*.

24 See *R v Clay,* 2003 SCC 75 at para 38, [2003] 3 SCR 735.

25 See *R v Khawaja,* 2012 SCC 69 at para 40, [2012] 3 SCR 555.

26 See *Bedford, supra* note 1 at para 107.

27 Elsewhere I have conducted more extensive analyses engaging with the relevant Supreme Court case law. See Fehr, "Individualistic," *supra* note 5 at 69–71; and Fehr, "Rethinking," *supra* note 6 at 144–47.

28 See *Bedford, supra* note 1 at para 134.

29 See *Canada (Attorney General) v Bedford,* 2012 ONCA 186 at para 221, 109 OR (3d) 1.

30 See *Bedford, supra* note 1 at paras 146–59.

31 See *Bedford v Canada,* 2010 ONSC 4264 at para 393, 102 OR (3d) 321.

32 *Ibid* at para 410.

33 See *Bedford, supra* note 1 at paras 123–26.

34 *Ibid* at para 159 (emphasis added).
35 *Ibid* at para 139.
36 *Ibid* at paras 139–45.
37 See *Bedford, supra* note 29 at paras 253–54.
38 See *Bedford, supra* note 1 at paras 161–62.
39 See Fehr, *Constitutionalizing Criminal Law, supra* note 9 at 109–10.
40 2015 ONCA 585, 127 OR (3d) 81 leave to appeal to SCC refused, 36706 (5 May 2016).
41 RSO 1990, s H8, s 68.1(1).
42 RRO 1990, Reg 587, s 14(1).
43 See *Michaud, supra* note 40 at para 1.
44 *Ibid* at para 73.
45 *Ibid* at paras 73–74.
46 *Ibid* at paras 144–45.
47 *Ibid* at para 148.
48 See Fehr, "Individualistic," *supra* note 5 at 61.
49 See Stewart, "*Bedford,*" *supra* note 4 at 590.
50 *Ibid*.
51 *Ibid*.
52 *Ibid*.
53 *Ibid*.
54 *Ibid*. For a competing view, see *R v AB*, 2015 ONCA 803, 333 CCC (3d) 382. For a rebuttal, see Hamish Stewart, *Fundamental Justice: Section 7 of the Canadian Charter of Rights and Freedoms,* 2nd ed (Toronto: Irwin Law, 2019) at 161–62.
55 See *Michaud, supra* note 40 at para 151.
56 *Ibid* at para 147.
57 See *Rodriguez v British Columbia (Attorney General),* [1993] 3 SCR 519 at 590, 107 DLR (4th) 342.
58 See *Canadian Foundation for Children, Youth and the Law v Canada (Attorney General),* 2004 SCC 4 at para 8, [2004] 1 SCR 76.
59 *Ibid*.
60 See Fehr, "Rethinking," *supra* note 6 at 140.
61 *Ibid* at 140–41, citing Michael Coenen, "Rules against Rulification" (2014) 124 Yale Law Journal 644 at 646; Louis Kaplow, "Rules versus Standards: An Economic Analysis" (1992) 42 Duke Law Journal 557; Duncan Kennedy, "Form and Substance in Private Law Adjudication" (1976) 89 Harvard Law Review 1685; Antonin Scalia, "The Rule of Law as a Law of Rules" (1989) 56 University of Chicago Law Review 1175; Pierre Schlag, "Rules and Standards" (1985) 33 UCLA Law Review 379; Kathleen Sullivan, "Foreword: The Justices of Rules and Standards"

(1992) 106 Harvard Law Review 22; Cass Sunstein, "Problems with Rules" (1995) 83 California Law Review 953; Robert Sharpe, *Good Judgment: Making Judicial Decisions* (Toronto: University of Toronto Press, 2018).

62 See *Michaud, supra* note 40 at para 149.

63 2003 SCC 74, [2003] 3 SCR 571.

64 *Ibid* at para 106, citing John Stuart Mill, *On Liberty and Considerations on Representative Government* (Oxford: Basil Blackwell and Mott, 1946) at 8–9.

65 See *Malmo-Levine, supra* note 63 at para 115.

66 *Ibid* at paras 116–22.

67 *Ibid* at paras 117–18, citing cannibalism, bestiality, cruelty to animals, and duelling.

68 See, e.g., Colton Fehr, "Vaccine Passports and the *Charter*: Do They Actually Infringe Rights?" (2022) 43 National Journal of Constitutional Law 93–113.

69 See *Reference re Section 94(2) of the Motor Vehicle Act*, [1985] 2 SCR 486 at para 29, 24 DLR (4th) 536.

70 See Fehr, *Constitutionalizing Criminal Law, supra* note 9 at 110.

71 See *Bedford, supra* note 1 at para 123.

72 *Ibid* at para 127.

73 *Ibid.*

74 See Stewart, "*Bedford*," *supra* note 4 at 587.

75 See Stewart, "Sex Work," *supra* note 8 at 82–83.

76 *Supra* note 2.

77 *Ibid* at para 19.

78 *Ibid* at para 129.

79 See Fehr, "Individualistic," *supra* note 5 at 62–64.

80 *Ibid* at 63–64, citing *R v Preston* (1990), 47 BCLR (2d) 273 at 15, 79 CR (3d) 61 (BCCA) ("[w]hile I am content to accept, at least for the purposes of this case, that sentences of incarceration can have a deterrent effect in cases of trafficking and trafficking related offences, including importing, where the offender or potential offender is not an addict, I have grave doubts that the same can be said in cases of possession where the offender who is to be specifically deterred, or the potential offender who is to benefit from the so-called general deterrent effect of such a sentence, is addicted to the substance in question").

81 See *PHS, supra* note 2 at para 133.

82 Recall that, if the law is presumed to achieve its objective, then an arbitrariness analysis is impossible. Even if such an analysis were conducted, however, the applicants could not reasonably contend that the law did not achieve its objective as applied to some individuals, namely pimps. This is enough to establish that the law is not arbitrary in either the logical or the empirical sense.

83 See Stewart, "Sex Work," *supra* note 8 at 83.

84 See *Bedford, supra* note 1 at para 127.

85 See Fehr, "Individualistic," *supra* note 5 at 68.
86 See Fehr, *Constitutionalizing Criminal Law*, *supra* note 9 at 113.
87 *Ibid.*
88 *Ibid.*
89 See, e.g., Jeremy Waldron, "The Core of the Case against Judicial Review" (2006) 115 Yale Law Journal 1346.
90 See, e.g., John Hart Ely, *Democracy and Distrust: A Theory of Judicial Review* (Cambridge, MA: Harvard University Press, 1980); and Ronald Dworkin, *Freedom's Law: The Moral Reading of the American Constitution* (Cambridge, MA: Harvard University Press, 1996).
91 See, e.g., Peter Hogg and Allison Bushell, "The *Charter* Dialogue between Courts and Legislatures (or Perhaps the *Charter of Rights* Isn't Such a Bad Thing after All)" (1997) 35 Osgoode Hall Law Journal 75; and Kent Roach, *The Supreme Court on Trial: Judicial Activism or Democratic Dialogue?* (Toronto: Irwin Law, 2016).
92 See, e.g., Melanie Murchison, "Making Numbers Count: An Empirical Analysis of 'Judicial Activism' in Canada" (2017) 40 Manitoba Law Journal 425 at 464, discussing post-9/11 applications of the dialogue metaphor. The article employs Margit Cohn and Mordechai Kremnitzer's "multidimensional model" for measuring judicial activism in "Judicial Activism: A Multi-Dimensional Model" (2005) 18 Canadian Journal of Law and Jurisprudence 333.
93 See Roach, *Supreme Court on Trial*, *supra* note 91 at 383–84.
94 *Ibid* at 393.
95 *Ibid* at 395.
96 *Ibid* at 404.
97 See, e.g., Richard Albert, "Advisory Review: The Reincarnation of the Notwithstanding Clause" (2008) 45 Alberta Law Review 1037; and Richard McAdam, "The Notwithstanding Taboo" (2009) 6 Federal Governance 1.
98 See Roach, *Supreme Court on Trial*, *supra* note 91 at 318–19; and Fehr, *Constitutionalizing Criminal Law*, *supra* note 9 at 166–69, citing various examples of criminal law cases in which Parliament feasibly could have employed the notwithstanding clause.
99 See Peter Hogg, *Constitutional Law of Canada*, 5th ed (Toronto: Thomson Reuters Canada, 2007) (loose-leaf supplement) at 53. See also Alana Klein, "The Arbitrariness in 'Arbitrariness' (and Overbreadth and Gross Disproportionality): Principle and Democracy in Section 7 of the *Charter*" (2013) 63 Supreme Court Law Review 377; Jamie Cameron, "From *MVR* to *Chaoulli v. Quebec:* The Road Not Taken and the Future of Section 7" (2006) 34 Supreme Court Law Review (2d) 105 at 105; and Hart Schwartz, "Circularity, Tautology and Gamesmanship: 'Purpose' Based Proportionality-Correspondence Analysis in Sections 15 and 7 of the *Charter*" (2016) 35 National Journal of Constitutional Law 105 at 108–9.

100   See Hogg, *Constitutional Law, supra* note 99 at 53.

101   See *M v H*, [1999] 2 SCR 3 at 70, 171 DLR (4th) 577.

102   Elsewhere I discuss the Supreme Court case law supporting Hogg's view. See Fehr, *Constitutionalizing Criminal Law, supra* note 9 at 128–30.

103   See *M v H, supra* note 101 at 70.

104   See Hogg and Bushell, "Dialogue," *supra* note 91 at 80.

105   See Roach, *Supreme Court on Trial, supra* note 91 at 308.

106   *Ibid.*

107   See *ibid* at chapter 13 for a more general review. See also Mark Tushnet, *Taking the Constitution Away from the Courts* (Princeton, NJ: Princeton University Press, 1999) at 33, 175, 186; Christopher Manfredi and James Kelly, "Six Degrees of Dialogue: A Response to Hogg and Bushell" (1999) 37 Osgoode Hall Law Journal 513 at 520; and Christopher Manfredi, "The Day the Dialogue Died: A Comment on *Sauvé v Canada*" (2007) 45 Osgoode Hall Law Journal 105.

108   *Ibid.*

109   *Ibid.*

110   See Roach, *Supreme Court on Trial, supra* note 91 at 272–73, 311.

111   *Ibid* at 273.

112   See Fehr, *Constitutionalizing Criminal Law, supra* note 9 at 115, 127.

113   See *R v Anwar*, 2020 ONCJ 103, 62 CR (7th) 402; and *R v NS*, 2021 ONSC 1628.

114   See Fehr, *Constitutionalizing Criminal Law, supra* note 9 at 120–21, citing *Respect for Communities Act*, SC 2015, c 22; and *PHS, supra* note 2.

115   See Fehr, *Constitutionalizing Criminal Law, supra* note 9 at 123–25, citing *An Act to Amend the Criminal Code and to Make Related Amendments to Other Acts (Medical Assistance in Dying)*, SC 2016, c 3; and *Carter v Canada (Attorney General)*, 2015 SCC 5, [2015] 1 SCR 331.

116   See Fehr, *Constitutionalizing Criminal Law, supra* note 9 at 125–26, citing *An Act to Amend the Corrections and Conditional Release Act and Another Act*, SC 2019, c 27, passed in response to *British Columbia Civil Liberties Association v Canada (Attorney General)*, 2019 BCCA 228, 377 CCC (3d) 420; and *Canadian Civil Liberties Association v Canada (Attorney General)*, 2019 ONCA 243, 144 OR (3d) 641.

117   See Fehr, *Constitutionalizing Criminal Law, supra* note 9 at 127. I cite the relevant case law, *supra* notes 114–16. The prior section 7 case that I am referring to is *R v Daviault*, [1994] 3 SCR 63, 118 DLR (4th) 469. That case involved a constitutional challenge to changing the common law intoxication rules. The Supreme Court responded by passing what is now section 33.1 of the *Criminal Code, supra* note 18, widely viewed as practically overturning the *Daviault* decision. Notably, section 33.1 was unanimously struck down by the Supreme Court in *R v Brown*, 2022 SCC 18, for reasons similar to those expressed in *Daviault*.

118 See *R v Ruzic*, 2001 SCC 24, [2001] 1 SCR 687.

119 See *Carter, supra* note 115 at para 72 ("[w]hile the Court has recognized a number of principles of fundamental justice, three have emerged as central in the recent s. 7 jurisprudence: laws that impinge on life, liberty or security of the person must not be arbitrary, overbroad, or have consequences that are grossly disproportionate to their object").

CHAPTER 6:
SUSPENDED DECLARATIONS OF INVALIDITY

1 See *Canada (Attorney General) v Bedford*, 2013 SCC 72 at paras 167–69, [2013] 3 SCR 1101.

2 *Ibid* at para 167.

3 *Ibid*.

4 *Ibid* at para 168.

5 *Ibid* at para 169.

6 See *Canada v Bedford*, 2010 ONSC 4264 at paras 513–35, 102 OR (3d) 321. Although this overlap is not complete – the communication provision most notably did not require proof of an actual nuisance – it was still a significant amount of overlap.

7 My comments are restricted to the substantive determination of whether a suspended declaration is appropriate. For discussion of the appropriate procedure for making such determinations, see Carolyn Mouland, "Remedying the Remedy: *Bedford*'s Suspended Declaration of Invalidity" (2018) 41 Manitoba Law Journal 281.

8 See, e.g., Bruce Ryder, "Suspending the *Charter*" (2003) 21 Supreme Court Law Review (2d) 267; Kent Roach, "Principled Remedial Discretion under the *Charter*" (2004) 25 Supreme Court Law Review (2d) 101; Grant Hoole, "Proportionality as a Remedial Principle: A Framework for Suspended Declarations of Invalidity" (2011) 49 Alberta Law Review 107; Robert Leckey, *Bills of Rights in the Common Law* (Cambridge, UK: Cambridge University Press, 2015); Robert Leckey, "The Harms of Remedial Discretion" (2016) 14 International Journal of Constitutional Law 584; and Robert Leckey, "Enforcing Laws That Infringe Rights" (2016) Public Law 206.

9 See, e.g., Kent Roach, "Polycentricity and Queue-Jumping in Public Law Remedies: A Two-Track Response" (2016) 66 University of Toronto Law Journal 3; and Kent Roach, "Dialogic Remedies" (2019) 17 International Journal of Constitutional Law 860.

10 See Sarah Burningham, "A Comment on the Court's Decision to Suspend the Declaration of Invalidity in *Carter v. Canada*" (2015) 78 Saskatchewan Law Review 201; Emmett Macfarlane, "Dialogue, Remedies, and Positive Rights: *Carter*

v. Canada as a Microcosm for Past and Future Issues under the *Charter of Rights and Freedoms*" (2017) 49 Ottawa Law Review 107; and Brian Bird, "The Judicial Notwithstanding Clause: Suspended Declarations of Invalidity" (2019) 42 Manitoba Law Journal 93.

11 See Bird, "Judicial Notwithstanding Clause," *supra* note 10 at 39.
12 Being Schedule B to the *Canada Act 1982* (UK), 1982, c 11.
13 See, e.g., Hoole, "Proportionality," *supra* note 8 at 110 ("[on] a plain reading of this provision, the invalidation of any law found to be *ultra vires* the Constitution should be immediate").
14 See *Reference re Remuneration of Judges of the Prov Court of PEI; Reference re Independence and Impartiality of Judges of the Prov Court of PEI*, [1997] 3 SCR 3 at para 99, 150 DLR (4th) 577 [*Provincial Judges Reference*].
15 [1985] 1 SCR 721, 19 DLR (4th) 1 [*Manitoba Language Reference*].
16 33 Vict, c 3 (Canada), reprinted in RSC 1985, App II.
17 See *Manitoba Language Reference*, *supra* note 15 at 747.
18 [1998] 2 SCR 217, 161 DLR (4th) 385 [*Secession Reference*].
19 *Ibid* at para 71. See also *Manitoba Language Reference*, *supra* note 15 at 749.
20 [1992] 2 SCR 679, 93 DLR (4th) 1.
21 *Ibid* at 715–16.
22 *Ibid* at 715.
23 [1991] 1 SCR 933, 63 CCC (3d) 481.
24 RSC 1985, c C-46, s 542(2).
25 See *Swain*, *supra* note 23 at 1021–22.
26 See *Schachter*, *supra* note 20 at 716.
27 *Ibid*.
28 See Ryder, "Suspending," *supra* note 8 at 273, 290–91, tracking this shift in rationale in the relevant case law. See also Kent Roach, "Remedial Consensus and Dialogue" (2002) 35 University of British Columbia Law Review 211 at 219; Sujit Choudhry and Kent Roach, "Putting the Past behind Us? Prospective Judicial and Legislative Constitutional Remedies" (2003) 21 Supreme Court Law Review (2d) 205 at 228; and Hoole, "Proportionality," *supra* note 8 at 114.
29 See Ryder, "Suspending," *supra* note 8 at 273, 290–91. Notably, this new direction was directly contrary to the Supreme Court's decision in *Schachter*, *supra* note 20 at 717 ("[t]he question whether to delay the application of a declaration of nullity should therefore turn not on considerations of the role of the courts and the legislature, but rather on considerations listed earlier relating to the effect of an immediate declaration on the public").
30 See Burningham, "Declaration of Invalidity," *supra* note 10 at 202, citing Hoole, "Proportionality," *supra* note 8 at 114; and Roach, "Remedial Consensus," *supra* note 28 at 218.
31 [1999] 2 SCR 203, 173 DLR (4th) 1.

32 *Ibid* at paras 116–18. It is possible that a suspended declaration of invalidity does facilitate dialogue. One study observes that 36 percent of Supreme Court decisions involving suspending declarations of invalidity resulted in a legislative response, whereas only 16 percent of immediate invalidity decisions received a legislative response. See Emmett Macfarlane, "Dialogue or Compliance? Measuring Legislatures' Policy Responses to Court Rulings on Rights" (2013) 34 International Political Science Review 39 at 49–50. However, this increased number is possibly affected by a tendency of the Supreme Court to issue suspended declarations of invalidity when a policy response is more likely. See Macfarlane, "Remedies," *supra* note 10 at 117.

33 See Peter Hogg, Allison Bushell Thornton, and Wade Knight, "*Charter* Dialogue Revisited – Or 'Much Ado about Metaphors'" (2007) 45 Osgoode Hall Law Journal 1 at 17–18. See also Peter Hogg and Ravi Amarnath, "Understanding Dialogue Theory" in Peter Oliver, Patrick Macklem, and Nathalie Des Rosiers, eds, *The Oxford Handbook of the Canadian Constitution* (Oxford: Oxford University Press, 2017) 1053 at 1054.

34 See Hogg, Bushell Thornton, and Knight, "Charter Dialogue Revisited," *supra* note 33 at 17–18.

35 See Choudhry and Roach, "Constitutional Remedies," *supra* note 28 at 233.

36 *Ibid.*

37 *Ibid.*

38 See Hoole, "Proportionality," *supra* note 8 at 132–34, 145–47. See also Burningham, "Declaration of Invalidity," *supra* note 10 at 203–7.

39 See Hoole, "Proportionality," *supra* note 8 at 109.

40 *Ibid* at 136.

41 *Ibid* at 109, 145–47.

42 *Ibid.*

43 *Ibid* at 118–23. As explained earlier, the *Bedford* case is a prime example.

44 *Ibid* at 123–28.

45 *Ibid* at 127. Minority government status provides one potential reason why a government might choose not to respond to a Supreme Court ruling.

46 *Ibid* at 128–31.

47 *Ibid* at 132. These first two factors track the rational connection branch of the section 1 test.

48 *Ibid.* This factor tracks the minimal impairment branch of the section 1 test.

49 *Ibid.* This factor tracks the proportionality branch of the section 1 test.

50 *Ibid* at 133.

51 *Ibid* at 134.

52 *Ibid.*

53 *Ibid* at 139.

54 See Roach, "Dialogic Remedies," *supra* note 9 at 867–68.
55 *Ibid* at 877.
56 *Ibid*.
57 *Ibid* at 862–63, citing William Blackstone, *Commentaries on the Laws of England*, vol 3 (Oxford: Clarendon Press, 1765–70) at 100–1; Albert Dicey, *Introduction to the Study of the Law of the Constitution*, 10th ed (London: Martin's Press, 1959) at 211–12.
58 See Roach, "Dialogic Remedies," *supra* note 9 at 877.
59 *Ibid* at 868.
60 *Ibid* at 877.
61 See Ryder, "Suspending," *supra* note 8 at para 32 (QL).
62 *Ibid*.
63 See, e.g., Kent Roach, "Principled Remedial Discretion under the *Charter*" (2004) 25 Supreme Court Law Review (2d) 101.
64 *Ibid* at 106–10.
65 *Ibid* at 112.
66 *Ibid* at 110. It is notable that Hoole's article was written seven years after Roach's article.
67 *Ibid*.
68 See Roach, "Dialogic Remedies," *supra* note 9 at 872.
69 See Albie Sachs, "The Judicial Enforcement of Socio-Economic Rights: The Grootboom Case" (2003) 56 Current Legal Problems 579 at 598.
70 See Leckey, *Bills of Rights*, *supra* note 8 at 99.
71 See Roach, "Dialogic Remedies," *supra* note 9 at 872.
72 *Ibid* at 872–73.
73 2015 SCC 5, [2015] 1 SCR 331; 2016 SCC 4, [2016] 1 SCR 13.
74 See Roach, "Dialogic Remedies," *supra* note 9 at 872–73.
75 See Burningham, "Declaration of Invalidity," *supra* note 10 at 204. See also Macfarlane, "Remedies," *supra* note 10 at 120.
76 See Macfarlane, "Remedies," *supra* note 10 at 120.
77 *Ibid*.
78 *Ibid*.
79 See Bird, "Judicial Notwithstanding Clause," *supra* note 10 at 32; *Manitoba Language Reference*, *supra* note 15 at 746–49; and *Provincial Judges Reference*, *supra* note 14 at para 9.
80 See Bird, "Judicial Notwithstanding Clause," *supra* note 10 at 35–36. Because these arguments do not appear to be rigorously defended in the scholarship, a complete review of their merits is unnecessary here.
81 *Ibid*.
82 *Ibid* at 39, 48, citing Burningham, "Declaration of Invalidity," *supra* note 10 at 204.

Notes to pages 125–33 | 233

83 See Bird, "Judicial Notwithstanding Clause," *supra* note 10 at 39.

84 *Ibid* at 39, 47.

85 For the process required to pass a federal bill, see Parliament of Canada, "The Process of Passing a Bill," *Library of Parliament,* online: <https://lop.parl.ca/About/Parliament/Education/ourcountryourparliament/html_booklet/process-passing-bill-e.html>.

86 See Robert Leckey, "Assisted Dying, Suspended Declarations, and Dialogue's Time" (2019) 69 University of Toronto Law Journal 64–83. See also Mouland, "Remedy," *supra* note 7 at 301–3.

87 *Ibid.* See also Dwight Newman, "Canada's Notwithstanding Clause, Dialogue, and Constitutional Identities" in Geoffrey Sigalet, Grégoire Webber, and Rosalind Dixon, eds, *Constitutional Dialogue: Rights, Democracy, Institutions* (Cambridge, UK: Cambridge University Press, 2019) 209 at 230–31.

88 *Ibid.*

89 See, e.g., Richard Albert, "Advisory Review: The Reincarnation of the Notwithstanding Clause" (2008) 45 Alberta Law Review 1037; Richard McAdam, "The Notwithstanding Taboo" (2009) 6 Federal Governance 1; Andrew Petter, "Legalize This: The Chartering of Canadian Politics" in James Kelly and Christopher Manfredi, eds, *Contested Constitutionalism: Reflections on the Canadian Charter of Rights and Freedoms* (Vancouver: UBC Press, 2010) at 33; and Jeremy Waldron, *Political Political Theory* (Cambridge, MA: Harvard University Press, 2016) at 354, note 30.

90 See Leckey, "Harms," *supra* note 8 at 595.

91 2020 SCC 38, [2020] 451 DLR (4th) 541.

92 *Ibid* at para 128.

93 *Ibid* at para 129.

94 *Ibid* at para 139.

95 *Ibid* at para 133.

96 *Ibid* at paras 237–41.

97 *Ibid* at para 121, citing *Koo Sze Yiu v Chief Executive of the HKSAR,* [2006] 3 HKLRD 455 at para 35.

98 See *Ontario v G, supra* note 91 at para 137.

99 See *Ibid* at para 239, citing *Constitution of the Republic of South Africa,* (1996), s 172(1)(b); and *Scotland Act, 1998* (UK), 1998, c 46, ss 102(2) and 102(3).

CHAPTER 7:
THE CASE FOR UPHOLDING THE SEX WORK LAWS

1 See *Canada (Attorney General) v Bedford,* 2013 SCC 72 at para 73, [2013] 3 SCR 1101.

2 *Ibid* at paras 79–92.
3 *Ibid* at para 86.
4 *Ibid* at para 92.
5 See *R v Ruzic*, 2001 SCC 24 at para 29, [2001] 1 SCR 687, citing George Fletcher, *Rethinking Criminal Law* (Boston: Little and Brown, 1978).
6 *Ibid*.
7 See *ibid* at para 47.
8 I defined this term in Chapter 1.
9 See *M v H*, [1999] 2 SCR 3 at 70, 171 DLR (4th) 577.
10 The court defines self-defence as a "rightful" act. See most recently *R v Ryan*, 2013 SCC 3 at para 31, [2013] 1 SCR 14. See also *R v Khill*, 2021 SCC 37 at paras 47–48.
11 Although the court has yet to provide a constitutional rationale for justification-based defences, commentators suggest that such a rationale must exist. Because excuses implicate for "wrongful" but morally involuntary conduct, it would be paradoxical to not also provide a constitutionally protected defence for justified conduct since such defences connote "rightful" (or at least "permissible") conduct. See Stephen Coughlan, "Duress, Necessity, Self-Defence, and Provocation: Implications of Radical Change?" (2001) 7 Canadian Criminal Law Review 147 at 157–58; Bruce Archibald, "*The General Part of Canadian Criminal Law and Criminal Law Reform*" (unpublished paper) 73 at 93; Don Stuart, *Canadian Criminal Law*, 3rd ed (Toronto: Carswell, 1995) at 475; Jeremy Horder, "Self-Defence, Necessity and Duress: Understanding the Relationship" (1998) 11 Canadian Journal of Law and Jurisprudence 143 at 160; Zoë Sinel, "The Duress Dilemma: Potential Solutions in the Theory of Right" (2005) 10 Appeal: Review of Current Law and Legal Reform 56 at 64; Hamish Stewart, "The Constitution and the Right of Self-Defence" (2011) 61 University of Toronto Law Journal 899; Alan Brudner, "Constitutionalizing Self-Defence" (2011) 61 University of Toronto Law Journal 867; Colton Fehr, "(Re-)Constitutionalizing Duress and Necessity" (2017) 42 Queen's Law Journal 99; and Colton Fehr, "Self-Defence and the Constitution" (2017) 43 Queen's Law Journal 85.
12 See *Bedford*, *supra* note 1 at para 86.
13 *Supra* note 5.
14 *Ibid* at para 29, citing Fletcher, *Rethinking Criminal Law*, *supra* note 5.
15 See *Bedford*, *supra* note 1 at para 86.
16 See *Ruzic*, *supra* note 5 at paras 29–30, citing *Perka v The Queen*, [1984] 2 SCR 232, 13 DLR (4th) 1; and *R v Hibbert*, [1995] 2 SCR 973, 99 CCC (3d) 193.
17 See, generally, *Perka*, *supra* note 16; and *R v Latimer*, 2001 SCC 1, [2001] 1 SCR 3.
18 By any "external threat," I mean to exclude threats deriving from the victim, which obviously implicate the defence of self-defence.

19 See *Ryan, supra* note 10 at para 17.

20 Despite having similar juristic foundations, the duress and necessity defences have different elements. For a persuasive criticism of the differences between duress and necessity, see Stanley Yeo, "Revisiting Necessity" (2010) 56 Criminal Law Quarterly 13.

21 See *Ruzic, supra* note 5 at para 29.

22 Although the court in *Ryan, supra* note 10 at para 55, concluded that "bodily harm" – defined as harm that is not "transient" or "trivial" – might form the basis for a moral involuntariness claim, it is difficult to see how such a low-level threat could deprive a person of their will. See Fehr, "Duress and Necessity," *supra* note 11 at 121.

23 See *Ruzic, supra* note 5 at para 90. Although imminence is a requirement in the necessity defence – see *Latimer, supra* note 17 at para 28 – requiring imminence for a duress claim might well be a death sentence for sex workers given the unique context of the threats that they face. As such, imminence is not a reasonable requirement to impose.

24 See *Ruzic, supra* note 5 at para 61. See also *Ryan, supra* note 10 at para 47.

25 See *Ryan, supra* note 10 at para 72. The court refers to this requirement as the nonutilitarian or "societal expectation" aspect of the proportionality requirement that it claims is "inherent" to the moral involuntariness principle. Although some maintain that this aspect of proportionality has no place within the moral involuntariness principle, I maintain that it serves a useful screening function for unpalatable emotions that ought not to form the basis of a defence. See Fehr, "Duress and Necessity," *supra* note 11, responding to Benjamin Berger, "Emotions and the Veil of Voluntarism: The Loss of Judgment in Canadian Criminal Defences" (2006) 51 McGill Law Journal 99; and Terry Skolnik, "Three Problems with Duress and Moral Involuntariness" (2016) 63 Criminal Law Quarterly 124.

26 See Fehr, "Duress and Necessity," *supra* note 11 at 109. In so doing, I respond in detail to a variety of other academic proposals in the literature, most notable of which are Stanley Yeo, "Challenging Moral Involuntariness as a Principle of Fundamental Justice" (2003) 28 Queen's Law Journal 335; Berger, "Veil of Voluntarism," *supra* note 25; Skolnik, "Three Problems," *supra* note 25; and Coughlan, "Implications of Radical Change?," *supra* note 11.

27 See Fehr, "Duress and Necessity," *supra* note 11 at 109, citing Coughlan, "Implications of Radical Change?," *supra* note 11 at 158, citing Bruce Archibald, Don Stuart, and Jeremy Horder, among other scholars, for a similar proposition.

28 See *Bedford, supra* note 1 at para 64.

29 At least this is true in the context of duress. See *Ryan, supra* note 10 at paras 48–52. See also the explanation that I offer, *supra* note 23, for why a temporal connection is all that is needed to support a moral involuntariness claim in the sex work context.

30 See *Bedford, supra* note 1 at para 66 (noting that street sex workers face an "alarming amount of violence").

31 *Ibid* at para 86.

32 It is notable that the federal government recently provided $20 million to help sex workers leave the trade after passing its reply law to *Bedford*. See Department of Justice Canada and Public Safety Canada, "Government of Canada Announces $20 Million to Help Victims Leave Prostitution," News Release (1 December 2014), online: <www.canada.ca/en/news/archive/2014/12/government-canada-announces-20-million-help-victims-leave-prostitution.html>.

33 See, e.g., Teela Sanders, "Becoming an Ex-Sex Worker: Making Transitions out of a Deviant Career" (2007) 2 Feminist Criminology 74; and Liz Kelly, Maddy Coy, and Rebecca Davenport, *Shifting Sands: A Comparison of Prostitution Regimes across Nine Countries* (London: London Metropolitan University, 2008) at 43–45.

34 See *Bedford, supra* note 1 at para 86.

35 *Ibid*.

36 See Monica O'Connor, "Choice, Agency, Consent and Coercion: Complex Issues in the Lives of Prostituted and Trafficked Women" (2017) 62 Women's Studies International Forum 8 at 8–9, citing Liz Kelly, "The Wrong Debate: Reflections on Why Force Is Not the Key Issue with Respect to Trafficking in Women for Sexual Exploitation" (2003) 73 Feminist Review 139; Janice Raymond, *Not a Choice, Not a Job: Exposing the Myths about Prostitution and the Global Sex Trade* (Sterling, VA: Potomac Books, 2013); and Jackie Turner, "Means of Delivery: The Trafficking of Women into Prostitution, Harms and Human Rights Discourse" in Maddy Coy, ed, *Prostitution, Harm and Gender Inequality: Theory, Research and Policy* (Farnham, UK: Ashgate, 2013) 33.

37 See O'Connor, "Choice," *supra* note 36 at 9.

38 *Ibid*, citing Melissa Ditmore, "Trafficking in Lives: How Ideology Shapes Policy" in Kamala Kempadoo, Jyoti Sanghera, and Bandana Pattanaik, eds, *Trafficking and Prostitution Reconsidered: New Perspectives on Migration, Sex Work and Human Rights* (Boulder, CO: Paradigm, 2005) 107; Kamala Kempadoo, "From Moral Panic to Global Justice: Changing Perspectives on Trafficking" in Kamala Kempadoo, Jyoti Sanghera, and Bandana Pattanaik, eds, *Trafficking and Prostitution Reconsidered: New Perspectives on Migration, Sex Work and Human Rights* (Boulder, CO: Paradigm, 2005) vii; Ronald Weitzer and Melissa Ditmore, "Sex Trafficking: Facts and Fictions" in Ronald Weitzer, ed, *Sex for Sale: Prostitution, Pornography and the Sex Industry* (New York: Routledge, 2010) 325.

39 See O'Connor, "Choice," *supra* note 36 at 9.

40 See Sanders, "Transitions," *supra* note 33 at 76.

41 See Jade Bilardi et al, "The Job Satisfaction of Female Sex Workers Working in Licenced Brothels in Victoria, Australia" (2011) 8 Journal of Sexual Medicine 116 at 119; J. Groves et al, "Sex Workers Working within a Legalized Industry: Their Side of the Story" (2008) 84 Sexually Transmitted Infections 393 at 394; Teela Sanders, "A Continuum of Risk? The Management of Health, Physical and Emotional Risks by Female Sex Workers" (2004) 26 Sociology of Health and Illness 557 at 561; and Cecilia Benoit and Alison Millar, *Dispelling Myths and Understanding Realities: Working Conditions, Health Status, and Exiting Experiences of Sex Workers* (Victoria: University of Victoria Press, 2001) at 22.

42 See Helga Hallgrimsdóttir et al, "Fallen Women and Rescued Girls: Social Stigma and Media Narratives of the Sex Industry in Victoria, B.C., from 1980–2005" (2006) 43 Canadian Review of Sociology 265 at 276.

43 See Leslie Jeffrey and Gayle MacDonald, "It's the Money Honey: The Economy of Sex Work in the Maritimes" (2006) 43 Canadian Review of Sociology and Anthropology 313 at 317–18.

44 See Bilardi et al, "Licenced Brothels," *supra* note 41 at 119.

45 See Marina McKeganey and Neil Barnard, *Sex Work on the Streets: Prostitutes and Their Clients* (Buckingham: Open University Press, 1996) at 26–27; Groves et al, "Legalized Industry," *supra* note 41 at 393; and Chris Bruckert et al, *Erotic Service/Erotic Dance Establishments: Two Types of Marginalized Labour* (Ottawa: Ottawa University Press, 2003) at 22–23.

46 See Melissa Petro, "Selling Sex: Women's Participation in the Sex Industry" in Melissa Ditmore, Antonia Levy, and Alys Willman, eds, *Sex Work Matters: Exploring Money, Power and Intimacy in the Sex Work Industry* (New York: Zed Books, 2010) 155 at 157; Benoit and Millar, *Dispelling Myths, supra* note 41 at 36–37; and Groves et al, "Legalized Industry," *supra* note 41 at 393.

47 See Bruckert et al, *Erotic Service, supra* note 45 at 22–23.

48 See Groves et al, "Legalized Industry," *supra* note 41 at 393–94.

49 See Bruckert et al, *Erotic Service, supra* note 45 at 22.

50 See Angela Campbell, *Sister Wives, Surrogates, and Sex Workers: Outlaws by Choice?* (London: Ashgate, 2013) at 151.

51 See Nikki Jeal et al, "The Multiplicity and Interdependency of Factors Influencing the Health of Street-Based Sex Workers: A Qualitative Study" (2008) 84 Sexually Transmitted Infections 381; and Judith Porter and Louis Bonilla, "The Ecology of Street Prostitution" in Ronald Weitzer, ed, *Sex for Sale: Prostitution, Pornography and the Sex Work Industry,* 2nd ed (New York: Routledge, 2010) 163 at 164.

52 See Linda Cusick and Matthew Hickman, "'Trapping' in Drug Use and Sex Work Careers" (2005) 12 Drugs Education, Prevention and Policy 369;

and Michael Gossop et al, "Sexual Behaviour and Its Relationship to Drug-Taking among Prostitutes in South London" (1994) 89 Addiction 961 at 967.

53 See Pivot Legal Society Sex Work Subcommittee, *Voices for Dignity: A Call to End the Harms Caused by Canada's Sex Work Laws* (Vancouver: Pivot Legal Society, 2004) at 22.

54 See Campbell, *Sister Wives, supra* note 50 at 150.

55 As outlined in Chapter 3, fines are most common for these types of sex workers.

56 See *Bedford v Canada*, 2010 ONSC 4264 at para 152, 327 DLR (4th) 52.

57 The Manitoba Court of Appeal contests whether murder can ever be committed in a morally involuntary manner. See *R v Willis*, 2016 MBCA 113, 344 CCC (3d) 443. For a rebuttal, see *R v Aravena*, 2015 ONCA 250, 323 CCC (3d) 54; and Colton Fehr, "The Constitutionality of Excluding Duress as a Defence to Murder" (2021) 44 Manitoba Law Journal 111.

58 See Campbell, *Sister Wives, supra* note 50 at 176.

59 *Ibid*.

60 I thank Terry Skolnik for raising this point.

61 One of the reviewers of the manuscript for this book took this approach. I thank this reviewer for comments that pushed me to think more deeply about the implications of relying on the law of criminal defences to weed out bad charges in the sex work context.

62 See *Bedford, supra* note 1 at para 75.

63 *Ibid* at para 76, citing *R v Khadr*, 2010 SCC 3 at para 21, [2010] 1 SCR 44.

64 *Ibid*.

65 See *Bedford, supra* note 1 at para 78.

66 *Ibid* at para 79.

67 *Ibid* at para 136. As mentioned in Chapter 1, I challenge this assumption in Chapter 9.

68 *Ibid* at para 80.

69 *Ibid* at paras 81–82. The court's previous jurisprudence determined that "lifestyle choices" do not engage the threshold section 7 interests. See *R v Malmo-Levine*, 2003 SCC 74 at para 86, [2003] 3 SCR 571.

70 See *Bedford, supra* note 1 at para 84.

71 *Ibid* at para 88.

72 *Ibid*.

73 *Ibid* at para 89.

74 *Ibid* at para 86.

75 *Ibid* at para 87.

76 *Ibid*.

77 Some have argued that the "moral" purpose underlying such a law is outside the boundaries of the criminal law, an argument that I expand upon in

Chapter 9. See, e.g., Sandra Ka Hon Chu and Rebecca Glass, "Sex Work Law Reform in Canada: Considering Problems with the Nordic Model" (2013) 51 Alberta Law Review 101 at 111–13. Writing in the context of Parliament's most recent decision to adopt the Nordic model of sex work regulation, Hamish Stewart notes that "[t]here is no support in the case law for the proposition that a moral purpose of this kind is constitutionally improper: indeed, the Supreme Court of Canada has stated the opposite." See Hamish Stewart, "The Constitutionality of the New Sex Work Law" (2016) 54 Alberta Law Review 69 at 85, citing *R v Butler*, [1992] 1 SCR 452 at 493, 89 DLR (4th) 449; and *Malmo-Levine, supra* note 68 at para 77. Similarly, see *Bedford, supra* note 56 at para 225; and *Bedford, supra* note 1 at para 136.

78 See *M v H, supra* note 9 at 70.
79 See *Reference re ss 193 and 195.1(1)(C) of the Criminal Code (Man.)*, [1990] 1 SCR 1123 at paras 92, 96, 56, CCC (3d) 65 [*Sex Work Reference*].
80 See Chapter 1.
81 I explained this argument in Chapter 5.
82 See *Bedford, supra* note 56 at para 152.
83 *Supra* note 68.
84 *Ibid* at para 177.
85 *Ibid*.
86 *Ibid* at para 178.
87 See *Bedford, supra* note 56 at para 152. Although operating a bawdy house typically resulted in stronger punishments, the sex work laws were not considered unconstitutional because of their effects on those operating a bawdy house.
88 See *Reference re Section 94(2) of the Motor Vehicle Act (British Columbia)*, [1985] 2 SCR 486 at 518, 531, 24 DLR (4th) 536.
89 *Ibid* at 518.
90 See *Bedford, supra* note 1 at para 162.
91 *Ibid* at para 129.
92 This conclusion is bolstered by the fact that the Supreme Court found neither law arbitrary. See *ibid* at paras 133–36, 148–59.
93 See *Alberta v Hutterian Brethren of Wilson Colony*, 2009 SCC 37 at para 48, [2009] 2 SCR 567.
94 *Ibid* at para 54, citing *RJR-MacDonald Inc v Canada (Attorney General)*, [1995] 3 SCR 199 at para 160, 127 DLR (4th) 1.
95 *Ibid*.
96 [1986] 1 SCR 103, 26 DLR (4th) 200.
97 *Ibid* at 140.
98 See Colton Fehr, "Instrumental Rationality and General Deterrence" (2019) 57 Alberta Law Review 53 at 54 (footnote 6), citing various sources.
99 *Ibid*.

100 Although Justice McLachlin (as she then was) suggested that this was the case in *R v Downey*, [1992] 2 SCR 10 at paras 78–80, 86–89, 90 DLR (4th) 449, she arrived at that conclusion in the context of determining whether the law's infringement of the presumption of innocence was rationally connected to its objective. Although a similar rationale might apply in the context of a section 7 challenge, McLachlin was writing for herself and one other member of the Supreme Court in *Downey*. Her refusal to rely on this argument in *Bedford* suggests that she abandoned this rationale.

101 See *Bedford*, *supra* note 1 at para 165. Although the Supreme Court's statement is the reverse of my argument, I see no reason why the principle ought not to apply in the same way.

102 *Ibid* at para 162.

103 *Supra* note 100.

104 See *Bedford*, *supra* note 1 at para 162.

105 *Ibid* at para 165.

106 See Janine Benedet, "*Bedford*: The Pimping Offence Should Have Been Upheld" (2014) 7 Criminal Reports (7th) 57 at 57–58.

107 *Ibid*.

108 See *Bedford*, *supra* note 1 at para 165.

CHAPTER 8: THE CONSTITUTIONALITY OF THE NEW SEX WORK LAWS

1 SC 2014, c 25 [*PCEPA*].

2 See Susana Mas, "Prostitution Law Comes into Force on Day of Action on Violence against Women," *CBC News* (5 December 2014), online: <https://www.cbc.ca/news/politics/prostitution-law-comes-into-force-on-day-of-action-on-violence-against-women-1.2862602>.

3 *Ibid*.

4 *Ibid*.

5 See Department of Justice, "Online Public Consultation on Prostitution-Related Offences in Canada – Final Results" (Department of Justice, 2014) online: <https://www.justice.gc.ca/eng/rp-pr/other-autre/rr14_09/p1.html> at 3 ("[w]hen asked whether purchasing sexual services should be a criminal offence, 56% of respondents said 'yes,' while 44% of respondents said 'no'").

6 See John Lowman and Christine Louie, "Public Opinion on Prostitution Law Reform in Canada" (2012) 54 Canadian Journal of Criminology and Criminal Justice 245 at 256, reporting results from studies conducted in 2009, 2010, and 2011. As the authors note at 254, support varied from 9% to 13% among women.

7 It is notable that Lowman and Louie, "Public Opinion," *supra* note 6, was written in 2012 before the *PCEPA*, *supra* note 1, was passed.

8 See Ella Bedard, "The Failures of Canada's New Sex Work Legislation," *Rank and File* (7 April 2015), online: <http://rankandfile.ca/the-failures-of-canadas-new-sex-work-legislation/>. See also Mike Blanchfield, "Supreme Court Strikes Down Canada's Anti-Prostitution Laws as *Charter* Breach," *Global News* (20 December 2013), online: <https://globalnews.ca/news/1042861/supreme-court-strikes-down-canadas-anti-prostitution-laws/>.

9 See Chris Bruckert, "*Protection of Communities and Exploited Persons Act*: Misogynistic Law Making in Action" (2015) 30 Canadian Journal of Law and Society 1 at 1–3; Leah Horlick, "Bill C-36: Two Steps Back" (2014) 48 Canadian Dimension 11; Natalie Snow et al, "The Right to Life, Liberty and Security for Prostitution: *Canada v. Bedford*" (2020) Women and Criminal Justice 1; Paula Simons, "Proposed Bill 'Is Going to Be a Disaster'; New Law Would Make Sex World More Dangerous," *Edmonton Journal* (7 June 2014); Michael Den Tandt, "Tories Make a Hash of New Prostitution Bill: Bill C-36 Can Only Put Sex Workers at Greater Risk," *Gazette* [Montreal] (6 June 2014); Andrew Coyne, "We Once Had to Wait Weeks for a New Harper Abuse of Power: Now We're Getting Them Two or Three Times a Day," *National Post* (6 June 2014), online: <https://nationalpost.com/opinion/andrew-coyne-we-once-had-to-wait-weeks-for-a-new-harper-abuse-of-power-now-were-getting-them-two-or-three-a-day>; and John Ivison, "MacKay's Weak Defence of His Prostitution Law Implies It Won't Survive the Courts," *National Post* (7 July 2014), online: <http://news.nationalpost.com/full-comment/john-ivison-mackays-weak-defence-of-his-prostitution-law-implies-it-wont-survive-the-courts>.

10 See Sex Workers United against Violence, "My Work Should Not Cost Me My Life: The Case against Criminalizing the Purchase of Sex in Canada" (Pivot Legal Society, 2014), online: <https://d3n8a8pro7vhmx.cloudfront.net/pivotlegal/pages/615/attachments/original/1401811234/My_Work_Should_Not_Cost_Me_My_Life.pdf?1401811234>; and "Legal Experts Oppose Bill C-36," *Herizons* [Winnipeg] (22 September 2014) 13.

11 See, e.g., Phoebe Galbally, "Playing the Victim: A Critical Analysis of Canada's Bill C-36 from an International Human Rights Perspective" (2016) 17 Melbourne Journal of International Law 35 at 67–68; Lauren Sampson, "'The Obscenities of This Country': *Canada v. Bedford* and the Reform of Canadian Prostitution Laws" (2014) 22 Duke Journal of Gender Law and Policy 137; Angela Campbell, "Sex Work's Governance: Stuff and Nuisance" (2015) 23 Feminist Legal Studies 27; Andrea Sterling, "'We Are Not Criminals': Sex Work Clients in Canada and the Constitution of Risk Knowledge" (2018) 33 Canadian Journal of Law and Society 291; Erica Kunimoto, "A Critical Analysis of Canada's Sex Work Legislation: Exploring Gendered and Racialized Consequences" (2018) 10 Stream: Interdisciplinary Journal of Communication 27; Natalie Snow, Mollee Steely, and Tusty ten Bensel, "The Right to Life, Liberty and Security for Prostitution: *Canada*

v. Bedford" (2020) Women and Criminal Justice 1; and Anna-Louise Crago et al, "Sex Workers' Access to Police Assistance in Safety Emergencies and Means of Escape from Situations of Violence and Confinement under an 'End Demand' Criminalization Model: A Five City Study in Canada" (2021) 10 Social Sciences 13.

12 See Benjamin Perrin, "Oldest Profession or Oldest Oppression? Addressing Prostitution after the Supreme Court of Canada Decision in *Canada v. Bedford*" (Ottawa: Macdonald-Laurier Institute Commentary Series, 2014). Carissima Mathen has also suggested that the Nordic model will be upheld under a Charter challenge. See Leslie MacKinnon, "Prostitution Law Changes Have Chance of Surviving Court Challenge," *CBC News* (10 June 2014), online: <https://www.cbc.ca/news/politics/prostitution-law-changes-have-chance-of-surviving-court-challenge-1.2669996>.

13 See Chapter 4.
14 RSC 1985, c C-46.
15 *Ibid*, s 787.
16 *Ibid*, s 21.
17 *Ibid*, ss 286.1(a–b).
18 *Ibid*, ss 286.2(5)(a–d).
19 *Ibid*, s 286.2(5)(e).
20 *Ibid*, s 286.2(1), 787.
21 See *R v Anwar*, 2020 ONCJ 103 at para 134, 62 CR (7th) 402.
22 See *R v Gallone*, 2019 ONCA 663 at para 61, 147 OR (3d) 225, citing *R v Deutsch*, [1986] 2 SCR 2 at 26–27, 30 DLR (4th) 435.
23 See *Gallone*, *supra* note 22 at para 47.
24 *Ibid* at para 86.
25 See Hamish Stewart, "The Constitutionality of the New Sex Work Law" (2016) 54 Alberta Law Review 69 at 71, 88.
26 See Campbell, "Stuff and Nuisance," *supra* note 11 at 29. See also Manpreet Abrol, "The Criminalization of Prostitution: Putting Women's Lives at Risk" (2014) 3 Journal of Historical Studies 1.
27 See Debra Haak, "The Initial Test of Constitutional Validity: Identifying the Legislative Objectives of Canada's New Prostitution Laws" (2017) 50 University of British Columbia Law Review 657 at 661, 672–77.
28 See *R v Safarzadeh-Markhali*, 2016 SCC 14 at para 26, [2016] 1 SCR 180.
29 *Ibid* at para 27.
30 *Ibid* at paras 26, 28.
31 *Ibid* at para 29.
32 *Ibid* at para 31.
33 *Ibid*.
34 *Ibid*.

35 See *R v Moriarity*, 2015 SCC 55 at para 32, [2015] 3 SCR 485.
36 See Canada, *House of Commons Debates*, 41st Parl, 2nd Sess, Vol 147, No 102 (12 June 2014) at 1150. See also Canada, *Debates of the Senate*, 41st Parl, 2nd Sess, Vol 149, No 86 (9 October 2014) at 1430–40.
37 See *House of Commons Debates*, No 102, *supra* note 36 at 1150.
38 See *Ibid* at 1700.
39 See Haak, "Legislative Objectives," *supra* note 27 at 685–86, 692.
40 See Department of Justice, *Technical Paper: Bill C-36, Protection of Communities and Exploited Persons Act* (Ottawa: Department of Justice, 2014) at 3.
41 *Ibid* at 6.
42 *Ibid*.
43 *Ibid* at 6, 8.
44 *Ibid* at 10.
45 See Haak, "Legislative Objectives," *supra* note 27 at 683.
46 See Department of Justice, *Technical Paper*, *supra* note 40 at 10–12.
47 See Haak, "Legislative Objectives," *supra* note 27 at 689.
48 2021 MBCA 101.
49 *Ibid* at para 14.
50 2022 ONCA 160.
51 *Ibid* at para 59.
52 *Ibid* (emphasis added).
53 *Ibid* (emphasis added).
54 See Haak, "Legislative Objectives," *supra* note 27 at 689.
55 See Chapter 5.
56 2021 ONSC 1628.
57 *Ibid* at para 145.
58 See *NS, supra* note 50 at paras 127–31.
59 See Stewart, "Sex Work," *supra* note 25 at 81. Although he makes this point in the context of the bawdy house law, it seems to apply with equal force to the communication law.
60 See James Gacek and Richard Jochelson, "Sex Work in Canada: Beginnings, *Bedford*, and Beyond" in Richard Jochelson and James Gacek, eds, *Sexual Regulation and the Law: A Canadian Perspective* (Bradford, ON: Demers Press, 2019) 57 at 78–79, citing various other sociolegal scholars with similar opinions.
61 See Haak, "Legislative Objectives," *supra* note 27 at 691.
62 See *Alberta v Hutterian Brethren of Wilson Colony*, 2009 SCC 37 at para 54, [2009] 2 SCR 567, citing *RJR-MacDonald Inc v Canada (Attorney General)*, [1995] 3 SCR 199 at para 160, 127 DLR (4th) 1.
63 *Ibid*.
64 See Stewart, "Sex Work," *supra* note 25 at 86, citing among others Campbell, "Stuff and Nuisance," *supra* note 11; and Lisa Dufraimont, "*Canada (Attorney*

General) v. Bedford and the Limits on Substantive Criminal Law under Section 7" (2014) 67 Supreme Court Law Review 483. See also Sylvia Machat et al, "Sex Workers' Experiences and Occupational Conditions Post-Implementation of End-Demand Criminalization in Metro Vancouver, Canada" (2019) 110 Canadian Journal of Public Health 575; Sandra Ka Hon Chu and Rebecca Glass, "Sex Work Law Reform in Canada: Considering Problems with the Nordic Model" (2013) 51 Alberta Law Review 101 at 103–8; Andrea Krüsi et al, "Criminalisation of Clients: Reproducing Vulnerabilities for Violence and Poor Health among Street-Based Sex Workers in Canada – A Qualitative Study" (2014) 4 British Medical Journal Open 1 at 2 ("[i]n an effort to avoid police, sex workers often move to outlying secluded areas to meet and service clients where there are few to no protections from violence and abuse, and reduced ability to refuse unwanted clients or services, including client demands for sex without a condom"), citing in support of this proposition Jerry Okal et al, "Sexual and Physical Violence against Female Sex Workers in Kenya: A Qualitative Inquiry" (2011) 23 AIDS Care 612; Kate Shannon et al, "Social and Structural Violence and Power Relations in Mitigating HIV Risk of Drug-Using Women in Survival Sex Work" (2008) 66 Social Science and Medicine 911; Kate Shannon et al, "Structural and Environmental Barriers to Condom Use Negotiation with Clients among Female Sex Workers: Implications for HIV-Prevention Strategies and Policy" (2009) 99 American Journal of Public Health 659; Lisa Maher et al, "Selling Sex in Unsafe Spaces: Sex Work Risk Environments in Phnom Penh, Cambodia" (2011) 8 Harm Reduction Journal 30; and Andrea Krüsi et al, "Negotiating Safety and Sexual Risk Reduction with Clients in Unsanctioned Safer Indoor Sex Work Environments: A Qualitative Study" (2012) 102 American Journal of Public Health 1154.

65 See Ka Hon Chu and Glass, "Sex Work Law Reform," *supra* note 64 at 106.

66 *Ibid* at 106–8, citing various sources.

67 *Ibid* at 107, citing Daniela Danna, "Client-Only Criminalization in the City of Stockholm: A Local Research on the Application of the 'Swedish Model' of Prostitution Policy" (2012) 9 Sexuality Research and Social Policy 80; *Legislation on the Purchase of Sexual Services* (Stockholm: Ministry of Education and Research, 2009), online: <http://www.government.se/sb/d/4096/a/119861>.

68 It is notable that even some supporters of the new sex work laws concede as much. See, e.g., Haak, "Legislative Objectives," *supra* note 27 at 690.

69 See *Bedford, supra* note 1 at para 125.

70 See Stewart, "Sex Work," *supra* note 25 at 82–84; Colton Fehr, "Rethinking the Instrumental Rationality Principles of Fundamental Justice" (2020) 58 Alberta Law Review 133; and Colton Fehr, "The 'Individualistic' Approach to Arbitrariness, Overbreadth, and Gross Disproportionality" (2018) 51 University of British Columbia Law Review 55.

71 See *PCEPA, supra* note 1, preamble.

72 See Perrin, "Oldest Profession," *supra* note 12.

73 See Dana Levy, "Israel Becomes the 8th Nordic Model Country as It Implements Its Prohibition of Consumption of Prostitution Services Act," *Nordic Model Now* (29 June 2020), online: <https://nordicmodelnow.org/2020/06/29/israel-becomes-the-8th-nordic-model-country-as-it-implements-its-prohibition-of-consumption-of-prostitution-services-act/>.

74 See *Bedford v Canada*, 2010 ONSC 4264 at para 207, 102 OR (3d) 321.

75 *Ibid.*

76 See Benjamin Perrin, *Invisible Chains: Canada's Underground World of Human Trafficking* (Toronto: Viking Canada, 2010) at 216.

77 *Ibid.*

78 See *Bedford, supra* note 74 at para 208.

79 See Perrin, "Oldest Profession," *supra* note 12 at 10–13.

80 *Ibid* at 14.

81 See *Bedford, supra* note 74 at para 187.

82 *Ibid* at para 204.

83 *Ibid* at para 196.

84 *Ibid* at para 201.

85 See Perrin, "Oldest Profession," *supra* note 12 at 14.

86 *Ibid.*

87 For more extensive reviews, readers should view the work of Melissa Farley (abolitionist) and Ronald Weitzer (decriminalization supporter). Obviously, many others have written in this field, but these two authors are widely considered to be leading scholars in it.

88 See Chapter 4.

89 In litigating the constitutionality of the sex work laws, scholars have shown that the harms to sex workers and to the public more generally are difficult to isolate and quantify. For an excellent review, see Debra Haak, "Re(de)fining Prostitution and Sex Work: Conceptual Clarity for Legal Thinking" (2019) 40 Windsor Review of Legal and Social Issues 67 at 76, citing Isabel Crowhurst, "Troubling Unknowns and Certainties in Prostitution Policy Claims-Making" in Marlene Spanger and May-Len Skilbrei, eds, *Prostitution Research in Context: Methodology, Representation and Power* (New York: Routledge, 2017) 47; and Hayli Millar, Tamara O'Doherty, and Katrin Roots, "A Formidable Task: Reflections on Obtaining Legal Empirical Evidence on Human Trafficking in Canada" (2017) 8 Anti-Trafficking Review 34.

90 See, e.g., Arend Lijphart, "Comparative Politics and Comparative Method" (1971) 65 American Political Science Review 682; and Luc Turgeon et al, eds, *Comparing Canada: Methods and Perspectives on Canadian Politics* (Vancouver: UBC Press, 2014).

91 *Criminal Code, supra* note 14, s 286.2(5)(e) (emphasis added).
92 See Stewart, "Sex Work," *supra* note 25 at 78.
93 *Ibid.*
94 *Ibid.*
95 *Ibid* at 79.
96 *Ibid* at 78. For a similar argument, see *NS, supra* note 56 at paras 88–113.

97 It is notable that the Ontario Superior Court pithily dismissed an application to strike down the new sex work laws in *R v Boodhoo*, 2018 ONSC 7205, 51 CR (7th) 207. As the court in *Anwar, supra* note 21 at paras 126–27, observed, the constitutional challenge proceeded even though the defence provided minimal evidence of the dangers posed to sex workers by the new sex work laws.

98 *Supra* note 21.
99 *Ibid* at para 200.
100 *Ibid* at para 201.
101 *Ibid* at para 203.
102 See *NS, supra* note 50 at paras 70–84.
103 See *Anwar, supra* note 21 at paras 204–10.
104 *Ibid* at paras 200–10.
105 See *NS, supra* note 56 at para 113.
106 *Ibid.*
107 See *NS, supra* note 50 at paras 70–84.

108 For the exclusion of economic rights from section 7 of the Charter, see, generally, *Gosselin v Québec (Attorney General)*, 2002 SCC 84, [2002] 4 SCR 429.

109 See *Anwar, supra* note 21 at paras 142–54.

110 See *NS, supra* note 56 at para 51. The main difference between the scenarios is that Justice Sutherland accounted for the possibility that the sex workers could also be male.

111 See *Anwar, supra* note 21 at paras 142–52.
112 *Ibid* at paras 153–55.

113 *Ibid* at para 137, citing *Deutsch, supra* note 22 at para 37. For a much narrower construction of the statute, see *NS, supra* note 50 at paras 102–14. Because I think the legislation is constitutional even on the broader interpretation, it is unnecessary to review other competing interpretations that effectively render the hypothetical scenarios irrelevant.

114 See *Anwar, supra* note 21 at para 166.
115 The Crown made a similar argument in *ibid* at paras 156–60.
116 *Ibid.*
117 See *NS, supra* note 50 at paras 99–100.
118 *Ibid* at para 113.

119 *Supra* note 22.

120 *Ibid* at para 98.

121 See *Reference re ss 193 and 195.1(1)(C) of the Criminal Code (Man)*, [1990] 1 SCR 1123 at 1187, 56 CCC (3d) 65 [*Sex Work Reference*].

122 See *Anwar, supra* note 21 at para 130.

123 *Ibid* at para 131.

CHAPTER 9: SEX WORK AND THE CRIMINAL LAW

1 I thank the reviewers for sharing their thoughts in this regard. Their comments pushed me to explain myself more thoroughly since my intention here – stated at the outset of the book – is not to take a side with respect to the regulation of sex work. Instead, my aim is to help Canadian lawmakers decide questions concerning the relationship between Canadian constitutional law and criminal law in a more structured and coherent manner.

2 The content of this chapter draws from personal interviews that I conducted on 7 and 30 July 2021.

3 2003 SCC 74, [2003] 3 SCR 571.

4 RSC 1985, c N-1, ss 3–4. Substantially similar offences were included in the *Controlled Drugs and Substances Act,* SC 1996, c 19, ss 4–5 [*CDSA*]. Marijuana was nevertheless mostly decriminalized with Parliament's adoption of the *Cannabis Act,* SC 2018, c 16.

5 See *Malmo-Levine, supra* note 3 at para 90, citing John Stuart Mill, *On Liberty and Considerations on Representative Government* (Oxford: Basil Blackwell, 1946).

6 See *Malmo-Levine, supra* note 3 at paras 40–62.

7 *Ibid* at paras 110–29.

8 See Patrick Devlin, *The Enforcement of Morals* (Oxford: Oxford University Press, 1965); and H.L.A. Hart, *Law, Liberty, and Morality* (Stanford, CA: Stanford University Press, 1977). The authors debated the Wolfenden Report's recommendation to decriminalize homosexuality. See United Kingdom, House of Commons, "Report of the Committee on Homosexual Offences and Prostitution," Cmnd 247 in *Sessional Papers,* vol 14 (1956–57) 85.

9 See *Malmo-Levine, supra* note 3 at para 238, citing Devlin, *Enforcement of Morals, supra* note 8.

10 See Devlin, *Enforcement of Morals, supra* note 8. For a concise review, see Bernard Harcourt, "The Collapse of the Harm Principle" (1999) 90 Journal of Criminal Law and Criminology 109 at 124–29.

11 See, e.g., Catharine A. MacKinnon, *Only Words* (Cambridge, MA: Harvard University Press, 1993); Catharine A. MacKinnon, *Toward a Feminist Theory of*

the State (Cambridge, MA: Harvard University Press, 1989) (arguing that there are harms in pornography); and George Kelling and James Wilson, "Broken Windows: The Police and Neighbourhood Safety" (1982) *The Atlantic* (identifying disorderly conduct such as loitering, panhandling, and squeegeeing as causing harm because those activities can lead to social disintegration).

12 The court further asserts that the harm principle did not pass a final factor: the principle must be a "legal principle." Since the court did not expand on this argument, I will not discuss it further. See *Malmo-Levine, supra* note 3 at para 114.

13 See *Rodriguez v British Columbia (Attorney General)*, [1993] 3 SCR 519 at 591, 107 DLR (4th) 342.

14 See Kelling and Wilson, "Broken Windows," *supra* note 11.

15 See *Malmo-Levine, supra* note 3 at para 127, citing Harcourt, "Collapse," *supra* note 10 at 113.

16 *Ibid.*

17 See *Malmo-Levine, supra* note 3 at paras 115–26.

18 *Canadian Foundation for Children, Youth and the Law v Canada (Attorney General)*, 2004 SCC 4 at para 8, [2004] 1 SCR 76.

19 *Ibid.*

20 See *Malmo-Levine, supra* note 3 at para 115.

21 *Ibid* at para 117, citing *Criminal Code of Canada*, RSC 1985, c C-46, s 182.

22 *Ibid*, citing *Criminal Code, supra* note 21, s 160.

23 *Ibid*, citing *Criminal Code, supra* note 21, s 155. For a discussion outlining why consensual incest does not result in harm, see Colton Fehr, "Consent and the Constitution" (2019) 42 Manitoba Law Journal 217 at 243–47.

24 See *Malmo-Levine, supra* note 3 at paras 116–22.

25 See Colton Fehr, *Constitutionalizing Criminal Law* (Vancouver: UBC Press, 2022) at 21–25.

26 See Joel Feinberg, *The Moral Limits of the Criminal Law* (Oxford: Oxford University Press, 1984), vol 1, *Harm to Others* at 12; vol 4, *Harmless Wrongdoing* at 323.

27 See Feinberg, *Moral Limits*, vol 4, *supra* note 26 at 323.

28 See Joel Feinberg, *The Moral Limits of the Criminal Law* (Oxford: Oxford University Press, 1985), vol 2, *Offense to Others* at 36.

29 *Ibid* at 26.

30 *Ibid.*

31 *Ibid* at 44.

32 *Ibid.*

33 *Ibid.*

34 *Ibid.*

35   For perhaps the most salient criticism – the offence principle does not require wrongdoing – see Andrew Simester and Andrew von Hirsch, "Rethinking the Offense Principle" (2002) 8 Legal Theory 269.

36   See, e.g., Brian Simpson, *Cannibalism and the Common Law: A Victorian Yachting Tragedy* (Chicago: University of Chicago Press, 1984) (reviewing the history of cannibalism and the legal rationale for its prohibition).

37   For a review of the rationale underlying bestiality legislation, see Brian James Holoyda, "Bestiality Law in the United States: Evolving Legislation with Scientific Limitations" (2022) 12 Animals 1525.

38   For an excellent critique of this and other more "harm-based" rationales, see Vera Bergelson, "Vice Is Nice but Incest Is Best: The Problem of a Moral Taboo" (2013) 7 Criminal Law and Philosophy 43. For my thoughts on how the criticisms related to incest might be constitutionally framed, see Fehr, "Consent," *supra* note 23 at 243–47.

39   (UK), 30 & 31 Vict, c 3, reprinted in RSC 1985, Appendix II, No 5. For a review of the current definition, see *Malmo-Levine, supra* note 3 at para 74 ("[t]he criminal power extends to those laws that are designed to promote public peace, safety, order, health or other legitimate public purpose").

40   See Hamish Stewart, "The Constitutionality of the New Sex Work Law" (2016) 54 Alberta Law Review 69 at 85, citing *R v Butler,* [1992] 1 SCR 452 at 493, 89 DLR (4th) 449; and *Malmo-Levine, supra* note 3 at para 77. See also *Bedford v Canada,* 2010 ONSC 4264 at para 225; and *Canada (Attorney General) v Bedford,* 2013 SCC 72 at para 136, [2013] 3 SCR 1101.

41   Public welfare offences enacted to protect people from themselves – such as the seatbelt and helmet laws cited in *Bedford, supra* note 40 at para 124 – are regulatory in nature, and I take no issue with whether regulatory law can be used to govern sex work.

42   [1985] 2 SCR 486, 24 DLR (4th) 536 [*Motor Vehicle Act Reference*].

43   See George Fletcher, *The Grammar of Criminal Law: American, Comparative, and International,* vol 1 (Oxford: Oxford University Press, 2007) at 101; and Kathleen Harris, "Experts Urge Liberals to Update 'Embarrassingly Bad' *Criminal Code,*" *CBC News* (18 November 2016), online: <https://www.cbc.ca/news/politics/criminal-code-outdated-justice-discrimination-1.3853810>.

44   See Fehr, *Constitutionalizing Criminal Law, supra* note 25.

45   *Ibid.*

CONCLUSION

1   Sonia Lawrence calls this belief a "contemporary reality" in "Expert-Tease: Advocacy, Ideology and Experience in *Bedford* and Bill C-36" (2015) 30 Canadian Journal of Law and Society 5 at 6.

2 See Beverley McLachlin, "Remarks of the Right Honourable Beverley McLachlin, P.C. Chief Justice of Canada," Conference on the Law and Parliament, Ottawa (22 November 2004), online: <https://www.scc-csc.ca/judges-juges/spe-dis/bm-2004-11-22-eng.aspx>.

3 *Ibid.*

4 See Angus Reid Institute, "Canadians Have a More Favourable View of Their Supreme Court Than Americans Have of Their Own" (17 August 2015), online: <http://angusreid.org/supreme-court/>.

5 See Janice Tibbetts, "Building Consensus," *Canadian Lawyer* (July 2013) 24 at 27.

6 See Jamie Cameron, "Law, Politics, and Legacy Building at the McLachlin Court in 2014" (2015) 71 Supreme Court Law Review (2d) 3 at 5.

7 See Tibbetts, "Building Consensus," *supra* note 5 at 28.

8 See David Vitale, "The Value of Dissent in Constitutional Adjudication: A Context-Specific Analysis" (2014) 19 Review of Constitutional Studies 83 at 85–86, citing William Brennand Jr., "In Defense of Dissents" (1986) 37 Hastings Law Journal 427 at 438; Michael Kirby, "Law at Century's End – A Millennial View from the High Court of Australia" (2001) 1 Macquarie Law Journal 1 at 12; Bora Laskin, "The Supreme Court of Canada: A Final Court of and for Canadians" (1951) 29 Canadian Bar Review 1038 at 1048; Andrew Lynch, "Is Judicial Dissent Constitutionally Protected?" (2004) 4 Macquarie Law Journal 81; Rory Little, "Reading Justice Brennan: Is There a 'Right' to Dissent?" (1999) 50 Hastings Law Journal 683; Claire L'Heureux-Dubé, "The Dissenting Opinion: Voice of the Future?" (2000) 38 Osgoode Hall Law Journal 495 at 503; and Antonin Scalia, "The Dissenting Opinion" (1994) 19 Journal of Supreme Court History 33.

9 See John Alder, "Dissents in Courts of Last Resort: Tragic Choices?" (2000) 20 Oxford Journal of Legal Studies 221 at 240.

10 See Carissima Mathen, "The Upside of Dissent in Equality Jurisprudence" (2013) 63 Supreme Court Law Review (2d) 111 at 113.

11 For a review of the literature on this point, see Vitale, "Value of Dissent," *supra* note 8 at 87–91.

12 See Charles Hughes, *The Supreme Court of the United States: Its Foundations, Methods and Achievements, an Interpretation* (New York: Columbia University Press, 1936) at 68.

13 See L'Heureux-Dubé, "Dissenting Opinion," *supra* note 8 at 517.

14 See Vitale, "Value of Dissent," *supra* note 8 at 88, citing Mathen, "Upside of Dissent," *supra* note 10. For the reference to the Constitution as a "living tree," see *Edwards v Canada (Attorney General)*, [1930] AC 124 (PC).

15 See Vitale, "Value of Dissent," *supra* note 8 at 90–91.

16 *Ibid* at 91.

17 See, e.g., Learned Hand, *The Bill of Rights (The Oliver Wendell Holmes Lectures, 1958)* (Cambridge, MA: Harvard University Press, 1958) at 72; Steven Peterson, "Dissent in American Courts" (1981) 43 Journal of Politics 412 at 429–30; and Mark Tushnet, ed., *I Dissent: Great Opposing Opinions in Landmark Supreme Court Cases* (Boston: Beacon Press, 2008) at xiii.

18 See Learned Hand, *Bill of Rights, supra* note 17 at 72.

19 See Vitale, "Value of Dissent," *supra* note 8 at 92, citing Richard Stephens, "The Function of Concurring and Dissenting Opinions in Courts of Last Resort" (1952) 5 University of Florida Law Review 394 at 395–96; and William Douglas, "Stare Decisis" (1949) 49 Columbia Law Review 735 at 754.

20 See Douglas, "Stare Decisis," *supra* note 19 at 754.

21 See Carissima Mathen, "Dissent and Judicial Authority in *Charter* Cases" (2003) 53 University of New Brunswick Law Journal 321 at 332.

22 *Ibid.*

23 See, e.g., Vitale, "Value of Dissent," *supra* note 8 at 93–94, citing Ruth Bader Ginsburg, "The Role of Dissenting Opinions" (2010) 95 Minnesota Law Review 95; Paul J. Wahlbeck, James F. Spriggs II, and Forrest Maltzman, "The Politics of Dissents and Concurrences on the US Supreme Court" (1999) 27 American Politics Quarterly 488 at 507; and Roscoe Pound, "Cacoethes Dissentiendi: The Heated Judicial Dissent" (1953) 39 American Bar Association Journal 794 at 795.

24 See Mathen, "Judicial Authority," *supra* note 21 at 328.

25 For an opinion from the Ontario government upholding the laws, see Allison Jones, "Ontario Review Finds Ottawa's Sex-Work Law Constitutional, Wynne Says," *Globe and Mail* (1 April 2015), online: <www.theglobeandmail.com/news/politics/ontario-review-finds-ottawas-sex-work-law-constitutional-wynne-says/article23734478/>. Unfortunately, the opinion has not been made public. For an argument that the Nordic model is unconstitutional, see Sandra Ka Hon Chu and Rebecca Glass, "Sex Work Law Reform in Canada: Considering Problems with the Nordic Model" (2013) 51 Alberta Law Review 101. For a commentary published shortly after the new sex work laws were passed, see Hamish Stewart, "The Constitutionality of the New Sex Work Law" (2016) 54 Alberta Law Review 69.

Bibliography

JURISPRUDENCE

Canadian

Alberta v Hutterian Brethren of Wilson Colony, 2009 SCC 37, [2009] 2 SCR 567
Bedford v Canada, 2010 ONSC 4264, 102 OR (3d) 321
British Columbia Civil Liberties Association v Canada (Attorney General), 2019 BCCA 228, 377 CCC (3d) 420
Canada (Attorney General) v Bedford, 2012 ONCA 186, 109 OR (3d) 1
Canada (Attorney General) v Bedford, 2013 SCC 72, [2013] 3 SCR 1101
Canada (Attorney General) v Downtown Eastside Sex Workers United against Violence Society 2012 SCC 45, [2012] 2 SCR 524
Canada (Attorney General) v PHS Community Services Society, 2011 SCC 44, [2011] 3 SCR 134
Canada v Pharmaceutical Society (Nova Scotia), [1992] 2 SCR 606, 93 DLR (4th) 36
Canadian Civil Liberties Association v Canada (Attorney General), 2019 ONCA 243, 144 OR (3d) 641
Canadian Foundation for Children, Youth and the Law v Canada (Attorney General), 2004 SCC 4, [2004] 1 SCR 76
Carter v Canada (Attorney General), 2015 SCC 5, [2015] 1 SCR 331
Carter v Canada (Attorney General), 2016 SCC 4, [2016] 1 SCR 13
Chaoulli v Quebec (Attorney General), 2005 SCC 35, [2005] 1 SCR 791
Clark v Hagar (1894), 22 SCR 510
Corbiere v Canada (Minister of Indian and Northern Affairs), [1999] 2 SCR 203, 173 DLR (4th) 1
David Polowin Real Estate v Dominion of Canada General Insurance Co (2005), 255 DLR (4th) 633, 76 OR (3d) 161 (ONCA)
Edwards v Canada (Attorney General), [1930] AC 124 (PC)
Gosselin v Quebec (Attorney General), 2002 SCC 84, [2002] 4 SCR 429
Harper v Canada, 2004 SCC 33, [2004] 1 SCR 827

Housen v Nikolaisen, 2002 SCC 33, [2002] 2 SCR 235
Irwin Toy v Quebec (Attorney General), [1989] 1 SCR 927, 58 DLR (4th) 577
M v H, [1999] 2 SCR 3, 171 DLR (4th) 577
Ontario (Attorney General) v G, 2020 SCC 38, 451 DLR (4th) 541
Perka v The Queen, [1984] 2 SCR 232, 13 DLR (4th) 1
R c Labaye, 2005 SCC 80, [2005] 3 SCR 728
R c Lemieux (1991), 70 CCC (3d) 434, 11 CR (4th) 224 (QBCA)
Re BC Motor Vehicle Act, [1985] 2 SCR 486, 24 DLR (4th) 536
Reference re Anti-Inflation Act, [1976] 2 SCR 373, 68 DLR (3d) 452
Reference re Remuneration of Judges of the Prov Court of PEI; Reference re Independence and Impartiality of Judges of the Prov Court of PEI, [1997] 3 SCR 3, 150 DLR (4th) 577
Reference re Residential Tenancies Act (Ontario), [1981] 1 SCR 714, 123 DLR (3d) 554
Reference re Secession of Quebec, [1998] 2 SCR 217, 161 LR (4th) 385
Reference re Section 293 of the Criminal Code of Canada, 2011 BCSC 1588, 279 CCC (3d) 1
Reference re ss 193 and 195.1(1)(C) of the Criminal Code (1987), 38 CCC (3d) 408, 49 Man R (2d) 1
Reference re ss 193 and 195.1(1)(C) of the Criminal Code (Man), [1990] 1 SCR 1123, 56 CCC (3d) 65
Re Manitoba Language Rights, [1985] 1 SCR 721, 19 DLR (4th) 1
RJR-Macdonald Inc v Canada (Attorney General), [1995] 3 SCR 199, 127 DLR (4th) 1
Rodriguez v British Columbia (Attorney General), [1993] 3 SCR 519, 107 DLR (4th) 342
R v AB, 2015 ONCA 803, 333 CCC (3d) 382
R v Abbey, 2009 ONCA 624, 97 OR (3d) 330
R v Alcorn, 2021 MBCA 101
R v Anwar, 2020 ONCJ 103, 62 CR (7th) 402
R v Aravena, 2015 ONCA 250, 323 CCC (3d) 54
R v Barrow (2001), 54 OR (3d) 417, 155 CCC (3d) 362 (ONCA)
R v Barrow, [2001] SCCA No 431
R v Bedford (2000), 184 DLR (4th) 727, 143 CCC (3d) 311 (ONCA)
R v Belnavis, [1997] 3 SCR 341, 151 DLR (4th) 443
R v Blais, 2008 BCCA 389, 85 BCLR (4th) 1
R v Boodhoo, 2018 ONSC 7205, 51 CR (7th) 207
R v Boudreault, 2018 SCC 58, [2018] 3 SCR 599
R v Brodie, [1962] SCR 681, 32 DLR (2d) 507
R v Brown, 2022 SCC 18
R v Buhay, 2003 SCC 30, [2003] 1 SCR 631

R v Butler, [1992] 1 SCR 452, 89 DLR (4th) 449
R v Clark, (1883) 2 OR 523 (ONQB)
R v Clay, 2003 SCC 75, [2003] 3 SCR 735
R v Corbeil, [1991] 1 SCR 830, 64 CCC (3d) 272
R v Cunningham (1986), 31 CCC (3d) 223 (MBPC)
R v Daviault, [1994] 3 SCR 63, 118 DLR (4th) 469
R v DD, 2000 SCC 43, [2000] 2 SCR 275
R v Deutsch, [1986] 2 SCR 2, 30 DLR (4th) 435
R v DiGiuseppe (2002), 161 CCC (3d) 424, 155 OAC 62 (ONCA)
R v Dominion News and Gifts (1962), [1964] SCR 251, [1964] 3 CCC 1
R v Downey, [1992] 2 SCR 10, 90 DLR (4th) 449
R v Edwards Books & Arts, [1986] 2 SCR 713, 35 DLR (4th) 1
R v Gallone, 2019 ONCA 663, 147 OR (3d) 225
R v Gareau, (1891) 1 CCC 66 (QBCA)
R v Grilo (1991), 64 CCC (3d) 53, 2 OR (3d) 514 (ONCA)
R v Hamilton (unreported)
R v Hayes, [1998] BC No 2752, 115 BCAC 22 (BCCA)
R v Head (1987), 36 CCC (3d) 562, 59 CR (3d) 80 (BCCA)
R v Heywood, [1994] 3 SCR 761, 120 DLR (4th) 348
R v Hibbert, [1995] 2 SCR 973, 99 CCC (3d) 193
R v Hicklin (1868), LR 3 QB 360
R v Hutt, [1978] 2 SCR 476, 82 DLR (3d) 95
R v Keegstra, [1990] 3 SCR 697, 61 CCC (3d) 1
R v Khadr, 2010 SCC 3, [2010] 1 SCR 44
R v Khawaja, 2012 SCC 69, [2012] 3 SCR 555
R v Khill, 2021 SCC 37
R v Latimer, 2001 SCC 1, [2001] 1 SCR 3
R v Lawrence, 2002 ABPC 189, 332 AR 188
R v Levesque, (1870) 30 UCQBR 509
R v Malmo-Levine, 2003 SCC 74, [2003] 3 SCR 571
R v Michaud, 2015 ONCA 585, 127 OR (3d) 81
R v Michaud, leave to appeal to SCC refused, 36706 (5 May 2016)
R v Morales, [1992] 3 SCR 711, 77 CCC (3d) 91
R v Morgentaler, [1988] 2 SCR 3, 51 DLR (4th) 481
R v Moriarity, 2015 SCC 55, [2015] 3 SCR 485
R v NS, 2021 ONSC 1628
R v NS, 2022 ONCA 160
R v Oakes, [1986] 1 SCR 103, 26 DLR (4th) 200
R v Patterson, [1968] SCR 157, 67 DLR (2d) 82
R v Pickton, 2006 BCSC 1090, 260 CCC (3d) 185
R v Pickton, 2007 BCSC 2039, [2007] BCJ No 3109

R v Preston (1990), 47 BCLR (2d) 273, 79 CR (3d) 61 (BCCA)
R v Remon, (1888) 16 OR 560 (ONQB)
R v Ruzic, 2001 SCC 24, [2001] 1 SCR 687
R v Ryan, 2013 SCC 3, [2013] 1 SCR 14
R v Safarzadeh-Markhali, 2016 SCC 14, [2016] 1 SCR 180
R v Searle (1994), 163 NBR (2d) 123 (NBPC)
R v Skinner, [1990] 1 SCR 1235, 56 CCC (3d) 1
R v Spence, 2005 SCC 71, [2005] 3 SCR 458
R v Swain, [1991] 1 SCR 933, 63 CCC (3d) 481
R v Towne Cinema Theatres, [1985] 1 SCR 494, 18 DLR (4th) 1
R v Whyte, [1988] 2 SCR 3, 51 DLR (4th) 481
R v Willis, 2016 MBCA 113, 344 CCC (3d) 443
R v Wong (1977), 2 Alta LR (2d) 90, 33 CCC (2d) 6 (ABCA)
R v Yu, 2002 ABCA 305, 171 CCC (3d) 90
Schachter v Canada, [1992] 2 SCR 679, 93 DLR (4th) 1
Schwartz v Canada, [1996] 1 SCR 254, 133 DLR (4th) 289
Shaw v Director of Public Prosecutions, [1962] AC 220 (HL)
Suresh v Canada (Minister of Citizenship and Immigration), 2002 SCC 1, [2002] 1 SCR 3
The Queen v Rehe, (1897) 1 CCC 63 (QBQB)
United States v Burns, 2001 SCC 7, [2001] 1 SCR 283

Foreign
Koo Sze Yiu v Chief Executive of the HKSAR, [2006] 3 HKLRD 455
Lochner v New York, 198 US 45 (1905)
Muller v Oregon, 208 US 412 (1908)

LEGISLATION

Canadian
An Act to Amend the Canadian Human Rights Act and the Criminal Code [Bill C-16], SC 2017, c 13
An Act to Amend the Corrections and Conditional Release Act and Another Act, SC 2019, c 27
An Act to Amend the Criminal Code (Prostitution), RSC 1985, c 51
An Act to Amend the Criminal Code and to Make Related Amendments to Other Acts (Medical Assistance in Dying), SC 2016, c 3
An Act to Make Provision for the Detention of Female Convicts in Reformatory Prisons in the Province of Quebec, 34 Vict (1871), c 30
An Act for the Prevention of Contagious Diseases at Certain Military and Naval Stations in This Province, 29 Vict (1865), c 8

An Act Respecting the Andrew Mercer Ontario Reformatory for Females, RSO 1887, c 239
An Act Respecting Offences of the Person, 32 & 33 Vict (1869), c 20
An Act Respecting Vagrants, 32 & 33 Vict (1869), c 28
Canada Evidence Act, RSC 1985, c C-5
Canadian Bill of Rights, SC 1960, c 44
Canadian Charter of Rights and Freedoms, being schedule B to the *Canada Act 1982* (UK), 1982, c 11
Cannabis Act, SC 2018, c 16
Constitution Act 1867 (UK), 30 & 31 Vict, c 3, reprinted in RSC 1985, Appendix II, No 5
Constitutional Questions Act, CCSM, c C180
Controlled Drugs and Substances Act, SC 1996, c 19
Criminal Code Amendment Act (1913), 3 & 4 Geo V, c 13
Criminal Code of Canada, RSC 1985, c C-46
Federal Courts Rules, SOR/98-106
Highway Traffic Act, RSO 1990, s H8
Highway Traffic Act Regulations, RRO 1990, Reg 587
Manitoba Act, 1870, 33 Vict, c 3 (Canada), reprinted in RSC 1985, App II
Narcotic Control Act, RSC 1985, c N-1
Protection of Communities and Exploited Persons Act, SC 2014, c 25
Respect for Communities Act, SC 2015, c 22
Rules of Civil Procedure, RRO 1990, Reg 194

Foreign

Basic Law for the Federal Republic of Germany (1949)
Civil Procedure Rules (UK), 2017
Constitution of the Republic of South Africa (1996)
Scotland Act, 1998 (UK), 1998, c 46

ARTICLES AND CHAPTERS

Abdulla, Adil. "The Circumstances of Change: Understanding the *Bedford/Carter* Exceptions to Vertical *Stare Decisis.*" (2020) 78 University of Toronto Faculty of Law Review 1.

Abrol, Manpreet. "The Criminalization of Prostitution: Putting Women's Lives at Risk." (2014) 3 Journal of Historical Studies 1.

Acker, James. "Social Science in Supreme Court Criminal Cases and Briefs: The Actual and Potential Contribution of Social Scientists as Amici Curiae." (1990) 14 Law and Human Behaviour 25.

Adams, Michael. "Escaping the 'Straitjacket': *Canada (Attorney General) v. Bedford* and the Doctrine of *Stare Decisis*." (2015) 78 Saskatchewan Law Review 325.

Albert, Richard. "Advisory Review: The Reincarnation of the Notwithstanding Clause." (2008) 45 Alberta Law Review 1037.

Alder, John. "Dissents in Courts of Last Resort: Tragic Choices?" (2000) 20 Oxford Journal of Legal Studies 221.

Alldridge, Peter. "Forensic Science and Expert Evidence." (1994) 21 Journal of Law and Society 136.

Anderson, Ken, and Tracy Ayodele. "Hot-Tubbing in Canadian Patent Litigation: A Preliminary Assessment." (2012) 24 Intellectual Property Journal 201.

Arvay, Joseph, and Alison Latimer. "Cost Strategies for Litigants: The Significance of *R. v. Caron*." (2011) 54 Supreme Court Law Review (2d) 427.

Backhouse, Constance. "Canadian Prostitution Law 1839–1972." In *Prostitution in Canada* (Ottawa: Canadian Advisory Council on the Status of Women, 1984), 7.

–. "Nineteenth-Century Canadian Prostitution Law: Reflection of a Discriminatory Society." (1985) 18 Social History 387.

Benedet, Janine. "*Bedford*: The Pimping Offence Should Have Been Upheld." (2014) 7 Criminal Reports (7th) 57.

Bergelson, Vera. "Vice Is Nice but Incest Is Best: The Problem of a Moral Taboo." (2013) 7 Criminal Law and Philosophy 43.

Berger, Benjamin. "Putting a Price on Dignity: The Problem of Costs in *Charter* Litigation." (2002) 26 Advocates' Quarterly 235.

–. "Emotions and the Veil of Voluntarism: The Loss of Judgment in Canadian Criminal Defences." (2006) 51 McGill Law Journal 99.

Bilardi, Jade, et al. "The Job Satisfaction of Female Sex Workers Working in Licenced Brothels in Victoria, Australia." (2011) 8 Journal of Sexual Medicine 116.

Binnie, Ian. "Science in the Courtroom: The Mouse That Roared." (2007) 56 University of New Brunswick Law Journal 307.

Bird, Brian. "The Judicial Notwithstanding Clause: Suspended Declarations of Invalidity." (2019) 42 Manitoba Law Journal 93.

Bird, Brian, and Michael Bookman. "*Stare Decisis* and the *Charter*." (2019) 92 Supreme Court Law Review (2d) 125.

Bloodworth, Michelle. "A Fact Is a Fact Is a Fact: *Stare Decisis* and the Distinction between Adjudicative and Social Facts in *Bedford* and *Carter*." (2014) 32 National Journal of Constitutional Law 193.

Brennand, William Jr. "In Defense of Dissents." (1986) 37 Hastings Law Journal 427.

Brooking, Lucy. "Conditions in Toronto." In Ernest Albert Bell, ed, *Canada's War on the White Slave Trade* (London: n.p., 1911).

Bruckert, Chris. "*Protection of Communities and Exploited Persons Act:* Misogynistic Law Making in Action." (2015) 30 Canadian Journal of Law and Society 1.

Brudner, Alan. "Constitutionalizing Self-Defence." (2011) 61 University of Toronto Law Journal 867.

Burningham, Sarah. "A Comment on the Court's Decision to Suspend the Declaration of Invalidity in *Carter v. Canada.*" (2015) 78 Saskatchewan Law Review 201.

Butler-Sloss, Elizabeth, and Ananda Hall. "Expert Witnesses, Courts and the Law." (2002) 95 Journal of the Royal Society of Medicine 431.

Cameron, Jamie. "Abstract Principle v. Contextual Conceptions of Harm: A Comment on *R. v. Butler.*" (1992) 37 McGill Law Journal 1135.

–. "From *MVR* to *Chaoulli v. Quebec:* The Road Not Taken and the Future of Section 7." (2006) 34 Supreme Court Law Review (2d) 105.

–. "Law, Politics, and Legacy Building at the McLachlin Court in 2014." (2015) 71 Supreme Court Law Review (2d) 3.

Campbell, Angela. "Sex Work's Governance: Stuff and Nuisance." (2015) 23 Feminist Legal Studies 27.

Carter, Mark. "Section 7 and 1 of the *Charter* after *Bedford, Carter,* and *Smith:* Different Questions, Same Answers?" (2017) 64 Criminal Law Quarterly 108.

Caudill, David, and Lewis LaRue. "Why Judges Applying the *Daubert* Trilogy Need to Know about the Social, Institutional, and Rhetorical – and Not Just the Methodological – Aspects of Science." (2003) 45 Boston College Law Review 1.

Champagne, Anthony, et al. "Are Court-Appointed Experts the Solution to the Problems of Expert Testimony?" (2001) 84 Judicature 178.

Champagne, Anthony, Daniel Shuman, and Elisabeth Whitaker. "An Empirical Examination of the Use of Expert Witnesses in American Courts." (1991) 31 Jurimetrics 375.

Choudhry, Sujit, and Kent Roach. "Putting the Past behind Us? Prospective Judicial and Legislative Constitutional Remedies." (2003) 21 Supreme Court Law Review (2d) 205.

Coenen, Michael. "Rules against Rulification." (2014) 124 Yale Law Journal 644.

Cohn, Margit, and Mordechai Kremnitzer. "Judicial Activism: A Multi-Dimensional Model." (2005) 18 Canadian Journal of Law and Jurisprudence 333.

Colvin, Eric. "Section Seven of the *Canadian Charter of Rights and Freedoms.*" (1989) 68 Canadian Bar Review 560.

Conrad, Geoffrey, and Jodi Lazare. "The Lawyer in Context: Toward an Integrated Approach to Legal Education." In Ruth Sefton-Green, ed, *Démoulages: Du carcan de l'enseignement du droit vers une éducation juridique* (Paris: Société de Législation Comparée, 2015) 45.

Cossman, Brenda. "Feminist Fashion or Morality in Drag? The Sexual Subtext of the *Butler* Decision" in Cossman et al, eds, *Bad Attitude/s on Trial: Pornography, Feminism and the Butler Decision* (Toronto: University of Toronto Press, 1997) 107.

–. "Disciplining the Unruly: Sexual Outlaws, *Little Sisters* and the Legacy of *Butler*." (2003) 36 University of British Columbia Law Review 77.

Coughlan, Stephen. "Duress, Necessity, Self-Defence, and Provocation: Implications of Radical Change?" (2001) 7 Canadian Criminal Law Review 147.

Coy, Maddy. "This Body which Is Not Mine: The Notion of the Habit Body, Prostitution and (Dis)embodiment." (2009) 10 Feminist Theory 61.

Crago, Anna-Louise, et al. "Sex Workers' Access to Police Assistance in Safety Emergencies and Means of Escape from Situations of Violence and Confinement under an 'End Demand' Criminalization Model: A Five City Study in Canada." (2021) 10 Social Sciences 13.

Crofts, Thomas. "Regulation of the Male Sex Industry." In Victor Minichiello and John Scott, eds, *Male Sex Work and Society* (New York: Columbia University Press, 2014) 178.

Crowhurst, Isabel. "Troubling Unknowns and Certainties in Prostitution Policy Claims-Making." In Marlene Spanger and May-Len Skilbrei, eds, *Prostitution Research in Context: Methodology, Representation and Power* (New York: Routledge, 2017) 47.

Cusick, Linda, and Matthew Hickman. "'Trapping' in Drug Use and Sex Work Careers." (2005) 12 Drugs Education, Prevention and Policy 369.

Danna, Daniela. "Client-Only Criminalization in the City of Stockholm: A Local Research on the Application of the 'Swedish Model' of Prostitution Policy." (2012) 9 Sexuality Research and Social Policy 80.

Da Silva, Michael. "Trial Level References: In Defence of a New Presumption." (2002) 2 Western Journal of Legal Studies 1.

Davis, Kenneth Culp. "An Approach to Problems of Evidence in the Administrative Process." (1942) 55 Harvard Law Review 364.

Derwin, Alexandra. "The Judicial Admission of Faulty Scientific Expert Evidence Informing Wrongful Convictions." (2018) 8 Western Journal of Legal Studies 1.

Ditmore, Melissa. "Trafficking in Lives: How Ideology Shapes Policy." In Kamala Kempadoo, Jyoti Sanghera, and Bandana Pattanaik, eds, *Trafficking and Prostitution Reconsidered: New Perspectives on Migration, Sex Work and Human Rights* (Boulder, CO: Paradigm, 2005) 107.

Dobbin, Shirley, et al. "Applying *Daubert*: How Well Do Judges Understand Science and Scientific Method?" (2002) 85 Judicature 244.

Douglas, William. "Stare Decisis." (1949) 49 Columbia Law Review 735.

Farley, Melissa, and Howard Barkan. "Prostitution, Violence, and Posttraumatic Stress Disorder." (1998) 27 Women and Health 37.

Farley, Melissa, Jacqueline Lynne, and Ann Cotton. "Prostitution in Vancouver: Violence and the Colonization of First Nations Women." (2005) 42 Transcultural Psychiatry 242.

Fehr, Colton. "Consent and the Constitution." (2019) 42 Manitoba Law Journal 217.

–. "The Constitutionality of Excluding Duress as a Defence to Murder." (2021) 44 Manitoba Law Journal 111.

–. "The 'Individualistic' Approach to Arbitrariness, Overbreadth, and Gross Disproportionality." (2018) 51 University of British Columbia Law Review 55.

–. "Instrumental Rationality and General Deterrence." (2019) 57 Alberta Law Review 53.

–. "(Re-)Constitutionalizing Duress and Necessity." (2017) 42 Queen's Law Journal 99.

–. "Rethinking the Instrumental Rationality Principles of Fundamental Justice." (2020) 58 Alberta Law Review 133.

–. "Self-Defence and the Constitution." (2017) 43 Queen's Law Journal 85.

–. "Vaccine Passports and the *Charter:* Do They Actually Infringe Rights?" (2022) 43 National Journal of Constitutional Law 93.

Ferris, Shawna. "Working from the Violent Centre: Survival Sex Work and Urban Aboriginality in Maria Campbell's *Halfbreed*." (2008) 34 English Studies in Canada 123.

Fisher, John. "Outlaws or In-Laws? Successes and Challenges in the Struggle for LGBT Equality." (2004) 49 McGill Law Journal 1183.

Fletcher, Tor. "Trans Sex Workers: Negotiating Sex, Gender, and Non-Normative Desire." In Elya M. Durisin, Emily van der Meulen, and Chris Bruckert, eds, *Selling Sex: Experience, Advocacy, and Research on Sex Work in Canada* (Vancouver: UBC Press, 2013) 98–113.

Friss, Eva, and Karsten Åström. "The Use of Court- and Party-Appointed Experts in Legal Proceedings in Sweden: Judges' Experiences and Attitudes." (2017) 3 Oslo Law Review 63.

Gacek, James, and Richard Jochelson. "Sex Work in Canada: Beginnings, *Bedford,* and Beyond." In Richard Jochelson and James Gacek, eds, *Sexual Regulation and the Law: A Canadian Perspective* (Bradford, ON: Demers Press, 2019) 57.

Galbally, Phoebe. "Playing the Victim: A Critical Analysis of Canada's Bill C-36 from an International Human Rights Perspective." (2016) 17 Melbourne Journal of International Law 35.

Ginsburg, Ruth Bader. "The Role of Dissenting Opinions." (2010) 95 Minnesota Law Review 95.

Gossop, Michael, et al. "Sexual Behaviour and Its Relationship to Drug-Taking among Prostitutes in South London." (1994) 89 Addiction 961.

Gotell, Lisa. "Shaping *Butler:* The New Politics of Anti-Pornography." In Brenda Cossman et al, eds, *Bad Attitude/s on Trial: Pornography, Feminism and the Butler Decision* (Toronto: University of Toronto Press, 1997) 48.

Graff, Harvey. "Pauperism, Misery and Vice Illiteracy and Criminality in the Nineteenth Century." (1977) 11 Journal of Social History 245.

Green, Leslie. "Pornographies." (2000) 8 Journal of Political Philosophy 27.

Groves, J., et al. "Sex Workers Working within a Legalized Industry: Their Side of the Story." (2008) 84 Sexually Transmitted Infections 393.

Haak, Debra. "The Initial Test of Constitutional Validity: Identifying the Legislative Objectives of Canada's New Prostitution Laws." (2017) 50 University of British Columbia Law Review 657.

–. "Re(de)fining Prostitution and Sex Work: Conceptual Clarity for Legal Thinking." (2019) 40 Windsor Review of Legal and Social Issues 67.

Hallgrimsdóttir, Helga, et al. "Fallen Women and Rescued Girls: Social Stigma and Media Narratives of the Sex Industry in Victoria, B.C., from 1980–2005." (2006) 43 Canadian Review of Sociology 265.

Harcourt, Bernard. "The Collapse of the Harm Principle." (1999) 90 Journal of Criminal Law and Criminology 109.

Hogg, Peter, and Allison Bushell. "The *Charter* Dialogue between Courts and Legislatures (or Perhaps the *Charter of Rights* Isn't Such a Bad Thing after All)." (1997) 35 Osgoode Hall Law Journal 75.

Hogg, Peter, Allison Bushell Thornton, and Wade Knight. "*Charter* Dialogue Revisited – Or 'Much Ado about Metaphors.'" (2007) 45 Osgoode Hall Law Journal 1.

Hogg, Peter, and Ravi Amarnath. "Understanding Dialogue Theory." In Peter Oliver, Patrick Macklem, and Nathalie Des Rosiers, eds, *The Oxford Handbook of the Canadian Constitution* (Oxford: Oxford University Press, 2017) 1053.

Holoyda, Brian James. "Bestiality Law in the United States: Evolving Legislation with Scientific Limitations." (2022) 12 Animals 1525.

Hoole, Grant. "Proportionality as a Remedial Principle: A Framework for Suspended Declarations of Invalidity." (2011) 49 Alberta Law Review 107.

Horder, Jeremy. "Self-Defence, Necessity and Duress: Understanding the Relationship." (1998) 11 Canadian Journal of Law and Jurisprudence 143.

Horlick, Leah. "Bill C-36: Two Steps Back." (2014) 48 Canadian Dimension 11.

Hughes, Jula, and Vanessa MacDonnell. "Social Science Evidence in Constitutional Rights Cases in Germany and Canada: Some Comparative Observations." (2013) 32 National Journal of Constitutional Law 23.

Jamel, Joanna. "An Investigation of the Incidence of Client-Perpetrated Sexual Violence against Male Sex Workers." (2011) 23 International Journal of Sexual Health 63.

Jeal, Nikki, et al. "The Multiplicity and Interdependency of Factors Influencing the Health of Street-Based Sex Workers: A Qualitative Study." (2008) 84 Sexually Transmitted Infections 381.

Jeffrey, Leslie, and Gayle MacDonald. "It's the Money Honey: The Economy of Sex Work in the Maritimes." (2006) 43 Canadian Review of Sociology and Anthropology 313.

Jenness, Valerie. "From Sex as Sin to Sex as Work: COYOTE and the Reorganization of Prostitution as a Social Problem." (1990) 37 Social Problems 403.

Jochelson, Richard. "After *Labaye:* The Harm Test of Obscenity, the New Judicial Vacuum, and the Relevance of Familiar Voices." (2009) 46 Alberta Law Review 741.

Ka Hon Chu, Sandra, and Rebecca Glass. "Sex Work Law Reform in Canada: Considering Problems with the Nordic Model." (2013) 51 Alberta Law Review 101.

Kaplow, Louis. "Rules versus Standards: An Economic Analysis." (1992) 42 Duke Law Journal 557.

Kelly, Liz. "The Wrong Debate: Reflections on Why Force Is Not the Key Issue with Respect to Trafficking in Women for Sexual Exploitation." (2003) 73 Feminist Review 139.

Kempadoo, Kamala. "From Moral Panic to Global Justice: Changing Perspectives on Trafficking." In Kamala Kempadoo, Jyoti Sanghera, and Bandana Pattanaik, eds, *Trafficking and Prostitution Reconsidered: New Perspectives on Migration, Sex Work and Human Rights* (Boulder, CO: Paradigm, 2005), 1.

Kennedy, Duncan. "Form and Substance in Private Law Adjudication." (1976) 89 Harvard Law Review 1685.

Kirby, Michael. "Law at Century's End – A Millennial View from the High Court of Australia." (2001) 1 Macquarie Law Journal 1.

Klein, Alana. "The Arbitrariness in 'Arbitrariness' (and Overbreadth and Gross Disproportionality): Principle and Democracy in Section 7 of the *Charter*." (2013) 63 Supreme Court Law Review 377.

Kloegman, Larissa. "A Democratic Defence of the Court Challenges Program." (2007) 16 Constitutional Forum 107.

Kristjanson, Freya. "Hot-Tubs and Concurrent Evidence: Improving Administrative Proceedings." (2012) 25 Canadian Journal of Administrative Law and Practice 79.

Krüsi, Andrea et al. "Criminalisation of Clients: Reproducing Vulnerabilities for Violence and Poor Health among Street-Based Sex Workers in Canada – A Qualitative Study." (2014) 4 British Medical Journal Open 1.

—. "Negotiating Safety and Sexual Risk Reduction with Clients in Unsanctioned Safer Indoor Sex Work Environments: A Qualitative Study." (2012) 102 American Journal of Public Health 1154.

Kunimoto, Erica. "A Critical Analysis of Canada's Sex Work Legislation: Exploring Gendered and Racialized Consequences." (2018) 10 Stream 27.

Laidlaw, Leon. "Challenging Dominant Portrayals of the Trans Sex Worker: On Gender, Violence, and Protection." (2018) 41 Manitoba Law Journal 351.

Larsen, Allison Orr. "The Trouble with Amicus Facts." (2014) 100 Virginia Law Review 1757.

Laskin, Bora. "The Supreme Court of Canada: A Final Court of and for Canadians." (1951) 29 Canadian Bar Review 1038.

Lawrence, Sonia. "Expert-Tease: Advocacy, Ideology and Experience in *Bedford* and Bill C-36." (2015) 30 Canadian Journal of Law and Society 5.

Lazare, Jodi. "Judging the Social Sciences in *Carter v Canada (AG)*." (2016) 10 McGill Journal of Law and Health S35.

—. "When Disciplines Collide: Polygamy and the Social Sciences on Trial." (2015) 32 Windsor Yearbook of Access to Justice 103.

Leckey, Robert. "Assisted Dying, Suspended Declarations, and Dialogue's Time." (2019) 69 University of Toronto Law Journal 64.

—. "Enforcing Laws That Infringe Rights." (2016) Public Law 206.

—. "The Harms of Remedial Discretion." (2016) 14 International Journal of Constitutional Law 584.

Lee, John, Tess Sheldon, and Roberto Lattanzio. "Law and Ordered C.H.A.O.S.: Social Science Methodology, and the *Charter* Claims of Persons with Disabilities." (2013) 32 National Journal of Constitutional Law 61.

L'Heureux-Dubé, Claire. "The Dissenting Opinion: Voice of the Future?" (2000) 38 Osgoode Hall Law Journal 495.

Lijphart, Arend. "Comparative Politics and Comparative Method." (1971) 65 American Political Science Review 682.

Little, Rory. "Reading Justice Brennan: Is There a 'Right' to Dissent?" (1999) 50 Hastings Law Journal 683.

Lowman, John. "Street Prostitution in Vancouver: Notes on the Genesis of a Social Problem." (1986) 28 Canadian Journal of Criminology 1.

Lowman, John, and Christine Louie. "Public Opinion on Prostitution Law Reform in Canada." (2012) 54 Canadian Journal of Criminology and Criminal Justice 245.

Lynch, Andrew. "Is Judicial Dissent Constitutionally Protected?" (2004) 4 Macquarie Law Journal 81.

Lyons, Tara, et al. "Negotiating Violence in the Context of Transphobia and Criminalization: The Experiences of Trans Sex Workers in Vancouver, Canada." (2017) 27 Qualitative Health Research 182.

Macfarlane, Emmett. "Dialogue, Remedies, and Positive Rights: *Carter v. Canada* as a Microcosm for Past and Future Issues under the *Charter of Rights and Freedoms.*" (2017) 49 Ottawa Law Review 107.

–. "Dialogue or Compliance? Measuring Legislatures' Policy Responses to Court Rulings on Rights." (2013) 34 International Political Science Review 39.

Machat, Sylvia, et al. "Sex Workers' Experiences and Occupational Conditions Post-Implementation of End-Demand Criminalization in Metro Vancouver, Canada." (2019) 110 Canadian Journal of Public Health 575.

Maher, Lisa, et al. "Selling Sex in Unsafe Spaces: Sex Work Risk Environments in Phnom Penh, Cambodia." (2011) 8 Harm Reduction Journal 30.

Mahoney, Kathleen. "Obscenity, Morals and the Law: A Feminist Critique." (1984) 17 Ottawa Law Review 33.

Manfredi, Christopher. "The Day the Dialogue Died: A Comment on *Sauvé v Canada.*" (2007) 45 Osgoode Hall Law Journal 105.

Manfredi, Christopher, and James Kelly. "Six Degrees of Dialogue: A Response to Hogg and Bushell." (1999) 37 Osgoode Hall Law Journal 513.

Mathen, Carissima. "Dissent and Judicial Authority in *Charter* Cases." (2003) 53 University of New Brunswick Law Journal 321.

–. "The Upside of Dissent in Equality Jurisprudence." (2013) 63 Supreme Court Law Review (2d) 111.

McAdam, Richard. "The Notwithstanding Taboo." (2009) 6 Federal Governance 1.

McGinnis, Janice. "Whores and Worthies: Feminism and Prostitution." (1994) 9 Canadian Journal of Law and Society 105.

McLaren, John. "Chasing the Social Evil: Moral Fervour and the Evolution of Canada's Prostitution Laws, 1867–1917." (1986) 1 Canadian Journal of Law and Society 125.

Millar, Hayli, Tamara O'Doherty, and Katrin Roots. "A Formidable Task: Reflections on Obtaining Legal Empirical Evidence on Human Trafficking in Canada." (2017) 8 Anti-Trafficking Review 34.

Mnookin, Jennifer. "Idealizing Science and Demonizing Experts: An Intellectual History of Expert Evidence." (2007) 52 Villanova Law Review 763.

–. "Expert Evidence, Partisanship, and Epistemic Competence." (2008) 73 Brooklyn Law Review 1009.

Monahan, John, and Laurens Walker. "Social Authority: Obtaining, Evaluating, and Establishing Social Science in Law." (1986) 134 University of Pennsylvania Law Review 477.

Moon, Richard. "*R. v. Butler:* The Limits of the Supreme Court's Feminist Re-Interpretation of Section 163." (1993) 25 Ottawa Law Review 361.

Moore, Marcus. "*R. v. Safarzadeh-Markhali:* Elements and Implications of the Supreme Court's New Rigorous Approach to Construction of Statutory Purpose." (2017) 77 (2d) Supreme Court Law Review 223.

Mouland, Carolyn. "Remedying the Remedy: *Bedford*'s Suspended Declaration of Invalidity." (2018) 41 Manitoba Law Journal 281.

Murchison, Melanie. "Making Numbers Count: An Empirical Analysis of 'Judicial Activism' in Canada." (2017) 40 Manitoba Law Journal 425.

Newman, Dwight. "Canada's Notwithstanding Clause, Dialogue, and Constitutional Identities." In Geoffrey Sigalet, Grégoire Webber, and Rosalind Dixon, eds, *Constitutional Dialogue: Rights, Democracy, Institutions* (Cambridge, UK: Cambridge University Press, 2019) 209.

–. "Judicial Method and Three Gaps in the Supreme Court of Canada's Assisted Suicide Judgment in *Carter*." (2015) 78 Saskatchewan Law Review 217.

O'Connell, Sheilagh. "The Impact of Bill C-49 on Street Prostitution: 'What's Law Got to Do with It?'" (1988) 4 Journal of Law and Social Policy 109.

O'Connor, Monica. "Choice, Agency, Consent and Coercion: Complex Issues in the Lives of Prostituted and Trafficked Women." (2017) 62 Women's Studies International Forum 8.

Okal, Jerry, et al. "Sexual and Physical Violence against Female Sex Workers in Kenya: A Qualitative Inquiry." (2011) 23 AIDS Care 612.

Paciocco, David. "Taking a 'Goudge' out of Bluster and Blarney: An 'Evidence-Based Approach' to Expert Testimony." (2009) 13 Canadian Criminal Law Review 135.

–. "Unplugging Jukebox Testimony in an Adversarial System: Strategies for Changing the Tune on Partial Experts." (2009) 34 Queen's Law Journal 565.

Parkes, Debra. "Precedent Revisited: *Carter v Canada (AG)* and the Contemporary Practice of Precedent." (2016) 10 McGill Journal of Law and Health S123.

Perryman, Benjamin. "Adducing Social Science Evidence in Constitutional Cases." (2018) 44 Queen's Law Journal 121.

Peterson, Steven. "Dissent in American Courts." (1981) 43 Journal of Politics 412.

Petro, Melissa. "Selling Sex: Women's Participation in the Sex Industry." In Melissa Ditmore, Antonia Levy, and Alys Willman, eds, *Sex Work Matters: Exploring Money, Power and Intimacy in the Sex Work Industry* (New York: Zed Books, 2010) 155.

Petter, Andrew. "Legalize This: The Chartering of Canadian Politics." In James Kelly and Christopher Manfredi, eds, *Contested Constitutionalism: Reflections on the Canadian Charter of Rights and Freedoms* (Vancouver: UBC Press, 2010) 33.

Porter, Judith, and Louis Bonilla. "The Ecology of Street Prostitution." In Ronald Weitzer, ed, *Sex for Sale: Prostitution, Pornography and the Sex Work Industry*, 2nd ed (New York: Routledge, 2010) 163.

Pound, Roscoe. "Cacoethes Dissentiendi: The Heated Judicial Dissent." (1953) 39 American Bar Association Journal 794.

Powell, Maria. "Moving beyond the Prostitution Reference: *Bedford v. Canada*." (2013) 64 University of New Brunswick Law Journal 187.

Roach, Kent. "Dialogic Remedies." (2019) 17 International Journal of Constitutional Law 860.

–. "Enforcement of the *Charter* – Subsections 24(1) and 52(1)." (2013) 62 Supreme Court Law Review (2d) 473.

–. "Polycentricity and Queue-Jumping in Public Law Remedies: A Two-Track Response." (2016) 66 University of Toronto Law Journal 3.

–. "Principled Remedial Discretion under the *Charter*." (2004) 25 Supreme Court Law Review (2d) 101.

–. "Remedial Consensus and Dialogue." (2002) 35 University of British Columbia Law Review 211.

Rotenberg, Lori. "The Wayward Worker: Toronto's Prostitute at the Turn of the Century." In Janice Acton, Penny Goldsmith, and Bonnie Shepard, eds, *Women at Work: Ontario, 1850–1930* (Toronto: Canadian Women's Educational Press, 1974), 57.

Russell, Stuart. "The Offence of Keeping a Common Bawdy-House in Canadian Criminal Law." (1982) 14 Ottawa Law Review 270.

Ryder, Bruce. "Suspending the *Charter*." (2003) 21 Supreme Court Law Review (2d) 267.

Sachs, Albie. "The Judicial Enforcement of Socio-Economic Rights: The Grootboom Case." (2003) 56 Current Legal Problems 579.

Sampson, Lauren. "'The Obscenities of This Country': *Canada v. Bedford* and the Reform of Canadian Prostitution Laws." (2014) 22 Duke Journal of Gender Law and Policy 137.

Sanders, Teela. "Becoming an Ex-Sex Worker: Making Transitions out of a Deviant Career." (2007) 2 Feminist Criminology 74.

–. "A Continuum of Risk? The Management of Health, Physical and Emotional Risks by Female Sex Workers." (2004) 26 Sociology of Health and Illness 557.

Scalia, Antonin. "The Dissenting Opinion." (1994) 19 Journal of Supreme Court History 33.

–. "The Rule of Law as a Law of Rules." (1989) 56 University of Chicago Law Review 1175.

Schlag, Pierre. "Rules and Standards." (1985) 33 University of California Los Angeles Law Review 379.

Schuck, Peter. "Why Don't Law Professors Do More Empirical Research?" (1989) 39 Journal of Legal Education 323.

Schwartz, Hart. "Circularity, Tautology and Gamesmanship: 'Purpose' Based Proportionality-Correspondence Analysis in Sections 15 and 7 of the *Charter*." (2016) 35 National Journal of Constitutional Law 105.

Scott, John. "A Prostitute's Progress: Male Prostitution in Scientific Discourse." (2003) 13 Social Semiotics 179.

Shannon, Kate, et al. "Social and Structural Violence and Power Relations in Mitigating HIV Risk of Drug-Using Women in Survival Sex Work." (2008) 66 Social Science and Medicine 911.

–. "Structural and Environmental Barriers to Condom Use Negotiation with Clients among Female Sex Workers: Implications for HIV-Prevention Strategies and Policy." (2009) 99 American Journal of Public Health 659.

Sharpe, Robert. "Access to *Charter* Justice." (2013) 63 Supreme Court Law Review (2d) 1.

Sharpe, Robert, and Vincent-Joël Proulx. "The Use of Academic Writing in Appellate Judicial Decision-Making." (2011) 50 Canadian Business Law Journal 550.

Shuman, Daniel, Elisabeth Whitaker, and Anthony Champagne. "An Empirical Examination of the Use of Expert Witnesses in the Courts – Part II: A Three City Study." (1994) 34 Jurimetrics 193.

Simester, Andrew, and Andrew von Hirsch. "Rethinking the Offense Principle." (2002) 8 Legal Theory 269.

Sinel, Zoë. "The Duress Dilemma: Potential Solutions in the Theory of Right." (2005) 10 Appeal: Review of Current Law and Legal Reform 56.

Skolnik, Terry. "Three Problems with Duress and Moral Involuntariness." (2016) 63 Criminal Law Quarterly 124.

Smiley, Cherry. "A Long Road behind Us, a Long Road Ahead: Towards an Indigenous Feminist National Inquiry." (2016) 28 Canadian Journal of Women and the Law 308.

Smith, Jesse. "Social Purity." In Ramsey Cook and Wendy Mitchinson, eds, *The Proper Sphere: Women's Place in Canadian Society* (Toronto: Oxford University Press, 1976) 234.

Smith-Rosenberg, Caroll. "Beauty, the Beast and the Militant Women: Study in Sex Roles and Social Stress." In Nancy Cott and Elizabeth Pleck, eds, *A Heritage of Her Own: Towards a New Social History of American Women* (New York: Simon and Schuster, 1979) 197.

Snow, Natalie, et al. "The Right to Life, Liberty and Security for Prostitution: *Canada v. Bedford*." (2020) Women and Criminal Justice 1.

Souter, Janelle. "'Clearly the Arc Bends': *Stare Decisis* and *Saskatchewan Federation of Labour v. Saskatchewan*." (2015) 78 Saskatchewan Law Review 397.

Sperlich, Peter. "Social Science Evidence and the Courts: Reading Beyond the Adversary Process." (1980) 63 Judicature 280.

Stephens, Richard. "The Function of Concurring and Dissenting Opinions in Courts of Last Resort." (1952) 5 University of Florida Law Review 394.

Sterling, Andrea. "'We Are Not Criminals': Sex Work Clients in Canada and the Constitution of Risk Knowledge." (2018) 33 Canadian Journal of Law and Society 291.

Stewart, Hamish. "*Bedford* and the Structure of Section 7." (2015) 60 McGill Law Journal 576.

—. "The Constitution and the Right of Self-Defence." (2011) 61 University of Toronto Law Journal 899.

—. "The Constitutionality of the New Sex Work Law." (2016) 54 Alberta Law Review 69.

Stridbeck, Ulf, Pål Grøndahl, and Cato Grønnerød. "Expert for Whom? Court-Appointed versus Party-Appointed Experts." (2015) 23 Psychiatry, Psychology and Law 246.

Stuart, Don. "*Bedford:* Striking Down Prostitution Laws and Revising Section 7 Standards to Focus on Arbitrariness." (2014) 7 Criminal Reports (7th) 52.

Sullivan, Kathleen. "Foreword: The Justices of Rules and Standards." (1992) 106 Harvard Law Review 22.

Sunstein, Cass. "Problems with Rules." (1995) 83 California Law Review 953.

Symons, Julian. "Orwell's Prophecies: The Limits of Liberty and the Limits of Law." (1984) 9 Dalhousie Law Journal 115.

Turner, Jackie. "Means of Delivery: The Trafficking of Women into Prostitution, Harms and Human Rights Discourse." In Maddy Coy, ed, *Prostitution, Harm and Gender Inequality: Theory, Research and Policy* (Farnham, UK: Ashgate, 2013) 33.

Valverde, Mariana. "The Harms of Sex and the Risks of Breasts: Obscenity and Indecency in Canadian Law." (1999) 8 Social and Legal Studies 181.

van der Meulen, Emily, and Elya M. Durisin. "Sex Work Policy: Tracing Historical and Contemporary Developments." In Elya M. Durisin, Emily van der Meulen, and Chris Bruckert, eds, *Red Light Labour: Sex Work Regulation, Agency, and Resistance* (Vancouver: UBC Press, 2018) 27.

Vitale, David. "The Value of Dissent in Constitutional Adjudication: A Context-Specific Analysis." (2014) 19 Review of Constitutional Studies 83.

Vuille, Joëlle. "Admissibility and Appraisal of Scientific Evidence in Continental European Criminal Justice Systems: Past, Present and Future." (2013) 45 Australian Journal of Forensic Sciences 389.

Wahlbeck, Paul J., James F. Spriggs II, and Forrest Maltzman. "The Politics of Dissents and Concurrences on the US Supreme Court." (1999) 27 American Politics Quarterly 488.

Waldron, Jeremy. "The Core of the Case against Judicial Review." (2006) 115 Yale Law Journal 1346.

Weitzer, Ronald, and Melissa Ditmore. "Sex Trafficking: Facts and Fictions." In Ronald Weitzer, ed, *Sex for Sale: Prostitution, Pornography and the Sex Industry* (New York: Routledge, 2010) 325.

Wesley, John. "Scientific Evidence and the Question of Judicial Capacity." (1984) 25 William and Mary Law Review 675.

Williams, Catherine. "Expert Evidence in Cases of Child Abuse." (1993) 68 Archives of Disease in Childhood 712.

Williams, D.H. "The Suppression of Commercial Prostitution in the City of Vancouver." (1941) 27 Journal of Social Hygiene 364.

Yeo, Stanley. "Challenging Moral Involuntariness as a Principle of Fundamental Justice." (2003) 28 Queen's Law Journal 335.

—. "Revisiting Necessity." (2010) 56 Criminal Law Quarterly 13.

Young, Alan. "Proving a Violation: Rhetoric, Research, and Remedy." (2014) 67 Supreme Court Law Review (2d) 617.

BOOKS

Anderson, Glenn. *Expert Evidence.* 2nd ed. (Toronto: LexisNexis, 2009).

Bacchi, Carol. *Liberation Deferred: The Ideas of English Canadian Suffragists 1877–1915* (Toronto: University of Toronto Press, 1983).

Bedford, Terri-Jean. *Dominatrix on Trial:* Bedford vs. Canada (Bloomington, IN: iUniverse, 2011).

Benoit, Cecilia, and Alison Millar. *Dispelling Myths and Understanding Realities: Working Conditions, Health Status, and Exiting Experiences of Sex Workers* (Victoria: University of Victoria Press, 2001).

Blackstone, William. *Commentaries on the Laws of England.* Vol 3 (Oxford: Clarendon Press, 1765–70).

Bristow, Edward. *Vice and Vigilantes: Purity Movements in Britain since 1700* (Dublin: Gill and MacMillan, 1977).

Brock, Deborah. *Making Work, Making Trouble: Prostitution as a Social Problem* (Toronto: University of Toronto Press, 1998).

Bruckert, Chris, et al. *Erotic Service/Erotic Dance Establishments: Two Types of Marginalized Labour* (Ottawa: Ottawa University Press, 2003).

Cameron, Stevie. *On the Farm: Robert William Pickton and the Tragic Story of Vancouver's Missing Women* (Toronto: Vintage Canada, 2011).

Campbell, Angela. *Sister Wives, Surrogates, and Sex Workers: Outlaws by Choice?* (London: Ashgate, 2013).

Connell, Judith, and Graham Hart. *An Overview of Male Sex Work in Edinburgh and Glasgow: The Male Sex Worker Perspective.* Medical Research Council, Social and Public Health Sciences Unit Occasional Paper No 8 (Glasgow: MRC, University of Glasgow, 2003).

Devlin, Patrick. *The Enforcement of Morals* (Oxford: Oxford University Press, 1965).

Dicey, Albert. *Introduction to the Study of the Law of the Constitution.* 10th ed (London: Martin's Press, 1959).

Dworkin, Ronald. *Freedom's Law: The Moral Reading of the American Constitution* (Cambridge, MA: Harvard University Press, 1996).

Ely, John Hart. *Democracy and Distrust: A Theory of Judicial Review* (Cambridge, MA: Harvard University Press, 1980).

Faigman, David. *Constitutional Fictions: A Unified Theory of Constitutional Facts* (Oxford: Oxford University Press, 2008).

Fehr, Colton. *Constitutionalizing Criminal Law* (Vancouver: UBC Press, 2022).

Feinberg, Joel. *The Moral Limits of the Criminal Law*. 4 vols (Oxford: Oxford University Press, 1984–85).

Fletcher, George. *The Grammar of Criminal Law: American, Comparative, and International*. Vol 1 (Oxford: Oxford University Press, 2007).

–. *Rethinking Criminal Law* (Boston: Little and Brown, 1978).

Gray, James. *Red Lights on the Prairies* (New York: Signet, 1971).

Hand, Learned. *The Bill of Rights (The Oliver Wendell Holmes Lectures, 1958)* (Cambridge, MA: Harvard University Press, 1958).

Hart, H.L.A. *Law, Liberty, and Morality* (Stanford, CA: Stanford University Press, 1977).

Hogg, Peter. *Constitutional Law of Canada*. 5th ed, loose-leaf (Toronto: Thomson Reuters Canada, 2007).

–. *Constitutional Law of Canada*. 5th ed, vol 2, loose-leaf (Scarborough, ON: Thomson Carswell, 2014).

Horowitz, Donald. *The Courts and Social Policy* (Washington, DC: Brookings Institution, 1977).

Hughes, Charles. *The Supreme Court of the United States: Its Foundations, Methods and Achievements, an Interpretation* (New York: Columbia University Press, 1936).

Kelly, Liz, Maddy Coy, and Rebecca Davenport. *Shifting Sands: A Comparison of Prostitution Regimes across Nine Countries* (London: London Metropolitan University, 2008).

Leckey, Robert. *Bills of Rights in the Common Law* (Cambridge, UK: Cambridge University Press, 2015).

MacKinnon, Catharine A. *Toward a Feminist Theory of the State* (Cambridge, MA: Harvard University Press, 1989).

–. *Only Words* (Cambridge, MA: Harvard University Press, 1993).

Martin's Annual Criminal Code 2010 (Aurora, ON: Canada Law Book, 2009).

McDiarmid, Jessica. *Highway of Tears: A True Story of Racism, Indifference and the Pursuit of Justice for Missing and Murdered Indigenous Women and Girls* (Toronto: Random House, 2019).

McKeganey, Marina, and Neil Barnard. *Sex Work on the Streets: Prostitutes and Their Clients* (Buckingham, UK: Open University Press, 1996).

Mill, John Stuart. *On Liberty and Considerations on Representative Government* (Oxford: Basil Blackwell and Mott, 1946).

Namaste, Viviane K. *Invisible Lives: The Erasure of Transsexual and Transgendered People* (Chicago: University of Chicago Press, 2000).

Palmegiano, Eugenia. *Women and British Periodicals 1832–1867: A Bibliography* (New York: Garland, 1976).

Perrin, Benjamin. *Invisible Chains: Canada's Underground World of Human Trafficking* (Toronto: Viking Canada, 2010).

Petter, Andrew. *The Politics of the Charter: The Illusive Promise of Constitutional Rights* (Toronto: University of Toronto Press, 2010).

Pivot Legal Society Sex Work Subcommittee. *Voices for Dignity: A Call to End the Harms Caused by Canada's Sex Work Laws* (Vancouver: Pivot Legal Society, 2004).

Purcell, Edward. *Brandeis and the Progressive Constitution: Erie, the Judicial Power, and the Politics of the Federal Courts in Twentieth-Century America* (New Haven, CT: Yale University Press, 2000).

Raymond, Janice. *Not a Choice, Not a Job: Exposing the Myths about Prostitution and the Global Sex Trade* (Sterling, VA: Potomac Books, 2013).

Roach, Kent. *Constitutional Remedies in Canada*. Loose-leaf (Aurora, ON: Canada Law Book, 2009).

–. *The Supreme Court on Trial: Judicial Activism or Democratic Dialogue?* (Toronto: Irwin Law, 2016).

Rosen, Ruth. *The Lost Sisterhood: Prostitution in America 1900–1918* (Baltimore: Johns Hopkins University Press, 1982).

Sharpe, Robert. *Good Judgment: Making Judicial Decisions* (Toronto: University of Toronto Press, 2018).

Simpson, Brian. *Cannibalism and the Common Law: A Victorian Yachting Tragedy* (Chicago: University of Chicago Press, 1984).

Stewart, Hamish. *Fundamental Justice: Section 7 of the Canadian Charter of Rights and Freedoms* (Toronto: Irwin Law, 2012).

–. *Fundamental Justice: Section 7 of the Canadian Charter of Rights and Freedoms.* 2nd ed (Toronto: Irwin Law, 2019).

Stuart, Don. *Canadian Criminal Law.* 3rd ed (Toronto: Carswell, 1995).

Stychin, Carl. *Law's Desire: Sexuality and the Limits of Justice* (London: Routledge, 1995).

Turgeon, Luc, et al, eds. *Comparing Canada: Methods and Perspectives on Canadian Politics* (Vancouver: UBC Press, 2014).

Tushnet, Mark, ed. *I Dissent: Great Opposing Opinions in Landmark Supreme Court Cases* (Boston: Beacon Press, 2008).

–. *Taking the Constitution Away from the Courts* (Princeton, NJ: Princeton University Press, 1999).

Van Kirk, Sylvia. *"Many Tender Ties": Women in Fur-Trade Society 1670–1870* (Winnipeg: Watson and Dwyer, 1980).

Waldron, Jeremy. *Political Political Theory* (Cambridge, MA: Harvard University Press, 2016).

Walkowitz, Judith. *Prostitution and Victorian Society: Women, Class and the State* (Cambridge, UK: Cambridge University Press, 1980).

West, D.J., and Buz de Villiers. *Male Prostitution: Gay Sex Services in London* (Binghampton, UK: Harrington Park Press, 1993).

OTHER

Angus Reid Institute. "Canadians Have a More Favourable View of Their Supreme Court Than Americans Have of Their Own." (17 August 2015), online: <http://angusreid.org/supreme-court/>.

Archibald, Bruce. "The General Part of Canadian Criminal Law and Criminal Law Reform" (unpublished).

Baron, Ethan. "Horrors of Pickton Farm Revealed in Graphic Detail." *National Post* (20 February 2007), online: <https://web.archive.org/web/20071123065221/http://www.canada.com/nationalpost/story.html?id=20941e5e-aae7-4c73-87bb-fbbb484e08d5&k=0>.

Bedard, Ella. "The Failures of Canada's New Sex Work Legislation." *Rank and File* (7 April 2015), online: <http://rankandfile.ca/the-failures-of-canadas-new-sex-work-legislation/>.

Bernhardt, Darren. "Winnipeg Police Pull Out of Project Devote, Create New Model for Investigating MMIWG Cases." *CBC News* (6 March 2020), online: <https://www.cbc.ca/news/canada/manitoba/winnipeg-police-project-devote-1.5488266>.

Blanchfield, Mike. "Supreme Court Strikes Down Canada's Anti-Prostitution Laws as *Charter* Breach." *Global News* (20 December 2013), online: <https://globalnews.ca/news/1042861/supreme-court-strikes-down-canadas-anti-prostitution-laws/>.

Canada. *Debates of the Senate,* 41st Parl, 2nd Sess, Vol 149, No 86 (9 October 2014).

–. Department of Justice. "Online Public Consultation on Prostitution-Related Offences in Canada – Final Results." (2014), online: <https://www.justice.gc.ca/eng/rp-pr/other-autre/rr14_09/p1.html>.

–. *Technical Paper: Bill C-36, Protection of Communities and Exploited Persons Act* (Ottawa: Department of Justice, 2014).

Casavant, Lyne, and Dominique Valiquet. "Legislative Summary of Bill C-36: An Act to Amend the *Criminal Code* in Response to the Supreme Court of Canada Decision in *Attorney General of Canada v. Bedford* and to Make Consequential Amendments to Other Acts." *Library of Parliament* (18 July 2014), online:

Bibliography | 273

<https://lop.parl.ca/staticfiles/PublicWebsite/Home/ResearchPublications/LegislativeSummaries/PDF/41-2/c36-e.pdf>.

The Challenge of Change: A Study of Canada's Criminal Prostitution Laws. Ottawa: Communication Canada, 2006.

Clancy, Clare. "RCMP KARE Team Broadens Mandate to Prevent Murders of At-Risk Individuals." *Edmonton Journal* (14 August 2017), online: <https://edmontonjournal.com/news/local-news/rcmp-kare-team-broadens-mandate-to-prevent-murders-of-at-risk-individuals>.

Committee on Sexual Offences against Children and Youths. *Sexual Offences against Children.* Vol 2 (Ottawa: Minister of Supply and Services Canada, 1984).

Coyne, Andrew. "We Once Had to Wait Weeks for a New Harper Abuse of Power: Now We're Getting Them Two or Three Times a Day." *National Post* (6 June 2014), online: <https://nationalpost.com/opinion/andrew-coyne-we-once-had-to-wait-weeks-for-a-new-harper-abuse-of-power-now-were-getting-them-two-or-three-a-day>.

Department of Justice Canada and Public Safety Canada. "Government of Canada Announces $20 Million to Help Victims Leave Prostitution." News Release (1 December 2014), online: <www.canada.ca/en/news/archive/2014/12/government-canada-announces-20-million-help-victims-leave-prostitution.html>.

—. *House of Commons Debates,* 41st Parl, 2nd Sess, Vol 147, No 102 (12 June 2014).

EGALE. "Sex Work in Canada: Research Brief." (April 2021), online: <https://adobeindd.com/view/publications/b04e7320-d7b9-418f-b32b-14bdce281ca0/1/publication-web-resources/pdf/Sex_Work_Brief_Updated.pdf>.

Fact Sheet on Prostitution and Trafficking in Human Beings (Stockholm: Ministry of Industry, Employment and Communications, Division for Gender Equality, 2005).

Gentile, Patrizia, et al. "Another Limited Bill: Gay and Lesbian Historians on C-75." (11 June 2018), online: <https://www.ourcommons.ca/Content/Committee/421/JUST/Brief/BR10002313/br-external/HooperTom-e.pdf>.

Goudge, Stephen. *Report of the Inquiry into Pediatric Forensic Pathology in Ontario: Policy and Recommendations.* Vol 3 (Toronto: Ontario Ministry of the Attorney General, 2008).

Harris, Kathleen. "Experts Urge Liberals to Update 'Embarrassingly Bad' *Criminal Code.*" *CBC News* (18 November 2016), online: <https://www.cbc.ca/news/politics/criminal-code-outdated-justice-discrimination-1.3853810>.

Ivison, John. "MacKay's Weak Defence of His Prostitution Law Implies It Won't Survive the Courts." *National Post* (7 July 2014), online: <http://news.nationalpost.com/full-comment/john-ivison-mackays-weak-defence-of-his-prostitution-law-implies-it-wont-survive-the-courts>.

274 | Bibliography

Jolly, Joanna. "Why I Failed to Catch Canada's Worst Serial Killer." *BBC News* (1 June 2017), online: <https://www.bbc.com/news/magazine-38796464>.

Jones, Allison. "Ontario Review Finds Ottawa's Sex-Work Law Constitutional, Wynne Says." *Globe and Mail* (1 April 2015), online: <www.theglobeandmail.com/news/politics/ontario-review-finds-ottawas-sex-work-law-constitutional-wynne-says/article23734478/>.

Jones, Deborah. "The Case of the Serial Killer." *Time* (26 January 2007), online: <http://content.time.com/time/world/article/0,8599,1582656,00.html>.

Kelling, George, and James Wilson. "Broken Windows: The Police and Neighbourhood Safety." *The Atlantic* (March 1982).

"Legal Experts Oppose Bill C-36." *Herizons* [Winnipeg] (22 September 2014) 13.

Legislation on the Purchase of Sexual Services (Stockholm: Ministry of Education and Research, 2009), online: <http://www.government.se/sb/d/4096/a/119861>.

Levy, Dana. "Israel Becomes the 8th Nordic Model Country as It Implements Its Prohibition of Consumption of Prostitution Services Act." *Nordic Model Now* (29 June 2020), online: <https://nordicmodelnow.org/2020/06/29/israel-becomes-the-8th-nordic-model-country-as-it-implements-its-prohibition-of-consumption-of-prostitution-services-act/>.

Loney, Heather. "Who Is Terri-Jean Bedford, the Dominatrix Fighting Canada's Prostitution Laws." *CBC News* (20 December 2013), online: <https://globalnews.ca/news/1043102/who-is-terri-jean-bedford-the-dominatrix-fighting-canadas-prostitution-laws/>.

Lowman, John. "Identifying Research Gaps in the Prostitution Literature." *Department of Justice* (March 2001), online: <https://www.justice.gc.ca/eng/rp-pr/csj-sjc/jsp-sjp/rr02_9/p1.html>.

MacInnes, Teresa, and Kent Nasan. *Buying Sex* (2013), online: <https://www.nfb.ca/film/buying_sex/>.

MacKinnon, Leslie. "Prostitution Law Changes Have Chance of Surviving Court Challenge." *CBC News* (10 June 2014), online: <https://www.cbc.ca/news/politics/prostitution-law-changes-have-chance-of-surviving-court-challenge-1.2669996>.

"Man Charged with Murder of Alberta Sex-Trade Worker." *CBC News* (10 May 2006), online: <https://www.cbc.ca/news/canada/man-charged-with-murder-of-alberta-sex-trade-worker-1.580752>.

Mas, Susana. "Prostitution Law Comes into Force on Day of Action on Violence against Women." *CBC News* (5 December 2014), online: <https://www.cbc.ca/news/politics/prostitution-law-comes-into-force-on-day-of-action-on-violence-against-women-1.2862602>.

McLachlin, Beverley. "Remarks of the Right Honourable Beverley McLachlin, P.C. Chief Justice of Canada." Conference on the Law and Parliament, Ottawa

(22 November 2004), online: <https://www.scc-csc.ca/judges-juges/spe-dis/bm-2004-11-22-eng.aspx>.

Nanda, Avnish. "Oral Arguments: Professor Alan Young on *Bedford*." *TheCourt.ca* (29 January 2014), online: <http://www.thecourt.ca/oral-arguments-professor-alan-young-on-bedford/>.

Native Women's Association of Canada (NWAC). *Sexual Exploitation and Trafficking of Aboriginal Women and Girls: Literature Review and Key Informant Interviews.* Final report (Ottawa: NWAC, 2014).

Oppal, Wally. *Forsaken: The Report of the Missing Women Commission of Inquiry.* Vol 3 (15 November 2012), online: <https://www2.gov.bc.ca/assets/gov/law-crime-and-justice/about-bc-justice-system/inquiries/forsaken-es.pdf>.

Parliament of Canada. "The Process of Passing a Bill." *Library of Parliament*, online: <https://lop.parl.ca/About/Parliament/Education/ourcountryourparliament/html_booklet/process-passing-bill-e.html>.

Perrin, Benjamin. "Oldest Profession or Oldest Oppression? Addressing Prostitution after the Supreme Court of Canada Decision in *Canada v. Bedford*" (Ottawa: Macdonald-Laurier Institute Commentary Series, 2014).

"Pickton Described How He Killed Women, Former Friend Says." *CBC News* (16 July 2007), online: <https://www.cbc.ca/news/canada/pickton-described-how-he-killed-women-former-friend-says-1.635605>.

Posner, Michael. "Meet the Dominatrix." *Globe and Mail* (16 September 2011), online: <https://www.theglobeandmail.com/news/national/meet-the-dominatrix/article594599/>.

Prime Minister of Canada, Justin Trudeau. "Remarks by Prime Minister Justin Trudeau to Apologize to LGBTQ2 Canadians" (28 November 2017), online: <https://pm.gc.ca/en/news/speeches/2017/11/28/remarks-prime-minister-justin-trudeau-apologize-lgbtq2-canadians>.

Roberts, Jennifer. "Why Experts Like 'Hot-Tubbing.'" *Globe and Mail* (19 April 2011), online: <www.theglobeandmail.com/report-on-business/industry-news/the-law-page/why-judges-like-hot-tubbing/article577733/>.

Sex Workers United against Violence. "My Work Should Not Cost Me My Life: The Case against Criminalizing the Purchase of Sex in Canada." *Pivot Legal Society* (2014), online: <https://d3n8a8pro7vhmx.cloudfront.net/pivotlegal/pages/615/attachments/original/1401811234/My_Work_Should_Not_Cost_Me_My_Life.pdf?1401811234>.

Simons, Paula. "Proposed Bill 'Is Going to Be a Disaster': New Law Would Make Sex World More Dangerous." *Edmonton Journal* (7 June 2014).

Special Committee on Pornography and Prostitution. *Pornography and Prostitution in Canada.* Vol 2 (Ottawa: Minister of Supply and Services Canada, 1985).

Street Prostitution: Assessing the Impact of the Law Synthesis Report (Ottawa: Department of Justice Canada, 1989).

Tandt, Michael Den. "Tories Make a Hash of New Prostitution Bill: Bill C-36 Can Only Put Sex Workers at Greater Risk." *Gazette* [Montreal] (6 June 2014).

Tibbetts, Janice. "Building Consensus." *Canadian Lawyer* (July 2013) 24.

Tyler, Tracey. "Prostitution Law Struck Down." *Toronto Star* (28 September 2010), online: <https://www.thestar.com/news/canada/2010/09/28/prostitution_laws_struck_down.html>.

United Kingdom. House of Commons. "Report of the Committee on Homosexual Offences and Prostitution." Cmnd 247 in *Sessional Papers,* vol 14 (1956–57) 85.

Victimization of Prostitutes in Calgary and Winnipeg (Ottawa: Department of Justice Canada, 1994).

Young, Alan. *The Costs of Charter Litigation* (Ottawa: Department of Justice Canada, Research and Statistics Division, 2016), online: <https://www.justice.gc.ca/eng/rp-pr/jr/ccl-clc/ccl-clc.pdf>.

Young, Chris. "Pressed on Prostitution Law, PM Jokes about Dominatrix." *Globe and Mail* (2 December 2010), online: <https://www.theglobeandmail.com/news/politics/ottawa-notebook/pressed-on-prostitution-law-pm-jokes-about-dominatrix/article613244/>.

Index of Cases

Alberta v Hutterian Brethren of Wilson Colony, 2009 SCC 37, [2009] 2 SCR 567, 239n93, 243nn62–63

Bedford v Canada, 2010 ONSC 4264, 102 OR (3d) 321, 1, 41–42, 49–77, 91, 93, 99–100, 114, 123, 148, 170–71, 201n77, 229n6, 238n56, 238n77, 239n87, 245nn81–84, 249n40

British Columbia Civil Liberties Association v Canada (Attorney General), 2019 BCCA 228, 377 CCC (3d) 420, 228n116

Canada (Attorney General) v Bedford, 2012 ONCA 186, 109 OR (3d) 1, 1, 49–51, 65–77, 84, 91, 99–100, 123, 214n108

Canada (Attorney General) v Bedford, 2013 SCC 72, [2013] 3 SCR 1101, 1–11, 26, 42–52, 65–77, 81–84, 88, 91, 95–101, 103, 105–7, 111–15, 118–19, 123, 128–30, 133–36, 139–42, 144–47, 149–50, 152–56, 158–59, 161, 165–67, 170–71, 179, 183–85, 187–94, 202n87, 244n69, 249n40

Canada (Attorney General) v Downtown Eastside Sex Workers United against Violence Society, 2012 SCC 45, [2012] 2 SCR 524, 47–48

Canada (Attorney General) v PHS Community Services Society, 2011 SCC 44, [2011] 3 SCR 134, 106, 220n46, 223n2, 228n114

Canada v Pharmaceutical Society (Nova Scotia), [1992] 2 SCR 606, 93 DLR (4th) 36, 208n34

Canadian Civil Liberties Association v Canada (Attorney General), 2019 ONCA 243, 144 OR (3d) 641, 228n116

Canadian Foundation for Children, Youth and the Law v Canada (Attorney General), 2004 SCC 4, [2004] 1 SCR 76, 225nn58–59

Carter v Canada (Attorney General), 2015 SCC 5, [2015] 1 SCR 331, 122–23, 220n46, 221n49, 228n115, 229n119

Carter v Canada (Attorney General), 2016 SCC 4, [2016] 1 SCR 13, 122–24

Chaoulli v Quebec (Attorney General), 2005 SCC 35, [2005] 1 SCR 791, 216n149

278 | Index of Cases

Clark v Hagar, (1894) 22 SCR 510, 200n65

Corbiere v Canada (Minister of Indian and Northern Affairs), [1999] 2 SCR 203, 173 DLR (4th) 1, 117

David Polowin Real Estate v Dominion of Canada General Insurance Co (2005), 255 DLR (4th) 633, 76 OR (3d) 161 (ONCA), 215n118

Edwards v Canada (Attorney General), [1930] AC 124 (PC), 250n14

Gosselin v Quebec (Attorney General), 2002 SCC 84, [2002] 4 SCR 429, 202n106, 246n108

Harper v Canada, 2004 SCC 33, [2004] 1 SCR 827, 215n131, 218n6

Housen v Nikolaisen, 2002 SCC 33, [2002] 2 SCR 235, 83, 218n5

Irwin Toy v Quebec (Attorney General), [1989] 1 SCR 927, 58 DLR (4th) 577, 202n100, 202n102

Koo Sze Yiu v Chief Executive of the HKSAR, [2006] 3 HKLRD 455, 233n97

Lochner v New York, 198 US 45 (1905), 203n113

M v H, [1999] 2 SCR 3, 171 DLR (4th) 577, 196n35, 228n101, 228n103, 234n9, 239n78

Muller v Oregon, 208 US 412 (1908), 88

Ontario (Attorney General) v G, 2020 SCC 38, 451 DLR (4th) 541, 127–28

Perka v The Queen, [1984] 2 SCR 232, 13 DLR (4th) 1, 199n33, 235nn16–17

R c Labaye, 2005 SCC 80, [2005] 3 SCR 728, 200n67

R c Lemieux (1991), 70 CCC (3d) 434, 11 CR (4th) 224 (QBCA), 201n78

R v AB, 2015 ONCA 803, 333 CCC (3d) 382, 225n54

R v Abbey, 2009 ONCA 624, 97 OR (3d) 330, 219n27

R v Alcorn, 2021 MBCA 101, 165

R v Anwar, 2020 ONCJ 103, 62 CR (7th) 402, 172–77, 196n30, 228n113, 242n21

R v Aravena, 2015 ONCA 250, 323 CCC (3d) 54, 238n57

R v Barrow (2001), 54 OR (3d) 417, 155 CCC (3d) 362 (ONCA), [2001] SCCA No 431, 25n88

R v Bedford (2000), 184 DLR (4th) 727, 143 CCC (3d) 311 (ONCA), 53n10, 210n68

R v Belnavis, [1997] 3 SCR 341, 151 DLR (4th) 443, 207n12

R v Blais, 2008 BCCA 389, 85 BCLR (4th) 1, 209n61

R v Boodhoo, 2018 ONSC 7205, 51 CR (7th) 207, 196n30, 246n97

R v Boudreault, 2018 SCC 58, [2018] 3 SCR 599, 197n36

R v Brodie, [1962] SCR 681, 32 DLR (2d) 507, 212n67

R v Brown, 2022 SCC 18, 228n117

Index of Cases | 279

R v Buhay, 2003 SCC 30, [2003] 1 SCR 631, 82, 218n12

R v Butler, [1992] 1 SCR 452, 89 DLR (4th) 449, 200n67, 206n204, 213n77

R v Clark, (1883) 2 OR 523 (ONQB), 21

R v Clay, 2003 SCC 75, [2003] 3 SCR 735, 224n24

R v Corbeil, [1991] 1 SCR 830, 64 CCC (3d) 272, 201n74

R v Cunningham (1986), 31 CCC (3d) 223 (MBPC), 202n96

R v Daviault, [1994] 3 SCR 63, 118 DLR (4th) 469, 228n117

R v DD, 2000 SCC 43, [2000] 2 SCR 275, 85

R v Deutsch, [1986] 2 SCR 2, 30 DLR (4th) 435, 242n22, 246n113

R v DiGiuseppe (2002), 161 CCC (3d) 424, 155 OAC 62 (ONCA), 209n61

R v Dominion News and Gifts (1962), [1964] SCR 251, [1964] 3 CCC 1, 200n67

R v Downey, [1992] 2 SCR 10, 90 DLR (4th) 449, 23, 26, 30–31, 35–37, 51–52, 60, 72, 153–56, 158–59, 195n7, 202n91, 240n100

R v Edwards Books & Arts, [1986] 2 SCR 713, 35 DLR (4th) 1, 203n115

R v Gallone, 2019 ONCA 663, 147 OR (3d) 225, 176, 242nn22–24

R v Gareau, (1891) 1 CCC 66 (QBCA), 22

R v Grilo (1991), 64 CCC (3d) 53, 2 OR (3d) 514 (ONCA), 25, 202n93

R v Hamilton (unreported), 47

R v Hayes, [1998] BC No 2752, 115 BCAC 22 (BCCA), 217n177

R v Head (1987), 36 CCC (3d) 562, 59 CR (3d) 80 (BCCA), 202n86

R v Heywood, [1994] 3 SCR 761, 120 DLR (4th) 348, 195n13, 43, 205n201, 216n150

R v Hibbert, [1995] 2 SCR 973, 99 CCC (3d) 193, 196n33, 234n16

R v Hicklin (1868), LR 3 QB 360, 200n67

R v Hutt, [1978] 2 SCR 476, 82 DLR (3d) 95, 24, 40, 55

R v Keegstra, [1990] 3 SCR 697, 61 CCC (3d) 1, 202n102, 206n204

R v Khawaja, 2012 SCC 69, [2012] 3 SCR 555, 224n25

R v Khadr, 2010 SCC 3, [2010] 1 SCR 44, 238n63

R v Khill, 2021 SCC 37, 234n10

R v Latimer, 2001 SCC 1, [2001] 1 SCR 3, 234n17, 235n23

R v Lawrence, 2002 ABPC 189, 332 AR 188, 202n85

R v Levesque, (1870) 30 UCQBR 509, 21, 200n51

R v Malmo-Levine, 2003 SCC 74, [2003] 3 SCR 571, 43–44, 104, 148–49, 180–83, 185–86, 195n13, 205n201, 216n151, 238n69, 238n77, 249n39

R v Michaud, 2015 ONCA 585, 127 OR (3d) 81, 101–4

R v Michaud, leave to appeal to SCC refused, 36706 (5 May 2016), 225n40

R v Morales, [1992] 3 SCR 711, 77 CCC (3d) 91, 205n200

280 | Index of Cases

R v Morgentaler, [1988] 2 SCR 3, 51 DLR (4th) 481, 205n201, 215n120, 216n137
R v Moriarity, 2015 SCC 55, [2015] 3 SCR 485, 243n35
R v NS, 2021 ONSC 1628, 167, 173–74, 196n30, 228n113, 246n96
R v NS, 2022 ONCA 160, 165–67, 173–74, 176, 199n30, 246n102, 246n113
R v Oakes, [1986] 1 SCR 103, 26 DLR (4th) 200, 31–37, 150–51
R v Patterson, [1968] SCR 157, 67 DLR (2d) 82, 201n73
R v Pickton, 2006 BCSC 1090, 260 CCC (3d) 185, 41
R v Pickton, 2007 BCSC 2039, [2007] BCJ No 3109, 207n22
R v Preston (1990), 47 BCLR (2d) 273, 79 CR (3d) 61 (BCCA), 226n80
R v Remon, (1888) 16 OR 560 (ONQB), 21
R v Ruzic, 2001 SCC 24, [2001] 1 SCR 687, 136, 138, 138nn23–24, 199n34, 229n118, 234nn5–7, 234n16, 235nn21
R v Ryan, 2013 SCC 3, [2013] 1 SCR 14, 234n10, 234n19, 235n22, 235nn24–25, 235n29
R v Safarzadeh-Markhali, 2016 SCC 14, [2016] 1 SCR 180, 242nn28–34
R v Searle (D.R.), (1994) 163 NBR (2d) 123 (NBPC), 202n85
R v Skinner, [1990] 1 SCR 1235, 56 CCC (3d) 1, 26, 195n11
R v Spence, 2005 SCC 71, [2005] 3 SCR 458, 196n17, 197n38, 218n4, 218n11, 223n92

R v Swain, [1991] 1 SCR 933, 63 CCC (3d) 481, 116–17, 230n29
R v Towne Cinema Theatres, [1985] 1 SCR 494, 18 DLR (4th) 1, 200n67
R v Whyte, [1988] 2 SCR 3, 51 DLR (4th) 481, 30
R v Willis, 2016 MBCA 113, 344 CCC (3d) 443, 238n57
R v Wong (1977), 2 Alta LR (2d) 90, 33 CCC (2d) 6 (ABCA), 201n78
R v Yu, 2002 ABCA 305, 171 CCC (3d) 90, 217n178
Re BC Motor Vehicle Act, [1985] 2 SCR 486, 24 DLR (4th) 536, 73, 185–86, 202n108, 203n117, 216n137, 226n69, 239n88
Re Manitoba Language Rights, [1985] 1 SCR 721, 19 DLR (4th) 1, 116, 125, 232n79
Reference re Anti-Inflation Act, [1976] 2 SCR 373, 68 DLR (3d) 452, 221nn53–54
Reference re Remuneration of Judges of the Prov Court of PEI; Reference re Independence and Impartiality of Judges of the Prov Court of PEI, [1997] 3 SCR 3, 150 DLR (4th) 577, 230n14, 232n79
Reference re Residential Tenancies Act (Ontario), [1981] 1 SCR 714, 123 DLR (3d) 554, 223n53
Reference re ss 193 and 195.1(1)(C) of the Criminal Code (1987), 38 CCC (3d) 408, 49 Man R (2d) 1, 27, 202n97
Reference re ss 193 and 195.1(1)(C) of the Criminal Code (Man), [1990] 1 SCR 1123, 56 CCC (3d) 65, 23, 26–34, 43, 51–52, 60, 68–69,

71–72, 147, 198n7, 198nn11–12, 201nn75–76, 216n137, 247n121
Reference re Secession of Quebec, [1998] 2 SCR 217, 161 LR (4th) 385, 116
Reference re Section 293 of the Criminal Code of Canada, 2011 BCSC 1588, 279 CCC (3d) 1, 220n40, 220n46, 221n53
RJR-Macdonald Inc v Canada (Attorney General), [1995] 3 SCR 199, 127 DLR (4th) 1, 213n131, 218n6, 239nn94–95, 243n62–63
Rodriguez v British Columbia (Attorney General), [1993] 3 SCR 519, 107 DLR (4th) 342, 216n137, 225n57, 248n13

Schachter v Canada, [1992] 2 SCR 679, 93 DLR (4th) 1, 116–17, 119–21, 124, 217n171
Schwartz v Canada, [1996] 1 SCR 254, 133 DLR (4th) 289, 83
Shaw v Director of Public Prosecutions, [1962] AC 220 (HL), 202n87
Suresh v Canada (Minister of Citizenship and Immigration), 2002 SCC 1, [2002] 1 SCR 3, 208n35, 216n151

The Queen v Rehe, (1897) 1 CCC 63 (QBQB), 22

United States v Burns, 2001 SCC 7, [2001] 1 SCR 283, 208n35, 216n151

Index

abuse of process, 143
An Act Respecting Offences of the Person, 18
adjudicative facts, 70, 81–83
advertisement of sexual services, 249
advertising prohibition, 176
advocacy-based testimony, 93
Alder, John, 191
American Constitution, 28; Fourteenth Amendment, 28
American Supreme Court, 28, 88
Anglo-American structure, 16, 9, 142–44
Angus Reid Institute, 157
appellate review, 70, 81, 88, 94
arbitrariness, 7, 69, 95–98,106, 112
arch-liberal principle, 43

Backhouse, Constance, 15, 19, 22, 199n27, 199n42
bad dates, 54, 60
bawdy houses, 1, 5, 21, 26, 39, 44, 52–56, 58–61, 65–66, 68, 72–76, 104, 135–37, 141, 143, 147–48, 150–55, 179, 184, 189, 209n61, 212n66; 239n87; keeping or running of, 18–19, 23–24, 29, 49, 53, 58, 99, 137–38, 139, 153, 154, 155, 159, 161, 173–74, 188. *See also* sex work laws

BDSM, 49, 54
Bedford, Terri-Jean, 1, 49, 52
Benedet, Janine, 154
Berger, Benjamin, 45
bias, 57, 85
Bill C-36, 4, 10, 157, 163–64, 166, 171, 194
Bill C-49, 33, 37, 55
Bird, Brian, 124, 232n80
Bondage Bungalow Dominatrix, 49
Brandeis briefs, 88–89
bright-line rule, 102–4, 112, 153
burden of proof, 3, 44, 74, 96, 105–7, 112, 187
Burningham, Sarah, 124
Bushell, Allison, 110

Cameron, Jamie, 191
Canada (Attorney General) v Downtown Eastside Sex Workers United Against Violence Society, 41, 47–48, 210n74
Canada (Attorney General) v PHS Community Services Society, 106
Canadian Bill of Rights, 214n102
Canadian Charter of Rights and Freedoms, 2, 3, 4, 10, 16, 23, 28, 31, 38, 45, 47, 51, 69, 74–75, 81, 105, 108–12, 117–19, 121–22, 127, 129–30, 133, 143–44, 159,

171, 177, 187, 191, 193, 248n12; section 1, 3, 5, 6, 31, 34, 36, 67, 73–74, 95, 101, 108, 119, 134, 149–50, 152, 155, 168, 188–89, 196n21, 206n2; section 2, 123–24; section 2(b), 26, 27, 68, 176, 177; section 2(d), 26; section 7, 3, 8, 15, 16, 26–28, 40, 43–44, 51, 67–73, 77, 101, 108, 111–12, 123–24, 130, 133–34, 144–45, 173–76, 183, 185–86, 221n61, 246n108; section 11(d), 26, 30; section 12, 43, 105; section 15, 123–24, 221n48; section 24(1), 124; section 33, 109, 113, 123–24, 196n24
Canadian Organization for the Rights of Prostitutes, 55
Carter v Canada (Attorney General), 122
causal connection, 71, 133, 188
causation, 144–45, 150
Charter remedies, 45
Chief Justice Dickson, 28–29, 31–34
Chief Justice Hughes, 192
Chief Justice McLachlin, 1, 10, 36–37, 42, 72, 133, 146, 152, 190–91, 240n100
choice-based framework, 9, 156
Choudhry, Sujit, 118
commercial enterprise, 161, 172–73
communication and bawdy-house offences, 68, 104, 148, 150–51, 188
concurrent expert testimony, 93
Conservative government, 62, 157, 190
Constitution, the, 8, 74, 115–16, 118, 124, 126–28, 130, 192, 250n14; section 52, 74, 116, 124, 127–28, 130

Constitution Act, section 91(27), 183
constitutional analysis, 6, 9, 135, 147, 149, 152, 166, 184–85, 188–89
constitutional harm, 71
constitutional litigation process, 2
constructive dialogue, 108
Contagious Disease Act, 16–17
coordinate construction, 110
coordinate interpretation, 110–11
Corbiere v Canada (Minister of Indian and Northern Affairs), 117
cost of litigation, The, 45
Criminal Code, 18–19, 23, 37, 53, 75, 104, 116; section 17, 141; section 150.1, 102; section 151, 75; section 152, 75; section 153, 75; section 170, 75; section 171, 75; section 172.1, 75; section 173(2), 76; section 174, 76; section 175, 76; section 177, 76; section 179, 23; section 180, 76; section 193(1), 23; section 193(2), 23, 24; section 195(1)(j), 25; section 195.1(1)(c), 24; section 195.1(2), 25; section 197, 23, 74; section 210(1), 23; section 210(2), 23; section 212(1)(a)–(i), 75; section 212(1)(j), 25; section 213, 234, 251; section 213(1)(a), 75; section 213(1)(b), 75; section 213(1)(c), 24; section 213(2), 159; section 213(1.1), 159; section 264, 76; section 264.1, 75; section 280, 75; section 286.1, 159, 161, 164, 168, 171; section 286.2, 160–61, 172–73; section 286.3, 161, 175–76; section 286.4, 161, 176; section 286.5, 159–61, 168, 171, 173; section 718(b), 97

284 | Index

criminal law theory, 43–44, 185

Davis, Kenneth Culp, 81
de novo, 83–84
declaration of invalidity, 4, 8, 51–52, 68, 75–76, 114–22, 124–30, 188, 193, 231n32
declaratory relief, 48, 84
decriminalization, 54–55, 63, 170–71, 190, 245n87
defences, 6, 9, 136–37, 141, 143, 179, 184–85, 234n11, 235n20, 238n61
deference, 2, 7, 9, 67, 70, 81–84, 86–87, 121, 152, 154, 158, 171, 177, 193
Department of Justice, 33, 164
deterrence, 34, 97–98, 147–48, 163–64
Devlin, Lord Patrick, 180
Douglas, William, 193
duress, 136–37, 141–43, 235nn20–25, 235n29

economic rights, 175, 246n108
efficacy, 190, 40, 72, 89, 94, 102, 105–8, 170, 178
empirical evidence, 7, 11, 36, 40, 111, 152, 154, 187, 209n61
equality interests, 2, 158, 200
escort agency, 25, 30, 52, 174
evidentiary presumption, 35
evidentiary record, 47, 51–52, 64, 67, 86–87, 91
exploitation, 1, 35–36, 75, 100, 107, 148, 163–64, 173, 189

Federal Court Rules, 93
Feinberg, Joel, 181–84
Fletcher, George, 133
France, 170
Fraser Report, 35, 40
freedom of expression, 26–28, 32, 34, 69, 176–77, 191, 202n99
fundamental justice, 2–3, 5–7, 15, 26, 28–29, 43–44, 51, 67, 69–74, 95–98, 101–6, 108, 112, 133, 167, 180–81, 183, 186–87, 199n34, 204n147, 229n119

Gacek, James, 167
Gary Ridgway, 42
general behavioural standard, 102
general deterrence, 97–98
Genesee River Killer, 42
German Constitutional Court, 90–91
German law, 90–91
Germany, 90, 170–71, 213n81
Graff, Harvey, 20
Green River Killer, 42
gross disproportionality, 3, 38, 44, 72, 96, 98, 100–1, 104–5, 112, 148, 150, 195n13, 205n201

Haak, Debra, 10, 162, 164–65, 168
harm avoided, 100; caused, 76, 100, 138, 163
harm principle, 43, 104, 180–81, 185, 190, 248n12
Hart, HLA, 180
Highway of Tears, 42
Highway Traffic Act, 101
Hogg, Peter, 109–10, 117
holistic: approach, 106–7; conception, 95, 103, 105, 107–8, 112
Hoole, Grant, 119–20, 122, 126, 128, 230n13
House of Commons, 55, 60, 157
Housen v Nikolaisen, 83
Hughes, Jula, 90–91

human fallibility, 103
human traffickers, 64, 170
hypothetical scenario, 30, 148, 175–77

Iceland, 170
immunity provision, 159
Indigenous, 20, 40, 42, 56, 60, 221n48
individualistic: approach, 72, 101, 106–7; conception, 96, 102, 104–7, 112–13, 135, 148
individualization, 95–97
inquisitorial justice systems, 92
instrumental rationality, 2–4, 7–9, 43–44, 51, 71–72, 74, 95–97, 99, 101–3, 105–13, 129, 135, 148, 166, 169, 184, 186–88, 193. *See also* means-ends rationality
international evidence, 62–63, 158, 171, 178
Ireland, 170
Israel, 170

Jack the Ripper, 42
Jochelson, Richard, 167
Joel Rifkin, 42
joint experts, 92
Judge Learned Hand, 192
judicial: activism, 3, 108; appointments, 91; interpretation, 20; overreach, 144; review, 3–4, 7, 43, 111, 113, 121, 144
Justice Armour, 21
Justice Binnie, 85–86, 90–91, 93, 220n45
Justice Brandeis, 88–89
Justice Brown, 124, 128
Justice Cory, 35
Justice Côté, 128
Justice Dorion, 22

Justice Himel, 1, 2, 10, 41, 49–51, 54, 57, 62–65, 68, 71, 75–76, 84, 91, 93, 114, 128, 134, 148, 170–71
Justice Hoy, 176
Justice Iacobucci, 36
Justice L'Heureux-Dube, 117, 192
Justice La Forest, 31, 36
Justice Lamer, 28–29, 31, 33–34, 73, 147, 191
Justice LeBel, 136
Justice Mainella, 165
Justice McKay, 172–73, 174–77
Justice McLachlin, 1, 10, 36–37, 42, 72, 133, 146, 152, 190–91, 240n100
Justice Sopinka, 31
Justice Sutherland, 167, 173–74, 246n110
Justice Wilson, 33–34, 73
Justice Wurtele, 22

Lambeth Poisoner, 42
Larsen, Allison Orr, 89
Lazare, Jodi, 86, 225nn40–44
Lebovitch, Amy, 1, 47–48, 50, 53–55, 158
Leckey, Robert, 122, 125–27
Legal Aid, 39, 45, 141
Legal Aid Ontario's Test Case Program, 45
legal moralism, 180, 182
legislative facts, 70, 81–89, 91–94, 147, 187, 193, 218n3
legislative intent, 6, 33
Leigh, Carol, 10
Liberal government, 62
living on the avails. *See* sex work laws, living on the avails
Lochner v New York, 28

Louie, Christine, 157, 240n6
Lowman, John, 40, 157, 207n13, 240nn6–7

MacDonnell, Vanessa, 90–91
Macfarlane, Emmett, 124, 231n32
Mahoney, Kathleen, 38
majoritarianism, 21, 108–9, 111, 113, 115
majority rule, 108
male sex workers, 67, 207n13
mandatory minimum fines, 160
mandatory minimum sentencing, 97–98
Manitoba Act, 1870, 116
Manitoba Court of Appeal, 26–27, 165, 238n57
Manitoba Language Reference, 116, 125
Manitoba Provincial Court, 26
marginalized, 15, 39, 41, 108, 129, 137–38, 144, 153
material benefit offence, 160, 164, 172–73
Mathen, Carissima, 191, 193, 242n12
McGinnis, Janice, 38
means-ends rationality, 38, 43, 70, 95. *See also* instrumental rationality
Member of Parliament Joy Smith, 157
Mill, John Stuart, 28, 43, 104, 180–81, 184
Minister of Justice Peter McKay, 163
Monahan, John, 84
moral blameworthiness, 143
moral involuntariness, 134, 136–39, 141–43, 149–50, 155–56, 165, 235n22, 235nn25–26, 235n29
morally involuntary, 5, 9, 112, 133–34, 136, 141, 179, 188, 234n11, 238n57
Muller v Oregon, 88
multiple objectives, 5, 135, 147–48, 150

Narcotic Control Act, 180
National Action Committee on the Status of Women, 55
National Judicial Institute, 90
necessity, 18, 137–38, 141, 176, 235n20, 235n23
Netherlands, 63, 170, 213n81
Nevada, 170, 213n81
New Zealand, 170, 213n81
Nordic model, 64, 156, 158, 166, 169–71, 178, 189, 242n12, 243n64, 251n25
Northern Ireland, 170
Norway, 170
notice of constitutional question, 91
notwithstanding clause, 4, 109–10, 115, 123–24, 126–27, 129–30, 188. *See also Canadian Charter of Rights and Freedoms,* section 33
nuisance, 32, 34, 42, 59, 73, 76, 99–100, 115, 139, 148, 164, 180, 184, 189–90, 229n6

obiter dicta, 68
offence principle, 182–84, 190, 249n35
Ontario (Attorney General) v G, 127
Ontario Court of Appeal, 25, 49–51, 65–66, 69–70, 84, 100–4, 165, 167, 173, 176, 210n1, 214n108
Ontario Court of Queen's Bench, 21
Ontario Superior Court of Justice, 1, 51, 197n36, 246n97

Index | 287

overbreadth, 7, 38, 44, 69, 72, 95–104, 106, 112, 147, 208n34, 224n14

Paciocco, David, 85
palpable and overriding error, 70, 81
Parliament, 2, 4, 8–9, 18–19, 22–24, 29–30, 32–33, 35–37, 42, 49, 55, 59, 68, 92, 99, 109, 111, 114, 117, 124–25, 129–30, 141, 145–46, 150, 152, 154, 156–59, 163, 165–69, 171, 173, 177, 185, 189, 194, 227n85, 227n98
party liability, 172
Perrin, Benjamin, 170–71
Perryman, Benjamin, 84, 87, 90
Petter, Andrew, 45
Pickton, Robert, 41–42, 129, 207n23, 208n38
policy justifications, 74
Powell, Maria, 37
presumption of innocence, 26, 30, 52, 240n100
Prime Minister Justin Trudeau, 66
Prime Minister Stephen Harper, 49
principles of criminal law theory, 43–44, 185
principles of moral philosophy, 185
private interest standing, 47, 49–50, 210n74
procuring, 9, 18, 75, 159, 161, 164, 174–75
Project Devote, 42
Project Even-Handed, 41
Project Kare, 42
promoting democratic discourse, 27, 32
proportionality principle, 106, 109, 119, 120, 128
Prostitution Reference, 37

Protection of Communities and Exploited Persons Act, 157–59, 162–65, 169, 189, 240n7
protective staff, 1, 64–65, 71, 73, 134, 148, 153–55, 173, 189
public interest litigation, 123
public or private interest standing, 47, 49

Quebec Court of Appeal, 22
Quebec Court of Queen's Bench, 22
Queensland, 170
queue jumping, 122

R v Alcorn, 165
R v Anwar, 174, 176, 196n30
R v Clark, 21
R v DD, 85
R v Downey, 23, 26, 30–31, 35, 51–52, 60, 72, 240n100
R v Gareau, 22
R v Grilo, 25
R v Hamilton, 47
R v Heywood, 43
R v Hutt, 24, 32, 40, 55
R v Levesque, 21
R v Malmo-Levine, 43, 104, 148, 180–81, 183, 185–86, 249n39, 249n41
R v Michaud, 102, 104
R v NS, 173–74, 176, 196n30
R v Oakes, 31, 150; Oakes test, 31
R v Remon, 21
R v Ruzic, 136, 138
R v Skinner, 26
R v Swain, 116–17
R v Whyte, 30
ratio decendi, 68
reasonable avenues of escape, 134, 138

Reference Re Secession of Quebec, 116
Reference re Section 94(2) of the Motor Vehicle Act, 73, 185–86
regulation of sex work, 2, 15, 62
rehabilitative principles, 16
Roach, Kent, 45, 76, 109–11, 118, 120–23, 129
Rosen, Ruth, 17
rule of law, 68–69, 75–76, 116, 124, 149
Ryder, Bruce, 121, 230n29

Sachs, Albie, 122
Schachter v Canada, 75, 116–17, 119–21, 124, 230n29
Schwartz v Canada, 83
Scott, John, 67
Scott, Valerie, 1, 47–48, 54
screen clientele, 1, 5, 54, 58, 65, 99, 134, 136–37, 139, 141, 143, 152, 154, 158, 177
self-defence, 136–37, 143
self-fulfillment, 27, 32
sentencing, 98, 142
Sex Professionals of Canada, 54–55
sex work governance, 2, 22–23, 33, 147
sex work laws, 1, 2, 4–11, 15–16, 19–20, 22–23, 26, 37–40, 42–44, 47–48, 51–53, 57–58, 61–62, 64–67, 69, 71, 76–77, 88–89, 93, 111, 114–15, 128–30, 133–35, 137, 139, 141–59, 161–69, 171, 173, 175–78, 180, 183, 187–90, 194, 201n69, 239n87, 244n68, 245n89, 246n97; communicating in public for the purpose of sex work, 1, 24, 31–32, 55, 72, 99, 159, 164, 168, 184; living on the avails of sex work, 18–19, 25–26, 30–31, 34–37, 39, 54–56, 58–60, 72–74, 76, 100, 106–7, 134, 148, 152–55, 159, 172–73, 189, 217n155; working out of bawdy houses, 1. *See also* bawdy houses
Sex Work Reference, 23, 26–29, 31, 43, 47, 51–52, 60, 68–69, 71–72, 147
sexual morality, 15, 17, 23
Sharpe, Robert, 45
single objective, 135
social science evidence, 3–7, 9, 51, 70, 83–84, 87, 106, 145, 151, 168, 171, 178, 220n40, 220n46
social science research, 40, 52, 57, 81, 90
sociolegal rationale, 39
special interest, 50
standard of review, 81
standing, 38, 47, 49, 50, 53, 123
stare decisis principle, 51, 68–69
Stewart, Hamish, 102, 106–7, 162, 167, 172, 183, 238n77, 243n59
Subcommittee Report, 60–61
Supreme Court, 1–11, 16, 24, 26–32, 34–37, 39–40, 42–51, 55, 60, 66–77, 81–86, 88–89, 94–108, 111–19, 121–22, 124–30, 133–40, 144–50, 152–55, 159, 162–63, 168, 174, 180, 181, 183, 185–92
survival sex worker, 11, 58, 112, 134–44, 146, 149, 152–54, 165, 167–68, 174–75, 177, 188–89
suspended declaration of invalidity, 8, 51–52, 76, 117–21, 124–30, 188, 229n7, 231n32
Sweden, 63–64, 169–70, 213n81
Synthesis Report, 59

Terri-Jean Bedford, 1, 47, 49, 52
The Badgley Report, 35, 40
The Queen v Rehe, 22
threshold interest, 28, 71
transgender, 65–67, 214n102
truth finding, 27, 32
two-track model, 115, 120–23, 126, 129

underinclusive, 117
United Kingdom, 92
unwritten constitutional principle, 8, 115–16, 118, 124–25, 130, 188
utilitarian proportionality, 138

vagueness, 26, 29, 38, 52, 69, 181
Victimization Study, 60
Vitale, David, 192
volition, 133, 135, 143

Walker, Laurens, 84
Walkowitz, Judith, 17
white slavery, 17, 19, 198n14
Women's Legal Education and Advocacy Fund, 38

Yorkshire Ripper, 42
Young, Alan, 3, 6, 37–39, 43–50, 87–89, 180, 186, 208n38, 209n48, 209n50, 210n69

Printed and bound by CPI Group (UK) Ltd, Croydon, CR0 4YY
Set in Garamond by Artegraphica Design Co.
Copy editor: Dallas Harrison
Proofreader: Judith Earnshaw

Printed and bound by CPI Group (UK) Ltd, Croydon, CR0 4YY
15/12/2024
14612408-0001